The *Mellah* of Marrakesh

Indiana Series in Middle East Studies

Mark Tessler,

general editor

The *Mellah* of Marrakesh

Jewish and Muslim Space in Morocco's Red City

Emily Gottreich

INDIANA UNIVERSITY PRESS
BLOOMINGTON AND INDIANAPOLIS

Grateful acknowledgment is made to the Jewish Studies Publications Program of the Koret Foundation.

This book is a publication of

Indiana University Press
601 North Morton Street
Bloomington, IN 47404-3797 USA

http://iupress.indiana.edu

Telephone orders 800-842-6796
Fax orders 812-855-7931
Orders by e-mail iuporder@indiana.edu

The paper used in this publication meets the minimum requirements of American National Standard for Information Sciences—Permanence of Paper for Printed Library Materials, ANSI Z39.48-1984.

Manufactured in the United States of America

Library of Congress Cataloging-in-Publication Data

Gottreich, Emily, date
The mellah of Marrakesh : Jewish and Muslim space in Morocco's red city / Emily Gottreich.
p. cm. — (Indiana series in Middle East studies)
Includes bibliographical references and index.
ISBN 0-253-34791-2 (cloth : alk. paper) — ISBN 0-253-21863-2 (pbk. : alk. paper)
1. Jews—Morocco—Marrakech—History. 2. Jewish ghettos—Morocco—Marrakech—History—19th century. 3. City and town life—Morocco—Marrakech—History—19th century. 4. Marrakech Region (Morocco)—Social conditions—19th century. 5. Marrakech (Morocco)—Ethnic relations. I. Title. II. Series.
DS135.M85M374 2007
305.892'406464—dc22 2006006669

1 2 3 4 5 12 11 10 09 08 07

To my parents

Two things are forgotten only with death
the face of one's mother and the face
of one's city

—from the poem "Straw-Blond" by Nazim Hikmet

If one were to say that Marrakesh is perfect, it is not due to the perfection of one of its parts, but to all of them together.

—ʿAbd al-Wahid al-Marrakushi, al-iʿlām bi-man halla Marrākush wa Aghmāt min al-aʿlām

CONTENTS

ACKNOWLEDGMENTS

In the field of Moroccan Jewish history, the diffusion of primary source materials tends to mirror the dispersal of the Jews themselves. For this reason, the various texts on which this study is based were amassed from libraries, archives, and private collections in Morocco, France, England, Israel, and the United States (the list could have gone on). There is little chance that I would have ever succeeded in collecting or attempting to interpret this quasi-*geniza* of the Jewish community of Marrakesh without the considerable help of many individuals in each of the places where I conducted research and wrote. It is to the scholars and staff of Harvard University, and particularly those affiliated with the Center for Middle Eastern Studies, that I give thanks for launching me on the very rewarding path of Moroccan history. Foremost among those individuals is Susan Gilson Miller, who has seen this project through from its most tentative beginnings to its current form, unstintingly offering comments, criticisms, contacts, meals, and local knowledge along the way. Quite simply, I owe much of what I know and continue to learn about Moroccan history (not to mention life in general) to her. Through the Morocco Studies Program at Harvard, of which Susan Gilson Miller is the founding director, I was introduced to some of Morocco's leading thinkers, including Abdellatif Bencherifa, Abdelhai Diouri, Abdelfattah Kilito, and Abdallah Laroui, all of whom generously shared their vast knowledge of Moroccan culture and society and inspired me to learn more. I was taken under the formidable wing of Isadore Twersky, who taught me the fundaments of Jewish history and historiography. Although a Maimonides scholar, he was never able to travel to Fez to see the house reputed to once have been the home of the great RAMBAM, and so had to make do with my vague descriptions. His vision of the Jewish past has strongly influenced my own, for which I am grateful.

The warm reception this project has received in Morocco has been gratifying to me both as an individual and as a practitioner of Jewish history. From the moment I first stepped off the plane in Rabat, Ed Thomas and his staff at the Moroccan-American Commission for Educational and Cultural Exchange (MACECE) made every effort to facilitate my research, while the directors and staff at the Direction des archives royales (Mudīrīya al-Wathā'iq al-Malakīya), the Bibliothèque générale (al-Khizānat al-ʿāmma), and the Bibliothèque royale (al-Khizānat al-Ḥasanīya) welcomed me with open archives. When the libraries were closed, Khalid Ben Srhir had the patience and good humor to teach me how to decipher the documents I'd found in these places. Ahmed Toufiq likewise made his good offices available to me on several occasions, while Sion Assidon helped me trace the etymology of Moroccan Jewish names and provided his unique insight into their bearers' histories. In Marrakesh, Jacky Kadoch, president of the Jewish community of Marrakesh-Essaouira, provided his full cooperation with this project, the importance of which cannot be overestimated. Whatever sense of place I have managed to convey in the following pages is owed in no small part to him. With Jacky's introduction, the inhabitants of Marrakesh opened doors both real and figurative to the *mellah* and let me gaze in. I am grateful to them and hope that this book in some small way honors their forebears. The mayor of Marrakesh, Mr. Omar El Jazouli, allowed me to sit in on meetings about urban renewal programs for the former Jewish quarter, while the architects and planners of the Marrakesh branch of the Agence urbaine and the Etablissement régional d'aménagement et de construction du Tensift graciously shared their expertise (as well as their maps) on several occasions.

My research in France was greatly facilitated by the staffs of the Bibliothèque nationale, the Archives du ministère des affaires étrangères, and especially the Library of the Alliance israélite universelle, whose director, M. Jean-Claude Kuperminc, helped me appreciate the almost overwhelming complexity of the relationship between Moroccan Jewry and this important institution. The capable staffs at the Public Records Office, the British Library, the Greater London Records Office, and Southampton University (where the records of the Anglo-Jewish Association are kept) ensured that my research in England was equally productive. In Israel, the librarians at Tel Aviv University and Hebrew University were most helpful, as were those of the Central Archive for the History of the Jewish People and especially the Ben Zvi Institute, most notably Robert Attal. Shlomo Elbaz was kind enough to spend an afternoon with me in Jerusalem recalling the Marrakesh *mellah* of his youth.

Financial support for this project came from the Moroccan Studies Program at Harvard University, the Fulbright-Hays Program of the U.S. Department of Education, and a Schmidt/American Historical Association African Studies grant. The completion of the manuscript was accomplished with a grant from the American Institute for Maghrib Studies. For its institutional support, I would like to recognize the Center for Middle Eastern Studies at U.C. Berkeley, and especially its chair, my friend and colleague Nezar AlSayyad, who has helped me try to articulate my understanding of space and cities despite my regrettable weaknesses in the field of architectural history. My colleagues in the field of Moroccan Jewish studies, Daniel Schroeter and Sarah Levin, deserve my warmest thanks for their endless supplies of goodwill, stray documents, gentle critiques, and prized tidbits of information on the most obscure of topics. Jonathan Zatlin read drafts of some chapters and offered useful comments. Dale Eickelman was a generous and kind reviewer whose suggestions helped improve this work on many levels. Mark Tessler and Janet Rabinowitch at Indiana University Press have been wonderfully supportive editors, while Miki Bird and Shoshanna Green have gently pushed me to confront my inconsistencies, at least in prose and citations. For help with the illustrations, I am indebted to Varun Kapur and Lily Cooc. Finally, I owe a tremendous and unrepayable debt of gratitude to my parents, for whom education has always been what matters most. I dedicate this book to them. I thank Albert for help with the correct placement of French accents and for carrying my books across several continents, repeatedly. And to Magda and Solal, the apples of my eye: I thank you for lending meaning to it all.

NOTE ON TRANSLITERATION, SPELLING, AND USAGE

The question of language is always a difficult one for scholars of Moroccan history, especially Moroccan Jewish history, who must contend not only with the usual blurry distinctions between Modern Standard Arabic and regional dialects but also with well-established French transliteration systems and Jewish accents on all of the above. Moreover, since the sources on which this study draws were written in several different languages and at different time periods, the renderings of the names of people and places, as well as technical terms, vary quite a bit in the original texts consulted. My solution, such as it is, has been to strive for consistency while still honoring established traditions of nomenclature in the field.

For the transliteration of Arabic terms, I have followed the *International Journal of Middle Eastern Studies,* while for Hebrew terms I have followed the Library of Congress, though I have omitted the "h" at the end of a word corresponding to the Hebrew letter "hé." With the exception of the ayn ʿ and the hamza ʾ, I have dispensed with all diacritical marks in the transliterations of personal and place names, which are, anyway, typically rendered in Moroccan Arabic dialect, in Judeo-Arabic, or in a combination thereof. (The names of authors of works in Arabic or Hebrew cited here are fully transliterated according to how they appear on the original work, however.) Terms well known in the French scholarship remain in their most familiar forms (for example, *mellah* rather than the Arabic transliteration *millāḥ* or *mallāḥ,* and *dahir* instead of *zahir*), as do recognized family names like Glaoui, Ghanjaoui, and Corcos. The words "ibn" in Arabic and "ben" in Hebrew, meaning "son of," are abbreviated as "b." when found in the middle of a name. For the sake of simplicity, terms that will be familiar to most readers are neither transliterated nor italicized, thus "medina" instead of "*madīna,*" and "Kasbah" instead of "*qaṣba.*" For words common to scholarship in the English language, (American) English spellings will be used in the place of French or Arabic spellings (Marrakesh instead of Marrakech or Marrākush, Fez instead of Fès or Fās), while place names will be given according to contemporary Moroccan usage (Essaouira rather than Mogador).

All translations from other languages into English are my own unless otherwise indicated.

The *Mellah* of Marrakesh

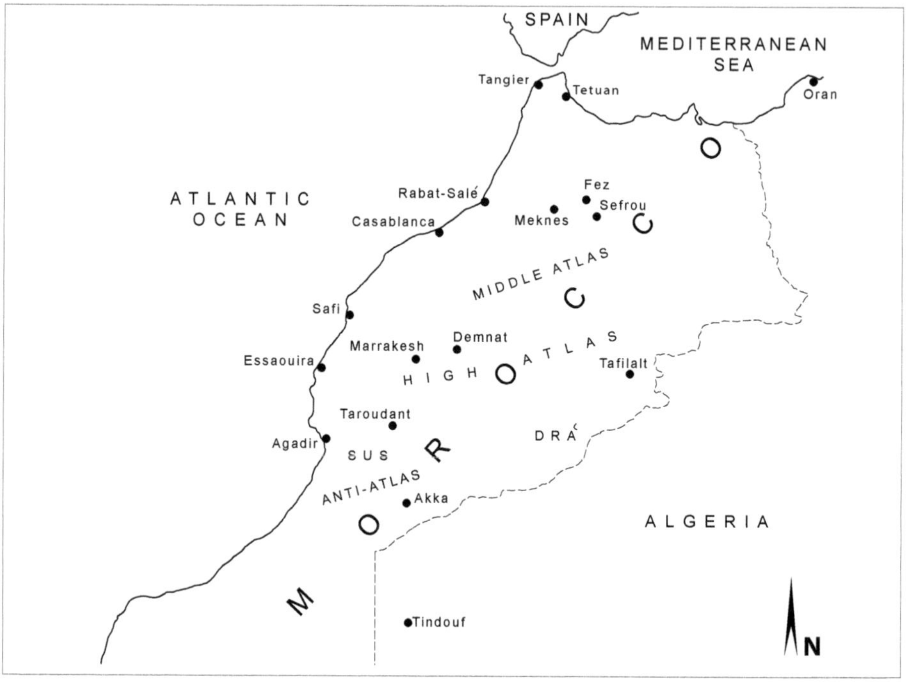

Figure i.1. Map of Morocco.

Introduction

The Jewish Quarter and the Moroccan Whole

In December of 1863, Moses Montefiore, the prominent British philanthropist, statesman, and self-styled defender of world Jewry, came to Morocco. Like his several previous trips to the Muslim world, his current visit was motivated by reports of the severe mistreatment of his coreligionists. In this instance, three Jews from the coastal town of Safi had been falsely accused of conspiring to murder a Spanish tax collector. By the time Sir Moses arrived on the scene, one of the men had been publicly executed in the main marketplace of Tangier, while the remaining two awaited judgment in the city's Kasbah.[1] Montefiore, thanks no doubt to his great diplomatic skills, was able to secure the prisoners' freedom after just one brief meeting with the Spanish consul. He then headed south to Marrakesh to plead the case of Moroccan Jews more generally at the royal court, where his efforts once again met with success: Sultan Muhammad IV was persuaded to enact a *dahir* (royal edict) ensuring that his Jewish subjects would henceforth be protected from oppression in accordance with Islamic law.[2] And so a satisfied Sir Moses returned home to England.

The Montefiore visit is often seen as a watershed in Moroccan Jewish history in that it set into motion a pattern of foreign diplomatic pressure intertwined with European Jewish concerns that would serve as a backdrop to Jewish-Muslim relations in Morocco from that point onward. Aside from its broader ramifications, however, Montefiore's visit also left its mark—in some sense quite literally—on an altogether more local level. For while in Marrakesh, Montefiore, despite being Jewish (not to mention of probable Moroccan descent[3]), opted not to reside in a house in the city's Jewish quarter that had been prepared for him and his (Christian) physician companion, Thomas Hodgkin, as would have been customary for foreigners, and especially a foreign Jew. Instead the two men stayed in a much finer house in the medina, the Muslim residential and commercial area. In so doing, however, they transgressed a fundamental rule of the so-called Islamic city: the segregation of non-Muslims from the living spaces of the Muslim population. The entrance to the house in question was accordingly sealed up upon Montefiore's departure, as "a house in which Jews or Christians had lived was regarded as unclean and unfit for the dwelling of a true believer."[4]

The term "Islamic city" as invoked above refers to the model developed in the 1920s and onward by colonial (mainly French) urbanists to describe the defining characteristics of cities in the Middle East and North Africa, implicitly if not explicitly in contrast to European cities.[5] Among its central tenets is that Islam, understood as a fundamentally urban religion, gave rise to cities whose morphologies were determined primarily by Muslims' need to fulfill the religious obligations of Islam. Thus a "real" city can be identified as such by the presence of institutions like a Friday mosque (*jāmiʿ*) for conducting prayers, communal baths (*ḥammām*) for maintaining ritual purity, and a market complex (*sūq*) in which are located the various "guilds," organized and regulated according to religious strictures. No less critical to the model's coherence than the presence of these institutions is the corresponding *absence* of any significant non-Muslim influence on city life. Such explanations for how cities look and function the way they do falter, however, when confronted with the long and multilayered history of Jews in Morocco. As the country's only surviving indigenous religious minority, Jews historically constituted up to (and in some locations more than) half the urban population and were by all accounts highly assimilated into Moroccan economic, social, and even political life. While such circumstances make it difficult to ignore Moroccan Jews' potential for historical agency, there nonetheless exists in Morocco an important institution to which one could point in order to restore a degree of analytic integrity to the "Islamic city," and particularly its insistence on the supposed marginality of non-Muslims. This institution is the *mellah*,[6] the walled Jewish quarter.

Despite its frequent comparison to the European ghetto (see below), the *mellah* is a purely Moroccan invention, indeed so much so that it has come to be synonymous with Moroccan Jewry itself, even though not all Moroccan cities actually contained one.[7] Walled Jewish quarters first appeared in the royal capitals, beginning with Fez in 1438, followed by Marrakesh in the sixteenth century, Meknes in the seventeenth century, and several smaller towns in the early nineteenth century. In each of these locations, the impetus for relocating the local Jewish community from religiously mixed neighborhoods to a separate quarter and the degree to which the new *mellah* then became integrated into urban life had everything to do with immediate exigencies and local circumstances and relatively little to do with defined Islamic precepts as such. (Muslim jurists themselves disagree widely on the matter of non-Muslim segregation, with some arguing that it is precisely through close, daily contact with Muslims that religious minorities can be induced to convert to Islam.[8]) But such discrepancies were of little concern to proponents of the "Islamic city." For them, the *mellah,* with its thick walls and gate that was locked nightly and throughout the Jewish Sabbath,[9] lent the appearance of strict non-Muslim isolation that made the corresponding myth of religious homogeneity, and hence "Islamic" agency in the ordering of the cityscape, possible. With the image of the *mellah* as a socially and physically introverted entity thus firmly imposed from without, it is not surprising that most studies of Jewish-Muslim relations in Morocco find their evidence outside the supposed isolation of the Jewish quarter (to the extent that this relationship is treated in structural as opposed to purely social terms at all, that is[10]), focusing on the minority group's acculturation into the broader parameters of Moroccan Muslim society, a process whose outcome is typically referred to as "symbiosis" or "syncretism." While Jews' usage and understanding of Muslim space is undoubtedly a significant factor in the history of Jewish-Muslim relations in Morocco and will be dealt with at some length here, it is only in relation to its complement—namely, Muslim usage and understanding of Jewish space (about which we know almost nothing in Morocco or elsewhere for that matter)—that the purported marginality of the *mellah* can be disproved. Nowhere is this more crucial than in Marrakesh, home to Morocco's largest Jewish community for most of its history, and where the Muslim presence in the *mellah* was often greater, in terms of both number and significance, than the Jewish presence in the medina.

The history that unfolds in the coming pages is that of a *mellah* fully invested with meaning as Jewish space and just as fully integrated into its urban setting. Following a model of concentric circles, chapter 1 will attempt to answer some of the fundamental questions related to the *mellah*'s origins. It will use a combination of Jewish oral and written sources, Arabic chronicles, travel narratives, and European captives' diaries to delve into the circumstances of Jewish life in sixteenth-century Marrakesh prior to the creation of the *mellah,* asking in particular what factors may have contributed to such an innovation and how it was explained or understood by its protagonists, Jews and Muslims alike, as well as by subsequent scholars. Within this context the larger question of periodization in Moroccan Jewish history is also raised. Slowly, a portrait of the *mellah* in the early years of its existence will begin to emerge: what did the *mellah* look like, smell like, and feel like? Close attention will be paid to its physical form, particularly in relation to the rest of the city, and how this form in turn influenced social relations among Jews within the *mellah* and between Jews and their Muslim neighbors. This portrait will serve as a basis for reading changes to the *mellah*'s environment in subsequent chapters. It also, incidentally, provides a means for comparing the nascent European ghetto with a contemporary example of a closed Jewish quarter in the Islamic world, though that topic shall not be of particular concern here.[11]

Chapter 2 augments the physical portrait of the *mellah* that has begun to take shape with important demographic information. Relying on an 1890 census of the Marrakesh *mellah*, I challenge common understandings of Moroccan Jewish population movements in the late nineteenth century while at the same time shedding important light on domestic arrangements in the *mellah*, including patterns of habitation, property ownership, and the problem of densification. Moving into the second circle, encompassing the relationship between the *mellah* and the Makhzan (the Moroccan government and administration), symbolically if not always physically located in the adjacent Kasbah, I link the overcrowded *mellah* to the larger crises facing the Moroccan state in the pre-Protectorate era, primarily during the reign of the sultan Mawlay Hassan (r. 1873–1894).

The city as a whole is the subject of chapters 3 and 4. Within this sphere, the notion of Jewish-Muslim "commensality"[12] in Morocco is reconsidered from the perspective of Muslim usages and understandings of Jewish space and vice versa. Beginning with the former, I show how the *mellah* fulfilled a necessary function in the daily lives of the inhabitants of Marrakesh as a liminal space where illicit activities could be pursued. Liminality worked in the other direction as well. While the city's Jews pursued many beneficial activities in the medina, particularly in the area of commerce, they nonetheless often held strongly negative feelings about Muslim space. Reflective of more than typical biases toward the "Other," these feelings developed directly out of specific experiences of inter-communal relations in Marrakesh. However, this mutual ambivalence was to a great extent counterbalanced by a shared sense of what it meant to be "*Marrākshī*." The basis for this identity and the extent to which local Jews participated in its formation will also be considered.

The last in the series of concentric circles encompasses the hinterland around Marrakesh (chapter 5). With Morocco's rural inhabitants constituting a full 89 percent of the country's total population at the beginning of the Protectorate era,[13] it is in many ways the most important. The Hawz plain in which Marrakesh sits and the High Atlas Mountains that border the city to the south and southeast were (and remain) areas of tremendous vitality. The Arab and Berber tribes of these areas, including the Ahmar, the Rehamna, the Sgharna, the Amizmiz, and the Misfiwa, along with the so-called Lords of the Atlas: the Goundafa, the Glaoua, and the M'tougga, were heavily involved in the life of the southern capital. While their dramatic (and frequent) attacks on the city naturally caught the notice of foreign observers, not all rural interaction with the city was hostile. Members of tribes came to

Marrakesh to visit the lodges of the religious brotherhoods (*zāwīyas*) with which they were affiliated,[14] to engage in the Moroccan pastime of *shirāʾ wa bayaʿ* (buying and selling), or simply for purposes of leisure, to amuse themselves at the never-ending carnival at Marrakesh's great plaza, the Jmaʿ al-Fna. The French historian Jean-Louis Miège described the special pull of Marrakesh on its rural neighbors:

> In the veneration the countryman feels for Marrakesh, there is the prestige the city always has for those who live in the country and also the respect for authority and for God. What attracts him is the all powerful chief whose sway extends over the far, distant country, the pasha[15] to whom all the upper country is submitted and the minaret and the most marvelous of mosques; then, too, there are the souk and the hope of driving a bargain and the city of sin, for Marrakesh is a city for pleasure.[16]

The tribes' contacts with the Jews of the *mellah* were likewise multifaceted. Such contacts were pursued sometimes in Marrakesh itself but also in the countryside, where Jews from the southern capital regularly traveled for reasons of commerce and pilgrimage. There they also met with their rural coreligionists, including members of some of the oldest Jewish settlements in Morocco, who date their arrival in the region to the destruction of the First Temple in the sixth century BCE, well before the introduction of Islam into North Africa. Small towns and villages like Demnat, Qalʿa, Intifa, Aghmat, Asni, Zagora, and Taroudant each contained dozens, and in some cases hundreds, of Jewish families. These satellite communities were officially linked to the Marrakesh *mellah* through their mutual submission to the same authority, the pasha of the Kasbah of Marrakesh.[17] Less officially, they also looked to their coreligionists in Marrakesh to supply them with everything from spouses and educations in normal times to food and refuge in times of upheaval. The great French historian of Marrakesh, Gaston Deverdun, has described the southern capital as "a closed city of Islam" permanently separated from the hostile countryside by its walls.[18] Yet the sustained interaction of the tribes and rural Jews of the Marrakesh hinterland with the denizens of the city's *mellah* suggests something quite different.

WHY MARRAKESH?

Soon after its founding in 1070,[19] Marrakesh emerged as the capital of the Moroccan south. Its location at the intersection of the major long-distance routes destined it to become an important trade emporium, especially with the demise of Sijilmasa in the sixteenth century, when it became the northern point for trans-Saharan caravan trade with Timbuktu. Marrakesh was also an intellectual center, boasting the Yusufiya, one of Morocco's two great mosque-universities, and claiming Averroes (Ibn Rushd) as an early visitor, who no doubt met with his contemporary the philosopher (and Marrakesh resident) Abubacer (Ibn Tufayl). And of course Marrakesh was a royal capital (*madīna makhzanīya*), with all the pomp and circumstance that the sultan's residence commanded. Marrakesh was no less important in the Jewish microcosm. As Morocco's largest city, Marrakesh was correspondingly home to the country's largest Jewish community, with late nineteenth-century observers estimating that Jews constituted up to one-third of the total population.[20] Though the Sephardic rite was not unknown in Marrakesh, local Jewish identity was for the most part unencumbered by the extra-Moroccan nostalgia that pulled at the *expulsado* communities to the north, and instead remained deeply rooted in the local Arab-Berber milieu. Jews' sense of being *Marrākshī* manifested itself in nearly all aspects of life, from the consistent use of Arabic and Berber[21] (as opposed to Hakétiya, the North African Judeo-Spanish dialect spoken by Jews in Morocco's northern towns) to reverence for the region's saints and holy figures (Muslim and Jewish alike), deep involvement in municipal politics, and the *mellah*'s high level of integration into the larger city. While many of these traits have been identified among the small Jewish conglomerations of the Atlas Mountains and pre-Saharan oases,[22] the imbrication of Jewish institutions and practices in Muslim social, religious, and economic space—and vice versa—has yet to be systematically investigated on the larger urban scale.[23]

Marrakesh also provides an excellent setting for addressing issues left unresolved by the "Islamic City" debates of the last several decades, in particular the influence of affinity groups on the shaping of city life. When it comes to the question of Jewish space, the most common approach is to conflate the *mellah* with the European ghetto. In such instances, the term "ghetto" and the European paradigm for Jewish-gentile relations it invokes is meant to reinforce the idea of the *mellah* as literally a form of punishment, created to "penalize" Jews for their "vulnerability and unpopularity."[24] Correspondingly, the narratives of Moroccan Jewish history that grow out of this approach are ones of degradation, though mitigated slightly by the economic benefits that accrue to the communities' elites as a result of their service to the royal court. The various deficiencies of the ghetto model as applied to a Moroccan context are beyond the scope of the current study. Suffice it to say that very little in the history of the Marrakesh *mellah*, either in terms of its origins, accruing history, or the patterns of Jewish-gentile relations that emerged there, conforms to any of its basic tenets. A more fruitful approach, I think, begins with the recognition that Moroccan society (like any society) acts on its environment in real, readable ways, one of which is the disposition of space. The ethnic quarter, long considered the foundation of city life in the Islamic world, is one such space, and of the twenty-four quarters (*ḥawmāt*) that made up Marrakesh during this period, none was more conspicuously ethnic than the *mellah*, particularly insofar as Jews were the city's only non-Muslim minority. Thus an inquiry into the circumstances of the *mellah*'s creation, subsequent alterations to its form, and its linkages to the rest of the city and the wider region not only reveals valuable information about the historical relationship between Jews and Muslims (as well as some Christians) in a fascinating setting, it also shows how the *mellah*—the concrete expression of that relationship—was constructed, understood, and accommodated in Morocco. To the extent that the *mellah* can then be read as a manifestation of the underlying social order of the Moroccan city, Jewish space is revealed as a typical, and not exceptional or aberrational, expression of the latter's logic.

In the process of presenting a more holistic treatment of so-called ethnic quarters in the Islamic world, perhaps some small part of a vibrant Jewish past will likewise be reintegrated into the history of this majestic Moroccan city, a city now almost entirely devoid of Jews. A particularly significant juncture in that history is the late nineteenth and early twentieth century, the end part of what Francophone historians call the "*longue dix-neuvième,*" when Moroccan society began experiencing the full impact of European imperialism. Almost no area of life was left undisturbed by the profound transformations that took place in Morocco during these decades. As Muhammad al-Nasiri, nineteenth-century Morocco's pre-eminent historian, put it at the time,

> We must note that the situation the present generation has come to find is entirely different from that of the previous generation. Everywhere the habits of the people have been turned upside down. The customs and practices of merchants and craftspeople have been altered in all ways, including the way they do business, earn and handle money, price goods and manage other types of expenditure. The primary cause of this state of affairs is the meddling of the Frenchmen and other foreigners with the population. Their habits smash violently into ours, and in the clash their ways defeat and absorb ours.[25]

Moroccan Jews found themselves deeply implicated in this "clash of civilizations." With their knowledge of foreign languages, extensive transnational economic and social networks, and aspirations for improved civil status,[26] they were the perfect intermediaries between the Europeans—who lacked sufficient local knowledge—and the Muslims with whom the Jews had lived in the closest proximity for centuries. Jews quickly found themselves disproportionately represented among the translators, agents, servants, and representatives of foreign powers. Their service in these capacities often earned them the much-coveted protégé status, providing them with immunity from the Moroccan government in most tax and judicial matters. The protégé system originated with the French-Moroccan commercial treaty of 1767, and eventually expanded to include most of the Western legations in Tangier, who used it to extend their own extraterritorial rights to local designates working in the legations and consulates or as employees of foreign busi-

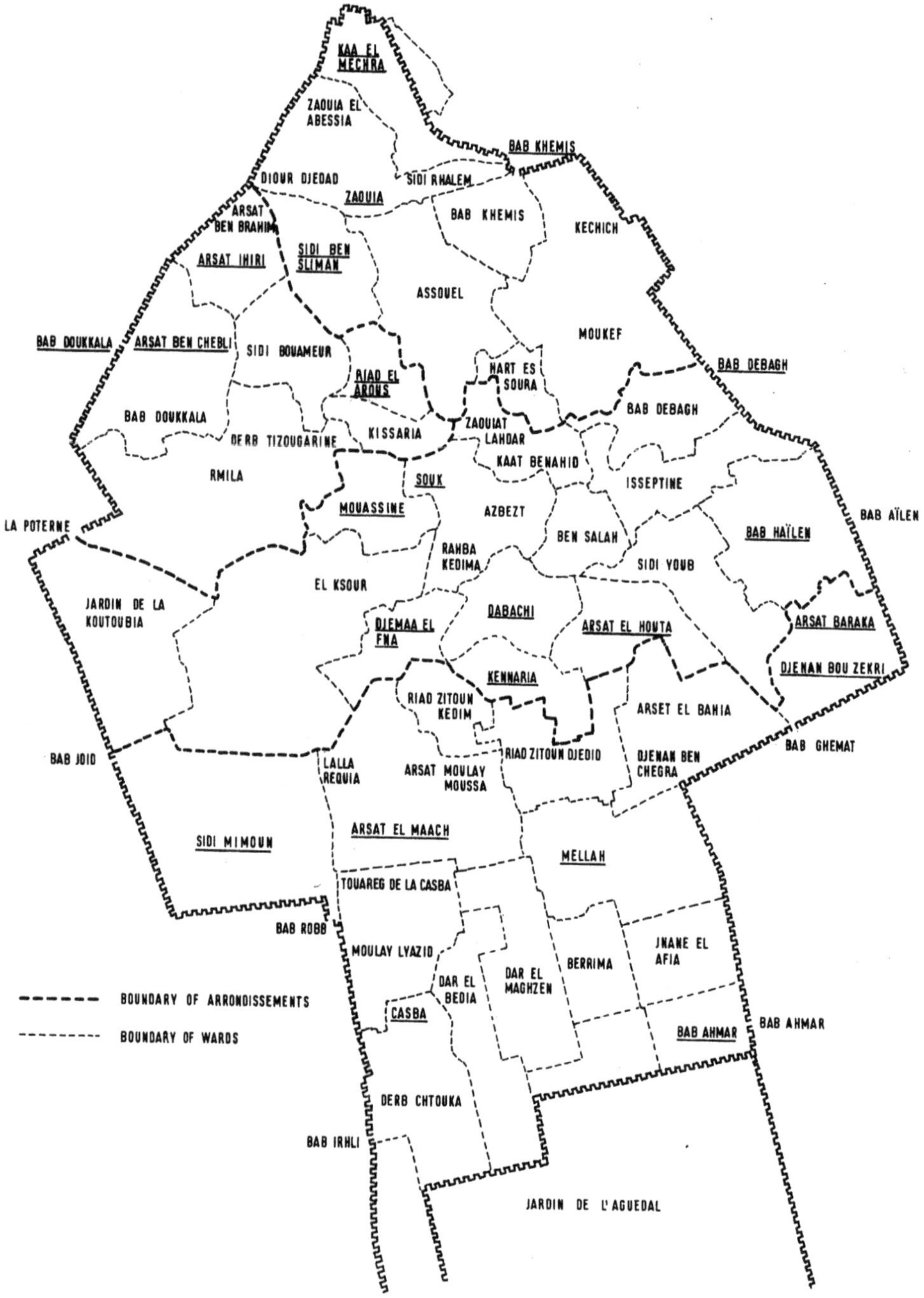

Figure i.2. Municipal divisions of Marrakesh. From Friedrich Schwerdtfeger, *Traditional Housing in African Cities* (New York: J. Wiley, 1982).

nessmen.[27] Despite multiple attempts at reforming the various abuses associated with the protégé system (most notably in the Tangier convention of 1863 and the Madrid convention of 1880), there was ultimately little will for enforcement, and its corrosion of Moroccan independence went largely unchecked. While it is true that Moroccan Jews were often the beneficiaries of the protégé system, it is also the case that being granted extraterritoriality but left physically in place ended up wreaking a sort of existential havoc with their sense of identity. In particular, the jealousy their special status inspired worked to the detriment of Jewish-Muslim relations such that when French rule over Morocco came to an end in 1956, Jews were perceived by many of their neighbors (and sometimes even by themselves) as being somehow less than fully Moroccan.

The cultural gap between Jews and Muslims was further widened by the "civilizing" efforts of European Jewish organizations, through whose efforts Jews became the first recipients of Western-style educations in pre-Protectorate Morocco, which included the French language and training in "modern" disciplines and vocations.[28] The organization that had by far the greatest influence on Moroccan Jews was the Alliance Israélite Universelle. Founded in 1860 in Paris by a group of liberal Jews, many of whom were originally from the Alsace region, the A.I.U. had as its mission nothing less than the intellectual, religious, and social regeneration of Jews in non-Westernized countries. Implicit in its platform lay the largely unstated goal of easing these Jews' own assimilation into European society by erasing any signs of "backwardness" among the "primitive" Jews living in parts of the world with which the colonial powers were increasingly coming into contact, lest any association be made between the two groups of Jews. In other words, the A.I.U. sought to de-Orientalize these communities, and by so doing de-Orientalize themselves as well.[29] To these ends, it opened modern schools throughout the Middle East, North Africa, the Balkans, and Eastern Europe. The A.I.U. opened its first school in Tetuan in 1862 and maintained a keen interest in Morocco throughout its history, eventually operating a total of eighty-three schools there, more than in all other countries combined.[30] The aspirations of the A.I.U. extended well beyond the classroom, however, with its teachers and directors constantly striving to inculcate Moroccan Jewish families with contemporary European ideas about hygiene, dress, and the practice of religion.

The improved ties to Europe and individual Europeans that came about during this period were generally encouraged by Jews living in Morocco's coastal towns, for whom commercial and consular relations with foreign powers were nothing new. Not only did such arrangements offer them immediate economic benefits, but the new closeness was also seen as a stepping-stone toward the ultimate goal of attaining European citizenship, particularly after Algerian Jews were granted French nationality en masse by the Crémieux decree of 1870. The situation, however, was significantly different in the interior of Morocco, where contact with outsiders, whether Christian or Jewish, came much later and was more limited. This was especially so in the royal capital of Marrakesh. Until 1867, individual European visitors were not even allowed to enter the city without the permission of the sultan, which was not always forthcoming. (Some foreigners, including the French explorer Charles de Foucauld, sought to circumvent the Makhzan's authority by disguising themselves as Eastern European Jews, who apparently cut less threatening figures than foreign Christians.) When Marrakesh began slowly opening to the West in the latter half of the century, few Europeans visited it, and even fewer sought to establish themselves there on a semi-permanent basis as they were beginning to do in other Moroccan cities. Those who did venture to Marrakesh were taken aback by the cold welcome they received from the denizens of the *mellah,* who treated even foreign Jews with suspicion. As the French observer Eugene Aubin observed in a passage about the southern capital,

> In the Maghreb the orthodoxy of the Jews is as strict and conservative as that of the Mohammedans. Religious forms are observed with the most fanatical ardour . . . This uncompromising religious attitude makes the Moroccan Jews as suspicious of Christians as they are of the Jews of other countries. The foreigner is looked upon, in the Mellahs as in the Medinas, with no kindly eye, and is forbidden to enter the synagogue, as he is forbidden to enter the mosque.[31]

Ethnographic descriptions of Moroccan Jews that emphasize their subjects' supposed xenophobia, like this one, have been shown to be parallels of common anti-Semitic tropes of the period.[32] With this in mind, it may be worth emphasizing that my point about the wariness Marrakesh's Jews showed toward foreigners is a relative one, and is intended as part of a larger corrective to the frequent blurring together of different Jewish communities in Morocco into a composite whole, i.e., a generalized "*mellah* society"[33] that does not take regional variations sufficiently into account. Thus the attitude of Jews in Marrakesh toward outsiders helps explain the great difficulty experienced by the A.I.U. in gaining a foothold in the southern capital compared to the coastal towns. From the arrival of its first emissary in Marrakesh, the Orientalist Joseph Halévy, in 1876, a full quarter of a century would pass—until nearly four decades after the first A.I.U. school opened in Morocco—before the A.I.U. would succeed in establishing a school in the southern capital. This came in December of 1900 under the directorship of Moïse Levy, soon joined by Messody Coriat to supervise the girls' school. Yet local Jews remained at best aloof from the institution, and at times violently opposed to it. Within a year of the school's opening, a special Saturday guard had to be hired to protect the school from Jews who took to laying siege to it.[34] As this and similar incidents show, Jews in Marrakesh were extremely ambivalent about growing European influence over Morocco. As I argue in the coming chapters, such ambivalence is in part traceable to the durability of traditional spatial and related social arrangements. Despite periodic modifications to the urban fabric, the blueprint for inter-communal relations, inscribed within the space of the city itself, allowed for long-established patterns of Jewish-Muslim exchange to persevere much longer in Marrakesh than they did in many other parts of Morocco, particularly the coastal towns, where they more quickly fell victim to the pressures and strategies of European colonialism. The current study will attempt to redraw some of the major aspects of this blueprint by outlining where and to what effect such exchanges took place in and around the *mellah* of Marrakesh during its four-hundred-year history, revising, in the process, what is at the very least an anachronistic assumption: that all Moroccan Jewish communities unequivocally supported the colonial project in the pre-Protectorate period.

1

Mellahization

The Juderea is also, as it were,
a citie of itselfe, where dwell the Jewes.
John Smith, English merchant in Marrakesh, 1604

In the summer of 1555, in compliance with a papal bull, the ghetto of Rome was created. Within less than half a decade, across the Mediterranean in the great, dry plain of the Hawz, the Jews of Marrakesh met a fate not unlike that of their Roman coreligionists when they too were transferred to their own "city within a city." Located where the royal stables had once stood, the new walled Jewish quarter of Marrakesh was in fact the second of its kind in Morocco after that of Fez, founded in 1438. Like its predecessor, the new Jewish quarter in Marrakesh was also called a "*mellah*," a name that originally referred to the salt-marsh area to which the Jews of the northern Moroccan capital had been transferred. Interestingly, the Roman ghetto had similarly inherited its name from its predecessor, the Venetian foundry (*getto* or *ghetto*) where a policy of Jewish confinement had been put into official practice in 1516. The two terms continued to follow parallel trajectories, moreover, with "ghetto" and "*mellah*" each eventually becoming a generic term for a Jewish quarter within their respective environments.

While such parallels may be striking, their significance should not be overstated. For just as Rome is not Marrakesh, the *mellah* is not a ghetto. The analogy often drawn between the two overlooks profound differences separating the North African Jewish experience from the European one, most notably the stark contrast between the Islamic principle of tolerance, formulated in the Pact of ʿUmar in the seventh century and known in Arabic as "*dhimma*,"[1] and Christian Europe's formative theological bias against its Jewish subjects. At the same time, it is important to recognize that Jewish quarters within the Islamic world, and even within Morocco itself, vary greatly in their spatial attributes, patterns of inter- and intra-communal relations, and social and economic development. While many recognizable continuities cut across Moroccan Jewish society, each of Morocco's *mellah*s (and by the early 1900s most Moroccan towns had one) was nonetheless created at a specific time and place and evolved according to local and regional exigencies. Understanding this process begins with understanding the origins of each *mellah*.

Prior to the founding of Marrakesh, Jews lived in the village of Aghmat Aylan, the one-time capital of the Rehamna tribe, about eight miles southeast of the city's future site. The first Jewish inhabitants of Marrakesh probably came from Aghmat and other nearby villages, though it is unclear exactly when they were allowed to settle in the city definitively,[2] and whether they were subsequently banished under the Almohads (Ar. *al-Muwaḥḥidūn*, 1147–1269), who rejected the concept of *dhimma* toleration altogether. By the Saʿdi period (1511–1659), however, it is clear that Jews were well-established residents of the Marrakesh medina. As indicated above, they were transferred to their new quarter a century or so after a similar event took place in Fez, within a few years of the establishment of the Roman ghetto, and during the reign of the Saʿdi dynasty in Morocco. But when exactly? Since the Moroccan chroniclers are all but silent on the subject of the *mellah* (as they are on most aspects of Jewish history), a good place to start is with the accounts of foreign visitors to Marrakesh during this period, beginning with the famous voyager Leo Africanus.[3]

Leo came to Marrakesh at least twice during his travels to Africa, in 1511–1512 and 1514–1515, and both times was struck by evidence of the city's being ravaged by war and famine. In fact, it seemed to Leo that Marrakesh had more ruins to its name than people:

> The city is sparsely populated. Only with great difficulty is one able to reach [the Kutubiya], because of the ruins of buildings blocking the route. The poor city is two-thirds uninhabited. One can truly say it has grown old before its time.[4]

Although Leo's comments may partly reflect elitist attitudes toward the south typical of a one-time denizen of Fez (he emphasizes the fact that there was only one bookstore in the city, and also that the sole professor to be found at the local *madrasa* [college] was "crassly ignorant"[5]) population decline and general decay were nevertheless real phenomena in early sixteenth-century Marrakesh. The power vacuum left by the Almohads and especially the misrule of the city by the Hintata emirs had all but devastated the city.[6] At the time of Leo's visit, Marrakesh had yet to recover. The revitalization and reordering of Marrakesh by the Saʿdis, in which the mellahization of the Jews was to play an important part, still lay several decades in the future. Accordingly, the Jews Leo encountered in and around Marrakesh appeared far from "contained." Among the more flagrant violations of *dhimma* precepts Leo witnessed was the freedom with which the Jewish mercenaries of tribal chiefs rode on horseback through the countryside, carrying arms.[7]

Jumping ahead a few decades from Leo, the respective works of Marmol and Torres,[8] classics of Spanish literature on the early modern Maghreb, bring us slightly closer to determining a date for the creation of the Marrakesh *mellah.* Luis del Marmol Carvajal left his home in 1535 to fight in the African Regiments with the Hapsburg king Charles V. A short time thereafter he was captured by corsairs off the coast of Tunisia, and like all captives seized in military encounters, he automatically became the property of the Moroccan state.[9] So it was as the prisoner of the Saʿdi sultan Ahmad al-Aʿraj that Marmol came to Marrakesh, where he spent at least the period 1541–1542 out of a total captivity of nearly eight years. When he was finally ransomed, Marmol chose to remain in Africa, improving the Arabic he had learned during his imprisonment and traveling widely to gather material for his *Descripción general de Africa.*[10] He returned to Spain to begin writing his work sometime around 1570.

Diego de Torres arrived in Marrakesh in 1546 charged with ransoming captives in the name of the Portuguese king. He remained there until 1550, possibly overlapping with Marmol's period of captivity. Like Marmol, Torres also learned Arabic, and was mostly on good terms with the new sultan, Muhammad al-Shaykh. Nonetheless, the sultan's son had Torres arrested for unpaid debts and sent to Taroudant as a prisoner. Upon Torres's release in 1553, he again passed through Marrakesh en route to Fez, where he stayed on for another year before returning to Spain.[11] The book based on his experiences was written sometime between his return to Spain and a later mission to Morocco in 1577. It was dedicated to Don Sebastian, and was meant to provide strategic information for the upcoming "Battle of the Three Kings," in which Torres himself took part. Portugal's defeat in 1578 delayed its publication until 1586.[12] In 1667 a French edition of his work appeared as the third volume of a translation of Marmol's *Descripción* under the title *Histoire des cherifs.*[13]

The significance of these two works for present purposes lies in the fact that in both cases the author resided in Marrakesh *before* the *mellah*'s creation, while the writing and publication of each book took place *after* it, upon the author's return to Europe (1554 in the case of Torres, c. 1570 in the case of Marmol). Such a dramatic change in the city's topography is naturally commented upon in the two works, providing useful chronological brackets for the creation of the *mellah.* A brief examination of the relevant passages will help clarify this point.

No *mellah* existed during Marmol's stay in Marrakesh during the early 1540s. Rather, Marmol tells us that at that time the local Jews inhabited more than three thousand households in the center of the city, that is, in the medina.[14] Nor did a *mellah* exist in 1553, the date of Torres's last glimpse of Marrakesh. He says that there were in fact two Jewish neighborhoods[15] in the medina at the time of his stay, comprising more than a thousand inhabitants.[16] While Marrakesh did not have a *mellah* when Torres departed in 1553, by the time he finally sat down to write, that was clearly no longer the case:

> [The sultan] ordered the creation of an enclosed *judéria* in a desolate area inside the city near the gate leading to Fez [to accommodate] more than two thousand inhabitants, so that the Jews would all live together, as in my time they lived in different Jewish neighborhoods and among the Moors.[17]

This same pattern is apparent in Marmol's *Descripción*, where the author appends the following statement to his earlier remarks: "The prince who reigns today [Mawlay al-Ghalib, see below] transferred the Jews out of the medina in order to separate them from the Muslim population."[18] Thus one can assume that the Marrakesh *mellah* was created sometime between 1553 and 1573, the former date marking the date of Torres's final departure from the city, the latter that of the publication of Marmol's book, the first of the two works to appear in print. Within this range, 1557 and 1560 are the years most often cited by scholars as the definitive date of the *mellah*'s creation. It remains to weigh their relative merits by investigating the particular foundation myths to which each date corresponds.

1557 AND JEWISH MEMORY

> This city is obviously the work of great masters.
>
> Luis del Marmol Carvajal, 1573

The Jews of Marrakesh have remembered and passed down their experience of mellahization exclusively in the form of oral narratives. Though the details of the story may vary in the telling, one remarkably consistent aspect is the date given for the *mellah*'s creation: 5317 in the Hebrew calendar (15 September 1556–4 September 1557 CE).[19] The following folk-tale is a typical rendition of the events. It not only reconfirms the oral date, but also hints at how the creation of the *mellah* was assimilated into some of the larger themes of Moroccan Jewish memory:

> In the year 1557 the King of Morocco turned to his vizier: "I pray you, find a suitable place in the city of Marrakesh for a new quarter for the Jews." His vizier said to him: "My Lord the King! I have a place near Tuzan al Afia [Jinan al-ʿAfiya], near the King's palace!" It came to pass that the place of residence of the Jews of Marrakesh was changed and the righteous King

> saw to it that the Jews did not lose thereby. Whoever wished to obtain a building in exchange for his own house could do so and whoever wished for money instead, could obtain it. Every man as he desired. At that time there lived in Marrakesh a widow who did not wish to leave her home and move to the new *mellah.* "I will not leave the place where my fathers and my fathers' fathers lived," she said. The King commanded that she be brought before him. "Woman! You must change the place of your residence. You must move to the new quarter!" "My lord the King!" said the woman. "I will not change the place of my residence. And if I am compelled to do so, my sin will be that of the King." "Leave her where she is," the King commanded his soldiers. "But tell me of the day of her death." When the old woman died, the Jews buried her in the cemetery, while the Moslems hurried to the King to inform him of her death. Then the King commanded: "Let the Jewess' room remain shut for ever. Let it never be opened!" And so it was. The room was closed and over the woman's grave they built a wall, which stands there to this day. And the place is still called: "The Jewess' Room."[20]

On the basis of this oral tradition, 1557 is often presented as the year of the *mellah*'s creation.[21] While the date is entirely plausible, a few notes of caution regarding it are nonetheless warranted. The first involves recognizing the special appeal that the year 1557 holds for marking transformations of the Marrakesh landscape. In other words, and especially in terms of the story above, it is worth asking which mnemonic chords the *mellah* strikes for Moroccan Jews and why. The second caveat concerns language, and is based on a discrepancy in the use of the term "*mellah*" in the Ibn Danan corpus, one of only a handful of surviving Jewish texts from the period of Saʿdi rule in Morocco.

Mawlay ʿAbdallah al-Ghalib and the Language of Monuments

An important precept in Judaism is that the law of the land is supreme; the temporal authority must be respected, even to the extent that it may contradict certain aspects of Jewish law. This attitude, combined with limited prospects for "horizontal" assimilation into broader social groups, helped foster the "vertical" relationship between Jews and rulers that is a basic characteristic of Jewish history. The paternalistic role of the ruler, whose importance was originally derived from the study of closed social corporations in feudal Europe, figures prominently in Moroccan Jewish history as well, as can be seen in the above story of the widow's room. With the exception of one Jew's opposition (and a woman's, at that), the sultan's orders were respected and, more importantly, respectable: "The righteous King saw to it that the Jews did not lose thereby." These sentiments are echoed in a second folk-tale that also takes place in Marrakesh, in which a Jew is wrongly accused of seducing a Muslim woman. He is about to be attacked by a furious mob when the sultan, who witnessed the Jew's virtue first-hand when he came to the *mellah* disguised as a beggar and received alms from him, intervenes just in time to save the Jew's life.[22] The obvious function of such stories is to reinforce Jews' allegiance to the temporal authority. But such allegiances are not unique to the Saʿdi era, nor even to Morocco. What ultimately ties the centrality of sultanic power in the worldview of Moroccan Jews to their experience of mellahization is the process by which one particular sultan, Mawlay ʿAbdallah al-Ghalib (r. 1557–1574), inscribed his authority onto the space of the city itself.

Although their close association with Jazulite Sufism and jihad against the Portuguese had won the Saʿdis the loyalty of large sectors of the local population,[23] when Mawlay al-Ghalib came to power in 1557 he was nonetheless faced with an urgent need to affirm Saʿdi rule. Most significantly, he lacked the strong tribal base that earlier Berber dynasties had been able to exploit in ruling Marrakesh, a notoriously difficult city to govern precisely because of its tribal divisions. His difficulties were compounded by nagging doubts about his dynasty's legitimacy. According to their critics, the Saʿdis were unfit to rule for the following reasons: first, their rise to power had circumvented the authority of the *ʿulamāʾ* (Muslim clerics); second, they were uncivilized as a result of their southern and rural origins; and finally, their claim to sharifism (descent from the prophet, a requirement for rule in Morocco) was seen as dubious at best.[24] The Saʿdi response to these challenges was based on counterclaims of sharifism, jihad, and mahdism. More important is how this response was articulated: namely, "*bi-lisān al-binyān,*" literally, "in the language of monuments."[25] By rebuilding Marrakesh into a spectacular capital, the Saʿdis sought to create a nucleus for their dynastic rule while also supplanting most of the city's architectural references to its Almoravid (Ar. *al-Murrābiṭ*) and Almohad past. The remarkable feat of urbanism that was required to accomplish such a program fell largely to Mawlay al-Ghalib, and it was during his rule that Marrakesh began to take on the form by which it is recognizable today. Decades before Henri IV transformed Paris through his commissioning of the Louvre, the Grand Palais, and the Hôpital Saint-Louis,[26] Mawlay al-Ghalib was busy reshaping Marrakesh with the first Saʿdi tombs, the Ibn Yusuf *madrasa* (the largest in the Maghreb at the time), and several important mosques. Among the latter, the two most notable were the mosque at Bab Dukkala, commissioned by the sultan's mother, and the mosque of the Muwwasin quarter, whose significance will be discussed in detail below. Only construction of the Badiʿ palace, painstakingly built during the years 1578–1593, was left to successors within the dynasty, though there too Mawlay al-Ghalib hand was apparent in the refurbishing of the surrounding Almohad-Almoravid Kasbah. Indeed so massive was the scope of these projects that the city was rife with rumors that Mawlay al-Ghalib had resorted to alchemy to pay for it all.[27]

There is no reason to think that the impact of Mawlay al-Ghalib's urbanism was felt any less keenly by Jews than by the rest of the city's population, and it is precisely this impact that causes the connection to be made in Jewish memory, already fixated on the centrality of sultanic authority,[28] between

Mawlay al-Ghalib's ascension to the sultanate in 1557 and the creation of the *mellah*, the Saʿdi construction that would most affect Jews' lives. For this reason, it is more than likely that 1557 resonates in Jewish memory primarily as the year when Mawlay al-Ghalib came to power. The *mellah*, meanwhile, is (literally) the concrete expression of the sultan's authority. In the absence of any external sources to confirm the oral accounts, mellahization in 1557 is best understood as a claim based on association.

On the Occurrence of the Term "Mellah" in the Ibn Danan Corpus

A second reason why 1557 cannot be considered the definitive date of the creation of the *mellah* stems from a reading of *Dibre ha-Yamim shel Fez*, a Judeo-Arabic chronicle covering the years 1552–1879 ascribed to the Ibn Danan family of Fez.[29] Specifically, discrepancies in its use of the term "*mellah*" give sufficient reason to doubt that such an entity existed in Marrakesh during the year in question.

The relevant passage occurs in a series of entries dated 5314–5321 (1553–1558). It concerns an epidemic that ravaged both Fez and Marrakesh, a far from uncommon occurrence in Morocco.[30] In describing the loss of life in the northern capital, the author explicitly uses the word "*mellah*": "In Shevat 5318 [January 1558] the epidemic began in the old city of Fez. In Adar I [c. February] of the same year it appeared in the *mellah*." As this excerpt makes clear, the concept of a *mellah* was readily available to the author. This is not altogether surprising, considering that the *mellah* of Fez had existed for well over a century at the time of this entry. The author even goes so far as to extend the term to the medina, calling it the "*mellah* of the Muslims."[31] When it comes to Marrakesh, however, the chronicler does not use the term. Instead, in the very same entry, we are told how many "Jews in Marrakesh" perished in the epidemic.[32] While this discrepancy does not prove that the Marrakesh *mellah* could not have been built in 1557, it is nonetheless striking. Would not the creation of a *mellah* in the southern capital have been remarkable enough to a Jew from Fez, whose own *mellah* until then was the first and only one in Morocco, for it to be mentioned by name?[33]

1560 AND THE MUWWASIN MOSQUE

The year 1560 is an alternative date for the creation of the Marrakesh *mellah*. It is preferred by both Bénech[34] and the *Encyclopaedia Judaica*,[35] yet it too is problematic, particularly in light of the lack of corroboration by any of the relevant primary sources. So where does this date come from? Once again, the built environment of Marrakesh, specifically the aforementioned Muwwasin mosque, may provide some answers.

The Muwwasin quarter (*Derb Mwāsīn* in Moroccan Arabic) is located in almost the exact center of the medina, adjacent to the street of dyers (*Derb*

Ṣabāghīn). This area was once home to a large Jewish population. It is most likely the Jewish neighborhood cited by Marmol and Torres, though neither mentions it by name or exact location.[36] In the year 970 AH (1562–1563), the date given by the seventeenth-century historian al-Ifrani, construction on a major mosque in the Muwwasin area began, and lasted until 980 (1572–1573).[37] Out of both practical and religious considerations, Jews living in that area would have been obliged to evacuate their homes to make way for the building of the new mosque.[38] According to al-Ifrani's chronology, this would have taken place by 1562 at the latest.[39] In this light, the notion that the *mellah* was created in 1560 to accommodate the displaced Jews of Muwwasin can be interpreted as a sort of compromise. It lies exactly midway between 1557, the year supplied by the Jewish oral tradition, and 1562–1563, the year in which construction on the Muwwasin mosque began. Al-Ifrani himself offers evidence of the quarter's Jewish past in relating that scrupulous Muslims would not pray in the new mosque because it was thought to have been built on top of a Jewish cemetery.[40] Jews themselves continued to avoid the Muwwasin quarter well into the modern period, as Jewish law forbids the priestly caste (Heb. *Kohanim*) from entering cemeteries for reasons of ritual purity.[41]

MELLAH AS PROCESS

Ultimately, neither 1557 nor 1560 can be deemed the definitive date of the creation of the Marrakesh *mellah*. In the first case, Jewish preoccupation with sultanic authority combined with evidence from the Ibn Danan corpus gives pause, as does the lack of corroboration from external sources. The significance of the Muwwasin mosque is correctly introduced in the second case, but the date marking the beginning of its construction can only serve as an end bracket for the chronology of the mellahization of Marrakesh's Jews. What results is a slightly modified range of plausibility, beginning with the Torres-supplied date of 1553 and ending with the construction of the Muwwasin mosque in 1562. Within this range 1557 is certainly a possibility, but cannot be confirmed. Any greater precision in this matter eludes us.

While frustrating, the impossibility of attaching a specific year to the *mellah*'s creation is also instructive, as it points to the fluidity of the institution itself. That is, insofar as Middle Eastern cities can be seen as processes rather than products,[42] the history of the *mellah* must be more than simply the byproduct of the construction of another Saʿdi monument. First, approaching the history of the *mellah* as a process acknowledges the obvious: In addition to the actual transfer of the Jews to their new quarter, mellahization required the creation of the fundamental physical elements of domestic and ritual life: walls, houses, bath complexes, fountains, communal ovens, slaughterhouses, markets, etc. Since this area had previously been a stable and not a residential quarter, these would have needed to be built from the ground up, and not adapted from pre-existing structures. Seen in this light, the period 1553–1562 should not be regarded as a range in which one date must be specified; rather, the transformation of this area into a Jewish quarter took place over the course of several years. On a deeper level, seeing the *mellah* as a process invites one to go beyond the relatively simple question of duration to the more complicated one of interpretation. In its most basic sense, the *mellah* was the sum of the people living in it and the materials used to build its institutions. But mellahization as such signifies something much more profound for the Jews of Marrakesh. It constitutes the major shift in their history, comparable only to their abandonment of the city altogether in the 1950s and 1960s. Seeing the *mellah* as a process brings into sharper focus the evolution of this shift and its repercussions, which pinpointing a particular date obscures. Michael Meyer makes a similar observation in his discussion of when the modern era begins in the context of European Jewish history. He argues that the impact of modernity on the Jews can be understood only as a transition resulting from an accumulation of events over time, including the breakdown of corporate society, Jewish participation in wider social spheres, a decrease in rabbinic authority, etc.[43] The nuances of this transition are lost by stressing one such event over others. From this sensibility comes his conscious choice of the term "modernization," echoed here in the similar if somewhat awkward neologism I have used to refer to the installation of the Jews in the *mellah* of Marrakesh. Finally, such an approach also does a much better job of explaining the *mellah*'s relationship to the rest of the city. Most importantly, it recognizes the continual Jewish presence in the medina in the decades and indeed centuries after 1562 as a natural occurrence. It helps make sense of a Hebrew epitaph on a grave unearthed near the Ibn Yusuf mosque bearing the Hebrew date 5358 (1598), four years after the *mellah*'s cemetery had come into use,[44] and also of the "Jewish widow" who refuses to relinquish her room. Indeed, our very understanding of the *mellah* and its place in the Moroccan city is transformed by reintegrating such "exceptions" into our perspective. Later sources support this view, with the Marrakesh *mellah* only slowly emerging as a recognizable entity in the eyes of visitors. In 1585 a "*judéria*" appears for the first time on a European (Portuguese) map of Marrakesh,[45] and a Jewish quarter as such is first remarked upon by European travelers at the turn of the sixteenth century.[46] The use of the specific term *mellah* is even slower to enter local and European vocabularies, appearing for the first time in Moroccan Jewish sources in 1639,[47] in Moroccan Muslim sources in 1680,[48] and in European sources in the 1760s.[49]

CAUSES OF MELLAHIZATION

Explanations for the phenomenon of mellahization in Morocco tend to fall into two main categories, one pragmatic and one ideational. In the first, the desire to keep the Jews in close proximity to the Kasbah is seen as the key motive, as this allows the sultan to protect "his" Jews from aggressors while at the same time giving the Makhzan easy access to their taxes and services. In Fez, for example, the creation of the *mellah* was directly preceded by an attack on the city's Jews.[50] But in Marrakesh, such concerns were more effect than cause. No attack on the Jews preceded its creation (indeed the mid-sixteenth century was a relatively calm period in Marrakesh), and we simply have no information about *jizya* (poll tax) collection during this period to support taxation claims one way or the other. As discussed above, an even more immediate reason for the relocation of the Jews in Marrakesh was the construction of the Muwwasin mosque. But Muwwasin only provides a partial explanation. It explains neither why *all* the city's Jews were uprooted (recall Torres's mention of two *judérias*), nor why they should then be regrouped within a single enclosed area.

In the second type of explanation, *mellahs* are seen as a form of collective punishment for specific transgressions. Though it is common in Muslim discourse, the theme of "*mellah* as punishment" has been adopted by Moroccan Jews as well to explain their own history.[51] In Marrakesh, the precipitating event was the supposed attack by a Jew on a Muslim woman whom he encountered while out at night calling his coreligionists to nocturnal prayers (Heb. *Seliḥot*).[52] The connecting of Jewish ritual with sexual deviation has long since been discredited as a standard element of anti-Semitic rhetoric, but the story is questionable on other grounds as well, including its similarity to a legend told about the creation of the Fez *mellah,* where the supposed catalyst was a Jew's being caught pouring wine into the lamps of a local mosque.[53] It seems that only by moving away from the generalities of Moroccan Jewish history toward the specificity of Saʿdi Marrakesh can we hope to understand why mellahization occurs when and where it does.

Population: Influx, Pressure, and Inter-Dhimmī Tensions

Of all the transformations Marrakesh underwent in the decades following Leo's visit, none was more striking than the city's repopulation. This factor alone would lead a Frenchman at the end of the Saʿdi period to deem Marrakesh more deserving of the title of "city" than Paris.[54] This population increase was to a certain extent a function of larger demographic patterns in the Mediterranean world of the sixteenth century, charted by Fernand Braudel.[55] But whatever natural growth may have occurred was surely supplemented by Mawlay al-Ghalib's ardent efforts to create a new capital, as Marmol confirms with his statement "Today the city is very populated. Thanks to the king it grows more attractive every day."[56]

All the splendid new monuments to the sultan's authority required an audience, and people duly poured into Marrakesh from far and wide. The new capital was first and foremost a magnet for "ordinary" Moroccans. Craftsmen, artisans, and financiers from throughout the country answered the call of the sultan who "loved beautiful buildings."[57] Many of these immigrants were *Fāsīs* (people from Fez), whose loyalty to their former governor, now sultan, endured. Others came from villages in the Atlas and beyond.[58] European Christians also settled in Marrakesh during the Saʿdi period. Like their Moroccan counterparts, some were artisans lured by the extravagance of the Saʿdi projects. As al-Ifrani marveled, "Even craftsmen from the Frankish countries flocked to [Marrakesh]."[59] A second group of immigrants consisted of English and Dutch merchants seeking to fill the gap left by the expulsion of the Portuguese from Morocco's chief Atlantic ports. English merchants first arrived in Marrakesh in 1551 in search of a market for their cloth and a steady supply of sugar and gold.[60] (The Dutch merchants in Marrakesh were mostly native Spaniards, the majority of whom were exiled Sephardic Jews.[61]) A third group of Christians consisted of Catholic participants in the religious struggles that so wracked the Mediterranean world during the sixteenth century. They included captives like Marmol who had either been taken prisoner in Mediterranean warfare or been kidnapped from the European mainland by corsairs. Between 1550 and 1651 the number of these individuals in Marrakesh grew from three thousand to five or six thousand.[62] Then there were the Franciscan friars sent to attend to the captives and prevent them from apostatizing. (In reality there was little danger of this, as the Moroccans discouraged conversion among their captives for fear of diminishing their ransom value.[63]) Last came the redemptionists, invested with sums so huge with which to buy back the Christians as to unwittingly stimulate the continuation of the very trade they so despised.[64]

The Christian population made its presence known in Marrakesh in a variety of ways, not least of all through its impact on the landscape. Many merchants and agents rented accommodations. Robert Lion, the agent of the Leicester partnership, and two other agents leased a headquarters for their business consisting of two counting houses, two warehouses, and a study.[65] Others owned property outright. One Gerard Gore was a fishmonger whose will specified that the house he and his brother owned in Marrakesh was to be inherited by his wife and sons.[66] Foreign merchants also required a customs house (Ar. *funduq*, Fr. *douane*) where tariffs could be collected, currencies exchanged, and merchandise destined for or coming from Europe held while awaiting inspection. There were in fact two customs houses in Marrakesh, which attests to the vitality of long-distance trade in the southern capital during this period. The older one was located within the Kasbah, while the second one, in operation from 1547 to 1612, was found in "the city's great plaza," possibly the area now known as Jmaʿ al-Fna, judging from the descriptions of Marmol and Torres.[67] Finally, the Christians maintained two cemeteries in Marrakesh. The fishmonger mentioned above stipulated in his will that he was to be buried in the first of these, the "Alhandiga [from Ar. *khandaq*, trench] of the Christians."[68] The second Christian cemetery was built in the

1640s, no doubt to accommodate victims of the plague epidemic that struck southern Morocco in 1639.

Two additional structures, missions and prisons, represented the Iberians specifically. A Franciscan mission and church had existed in Marrakesh as early as the thirteenth century,[69] and a nearby site was put to similar use during the Saʿdi period. Because much of the Catholics' religious life revolved around the captives, the two *sagènes* (from Ar. *sijn,* prison) were where the true "government of the church"[70] was located. Both prisons were in the Kasbah, though the larger one was transferred from its original site facing the great mosque to the defunct Almohad granaries when a gunpowder explosion destroyed the area in 1573–1574.[71]

Marrakesh was also a haven for many of the original objects of the Catholics' prejudice, the exiled Muslims and Jews from the Iberian Peninsula. How many of these individuals immigrated to Morocco, let alone to Marrakesh, remains speculative, though Braudel contends that all North African cities received a share of these "precious Spanish immigrants."[72] Although the Muslims and Moriscos who came to Morocco certainly contributed to the population increase in Marrakesh, the Jewish exiles are more directly relevant to our story here. The vast majority of the *megorashim* (the Hebrew term for the Spanish exiles, as distinct from the autochthonous *toshavim*) settled in the north of Morocco. Fez alone absorbed as many as twenty thousand Jews in the decades after the expulsion.[73] While Marrakesh received far fewer immigrants, they made up for their small number with an exceptionally high level of visibility. Within the *mellah,* the exiles quickly came to dominate the office of *shaykh al-yahūd* (literally the *shaykh* of the Jews, the political head of the local Jewish community).[74] They also formed one of the city's most dynamic corps of merchants.[75]

Deverdun has remarked that all that is good and beautiful in Marrakesh is the direct result of the fall of Granada and the consequent flow of Muslim and Jewish creativity into Morocco.[76] But one might also consider the possibility that the arrival of so many exiles, albeit relatively skilled, may have also been a source of destabilization.[77] In the case of the pre-Saharan oasis town of Tuwat, for example, Hunwick argues that the arrival of the refugees of 1492 created significant demographic pressure.[78] The ensuing political instability was a catalyst for virulent anti-*dhimma* activities, and eventually the town's entire Jewish community was destroyed. Repercussions were felt as far away as Timbuktu, where many Jewish refugees from Tuwat settled. The Jewish community of Marrakesh did not suffer quite so extreme a fate as a result of the influx of Iberian immigrants. But to the extent that population pressure existed in Marrakesh, it was greatly compounded by the hostile relations that developed between the two sets of *dhimmīs*, for which the Catholics' strenuous (and often successful) proselytizing efforts were largely to blame. While the Church's crusade against Islam could not be actively pursued in a sovereign Muslim country, Jews remained an acceptable target, and hence the battle for Jewish souls raged on in Morocco. (As a visitor to Fez bitterly remarked, "The Jews, just like the Muslims, detest the Christians and know nothing of us other than that we burn Jews with great ardor."[79]) The situation became particularly dramatic during the frequent waves of famine, when the promise of grain (which meant the difference between life and death) was held out in exchange for conversion.[80] But in Morocco, the local Jews did not hesitate to fight back against the missionaries. They even did so by using the offices of the Makhzan, as when the local rabbis urged the sultan to fine the Franciscan mission a debilitating sum on the grounds of a less than convincing accusation that a priest had seduced a young Jewish girl. (The more likely culprit was her Portuguese boss, who died leaving her both pregnant and without a patron.[81]) Finally, inter-*dhimmī* tensions can only have risen as Marrakesh gained a reputation as a major center for Marranos to return to Judaism.[82] Torres himself remonstrates fiercely against one such ex-Christian, calling him a "cheating Jew," ostensibly for having bilked a Muslim in business though obviously implying a broader reproach.[83]

The high visibility of non-Muslim immigrants and the intensification of Jewish-Christian hostilities among the city's increased population were two compelling reasons for imposing clear hierarchies of space. Ideally, these hierarchies were articulated in terms of religion. First came the medina, the Muslim residential quarter, where every effort was made to exclude Jewish or Christian habitation. Next came the Kasbah, in or near which customs houses, prisons, churches, and cemeteries were located to allow the sultan to monitor the lives of resident Christians. (Renegades also had a separate quarter and cemetery, from which they were forbidden to stray too far on pain of fines or death, though its exact location is not known.[84]) And last came the *mellah*. But the *mellah* never quite achieved the ideal (if that is the right word) of an exclusively Jewish space. For one thing, it was extremely porous: from the moment of the *mellah*'s creation, Muslims passed through its gate on an almost daily basis to pursue all manner of activities. For another, Jewish space and Christian space were in many cases contiguous, because the *mellah* and the Kasbah shared a wall. According to Thomas Legendre, a French merchant who visited Marrakesh in 1665, the prison in which Christian captives were kept was located a mere fifty steps from the *mellah*.[85] (Jewish and Christian merchants had in fact shared a prison in the Kutubiya quarter in pre-*mellah* times, where they were put "when they deserved it," according to Torres.[86]) The customs house was also nearby. Jean Mocquet, an official agent of the French king Henri IV in Marrakesh, measured the direct distance between the two as a league at most.[87] Moreover, according to Saʿdi regulations, all non-Muslim foreigners were required to be housed in the *mellah* itself. (But even without pressure from the Makhzan, any foreigners who could afford to avoid sleeping in the *funduq*, usually the representatives of larger European firms, did not hesitate to do so.) The Barbary Company's factor, Henry Roberts, was one such merchant, who conducted a lively trade in armaments from his home in the *mellah*.[88] According to Mocquet, who was also lodged in the *mellah*, the Jewish quarter was also where "ambassadors and foreign princes" typically stayed.[89] Meanwhile, the number of Iberian Catholics living in the *mellah* was significant enough to warrant its own neighborhood, known as "Amit," according to the recollections of one captive.[90] Indeed there was a long tradition of housing captives inside the *mellah*'s walls,[91] and in 1660 the Franciscan church was definitively relocated to the Jewish quarter when the sultan objected to its high towers, seen as potential citadels, located so close to the royal palace. Once established in the *mellah*, the Franciscans occupied the "most beautiful" houses the Jewish quarter had to offer.[92] That upper-class foreigners preferred to reside in the *mellah* indicates that it was, at least in its early days, a desirable abode, while the fact that non-Jews maintained a continual presence in the *mellah* throughout its history suggests an entity very unlike the European ghetto, where much greater isolation led to the development of a distinct language (Yiddish) and culture.

The Saʿdi Search for Legitimacy

Even greater than the challenge posed to the Saʿdis by the deluge of immigrants into their new capital was the entrenched resistance to their rule by the city of Fez. The north's opposition, especially when it erupted in military skirmishes, drained Saʿdi resources, while on the symbolic level, Fez's Idrisid legacy combined with the strict orthodoxy of its *ʿulamāʾ* (clerics) were a constant reminder of the Saʿdis' more tenuous qualifications. The Marrakesh-Fez rivalry played itself out in a variety of ways. Its most obvious manifestation was out-and-out warfare. But other, more subtle, forms of competition had just as serious consequences. In this second arena, architecture and urbanism were once again the Saʿdis' preferred tools of strategy.

The resentment and distrust between north and south was due to a series of events that took place during the Saʿdis' long and bloody struggle to dominate the whole of Morocco. Although by 1524 Saʿdi rule was successfully established in Marrakesh, another thirty years would pass before the Marinid-Wattasids' fierce hold over Fez would finally be broken. The brutality involved in subduing Fez permanently alienated the north from the Saʿdi cause, resulting in a psychological rift between the two cities that remains a feature of Moroccan society today.

The Saʿdis' first siege of Fez lasted two years and caused terrible damage to the region.[93] The Saʿdi sultan at the time, Muhammad al-Shaykh, had promised the people of Fez that if he entered their city as a result of their capitulation, he would "fill the streets with justice."[94] But he also warned that should he be obliged to enter by force, he would fill those same streets with dead bodies (which is precisely what came to pass when the authorities of

Fez steadfastly refused to grant al-Shaykh the *bayʿa* [oath of allegiance]). The Saʿdis were forced to beat a hasty retreat, however, when the vanquished Wattasid Abu Hassun returned to his city in January 1554 at the head of a contingent of Ottoman troops. The *Fāsīs* opened their gates for Abu Hassun and his men, and received them with "great joy."[95] When Muhammad al-Shaykh returned eight months later to conquer the city once and for all, the *Fāsīs*' snub, and particularly their willingness to ally themselves with non-Moroccan powers, and even non-Muslim ones if the latter had been willing, had diminished not at all in his memory. Fez was to pay dearly for its rejection of the Saʿdis. Ahmad al-Wattasi was put to death, along with "all the local *shaykhs* and judges."[96] According to Spanish sources, some two thousand members of the city's elite perished in the putsch.[97]

By September 1554 Saʿdi power had been consolidated. The war against the Marinid-Wattasids had been won, but bitter resentment still lingered on both sides. Realizing that he would never be fully accepted in the north, al-Shaykh gave up any hope of ruling from Fez and withdrew to Marrakesh, making it the definitive Saʿdi capital and the country's economic and political center. For the northerners, this was simply adding insult to injury. According to Deverdun, "Fez would never pardon the new dynasty for its decision,"[98] which threatened to transform the northern capital into a backwater.

With Fez finally conquered and the sultan safely installed in Marrakesh, the Saʿdis were still bothered by residual symbolic challenges to their rule and especially to their claim of sharifism. A rhyme circulating in Fez during the 1549 siege of the city perfectly conveys the Fez *ʿulamā*'s attitude toward the Saʿdis: "To kill a *Sūsī* [someone from the Sus region, i.e., a Saʿdi] is to kill a *majūsī* [pagan]."[99] The Saʿdis' preferred method for meeting such challenges to their legitimacy was to construct buildings and monuments, which translated into the near total neglect of Fez compared to the lavish building projects undertaken in Marrakesh. The Saʿdis built only one major edifice in Fez, the pavilions at the court of the mosque of al-Qarawiyyin.[100] Rather than further embellish Fez, the Saʿdis instead sought to recreate its grandeur in Marrakesh, and by so doing perhaps appropriate some of its status for themselves. Indeed the emulation of *Fāsī* ways was already apparent during the rule of Muhammad al-Shaykh, according to al-Ifrani:

> It is said that from the time of their entrance into Fez, the prince [al-Shaykh] and his courtesans, who had been dressed in yellow [robes] and exhibited visible traces of their Bedouin lifestyle, made every effort to acquire the manners and customs of the people of the city.[101]

Further on in the same work, al-Ifrani tells of the visit of Mawlay al-Ghalib's grand vizier to Fez in the company of a great *qāḍī* (judge) and an imam. When the three men from Marrakesh laid their eyes on the monuments there, "a jealous desire inflamed their entrails," moving them to recite poetry, to which they added their own lines to commemorate the vision before them.[102] But a checklist of the two cities' attributes would quickly reveal that a crucial element of *Fāsī* urban life was lacking in Marrakesh: a *mellah*. In the earlier discussion of the Saʿdis' use of "*bi-lisān al-binyān*," the creation of the *mellah* was shown to be one facet in a larger preoccupation with sultanic authority in Jewish memory. When the changes in the city's topography are viewed through the lens of the Saʿdi struggle for legitimacy, however, the *mellah* becomes absolutely central. By adopting an unambiguous position of authority toward the *ahl al-dhimma*, one that could be clearly read on the landscape of the capital, the Saʿdi sultan could successfully buttress his claims against his detractors. With its new *mellah*, Marrakesh looked more like Fez, its *dhimmī* population was contained, and the actual protection the new Jewish quarter afforded its inhabitants reinforced the sultan's paternalistic image. That the Saʿdis viewed the process of mellahization as a means of legitimating their rule is underlined by the name initially given to the Muwwasin mosque, which, as seen above, replaced one of the medina's former Jewish neighborhoods: *jāmiʿ al-ashrāf*, the sharifian mosque.[103]

DAILY LIFE IN THE EARLY *MELLAH*

Physical Space

If the twentieth-century *mellah* could be described by a less than sympathetic observer as a circle belonging in Dante's vision of hell,[104] then the Saʿdi *mellah* was, by comparison, paradisiacal. Upper-class Europeans' preference for residing there has already been established. As one such visitor remarked, "I was lodged by the Emperor's appointment in a faire house in the Judaria or Jurie, which is the place where the Jewes have their abode, and is the fairest place and quietist lodging in all the citie."[105] A Frenchman similarly praised the "*beau logis*" found for him in the *mellah* during his visit to Marrakesh in 1606.[106] The size of the *mellah* impressed Europeans, who compared it to small European cities like Meaux[107] and Magny.[108] Within this area lived between two and six thousand Jews during the Saʿdi era, with more space allotted to them then they needed at the time (this would change dramatically in later years).

The *mellah* was walled on all sides, with one gate on the northwestern perimeter giving access to the rest of the city via the Kasbah. The gate (*bāb al-millāḥ*) was guarded by the sultan's soldiers, though if their devotion to playing games while on watch is any indication, they were rarely pressed into actual defense of the *mellah* during this early period.[109] The eastern wall of the Almohad-Saʿdi Kasbah served as the *mellah*'s western limit. The Portuguese map of 1585 (see figure 1.1) and the engravings of the Dutch painter Adriaen Matham (see figure 1.2)[110] indicate the original southern wall, which extended eastward from the southeast corner of the Kasbah to Jinan al-ʿAfiya,

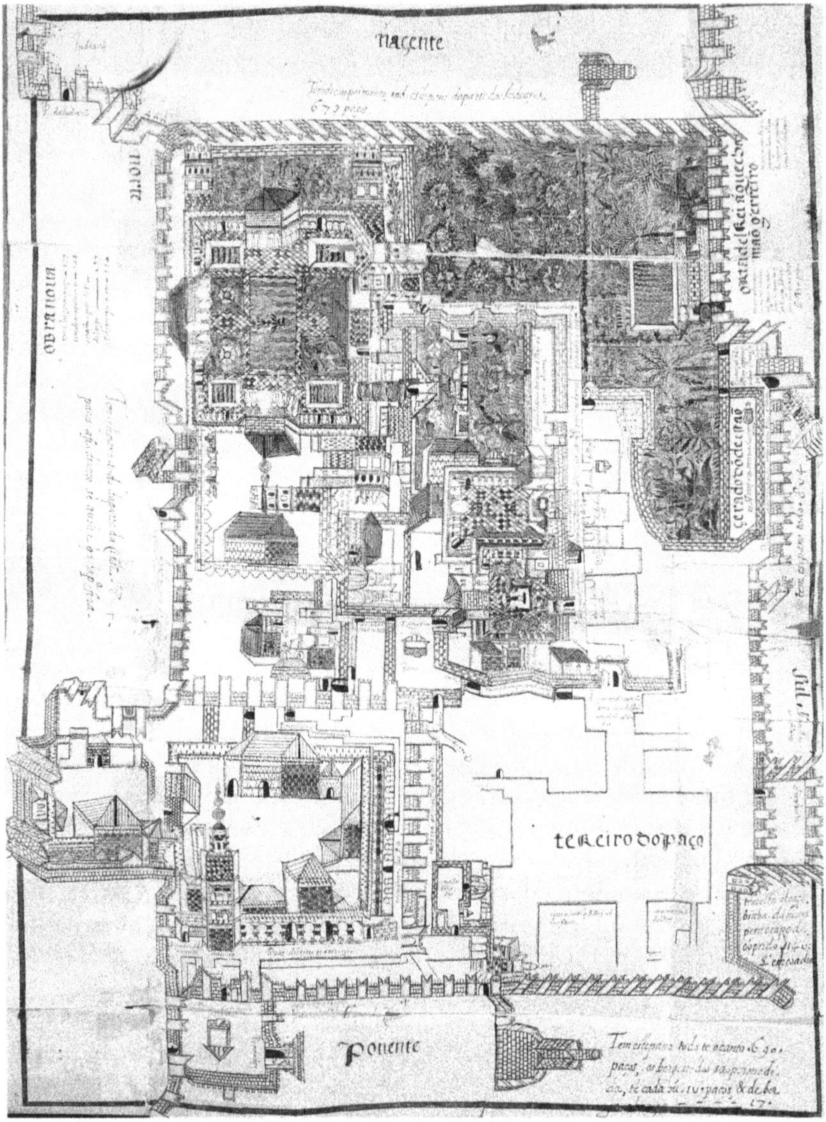

Figure 1.1. Portuguese map of Marrakesh, 1585. From Quentin Wilbaux, *Marrakech* (Paris: ARC Edition Internationale, 1999).

Vue de Merrakech en 1641 (2de Gedeelte), d'après le dessin original d'Adrien Matham, conservé à Vienne, à la K. K. Hof-Bibliothek.

Figure 1.2. Engraving by Adriaen Matham, 1641. The *mellah* is in the right foreground. The second, shorter cupola is a synagogue. From *Les sources inédites de l'histoire du Maroc*, première série, *Archives et bibliothèques des Pays-Bas*, ed. Henry de Castries (Paris: E. Leroux, 1906–1923), vol. 4.

the gardens just below the Jewish cemetery. The placement of the western and southern walls indicates that the Saʿdi *mellah* included the area known as Berrima, which in the later period was inhabited by Muslims.[111] Only part of the eastern wall of the *mellah* built by the Saʿdis is still observable today. Originally, this wall probably extended to meet the northern rampart of the *mellah* (of Almoravid construction). The most likely explanation for the disappearance of such a large segment is the severe flooding known to have occurred in Marrakesh during the late sixteenth century.[112]

The *mellah* was roughly rectangular, measuring 700 by 250 meters, with an area of seventeen and a half hectares. Eight additional hectares were appended for a cemetery, though they were used for growing vegetables until 1594. The most striking topographic feature of the *mellah* is its grid-like pattern of streets, laid out in four distinct quadrants. The intention behind this form is difficult to know. Throughout history, the grid's advantages for defense and surveillance have made it a standard scheme of planned cities in both the East and the West.[113] Bénech's statement that Murdukhai b. ʿAttar, the *mellah*'s first *shaykh al-yahūd*, was charged with the task of building the *mellah* and given the funds to do so suggests at least the possibility of a recognizably Jewish architecture, though any certainty in this matter will require a comparative study of Morocco's *mellahs* by future scholars.[114] In any event, it should be noted that the form of the *mellah* in Marrakesh is unlike any other part of the city.

Bab Aghmat was the nearest of the city's gates to the *mellah* (see figure 1.5) and, in good Marrakesh tradition, recalled the origins of its nearest inhabitants.[115] The *mellah* itself was divided into two distinct neighborhoods in this early period. They are mentioned by name in the Ibn Danan chronicle in an entry concerning flooding in the area.[116] The smaller of the two

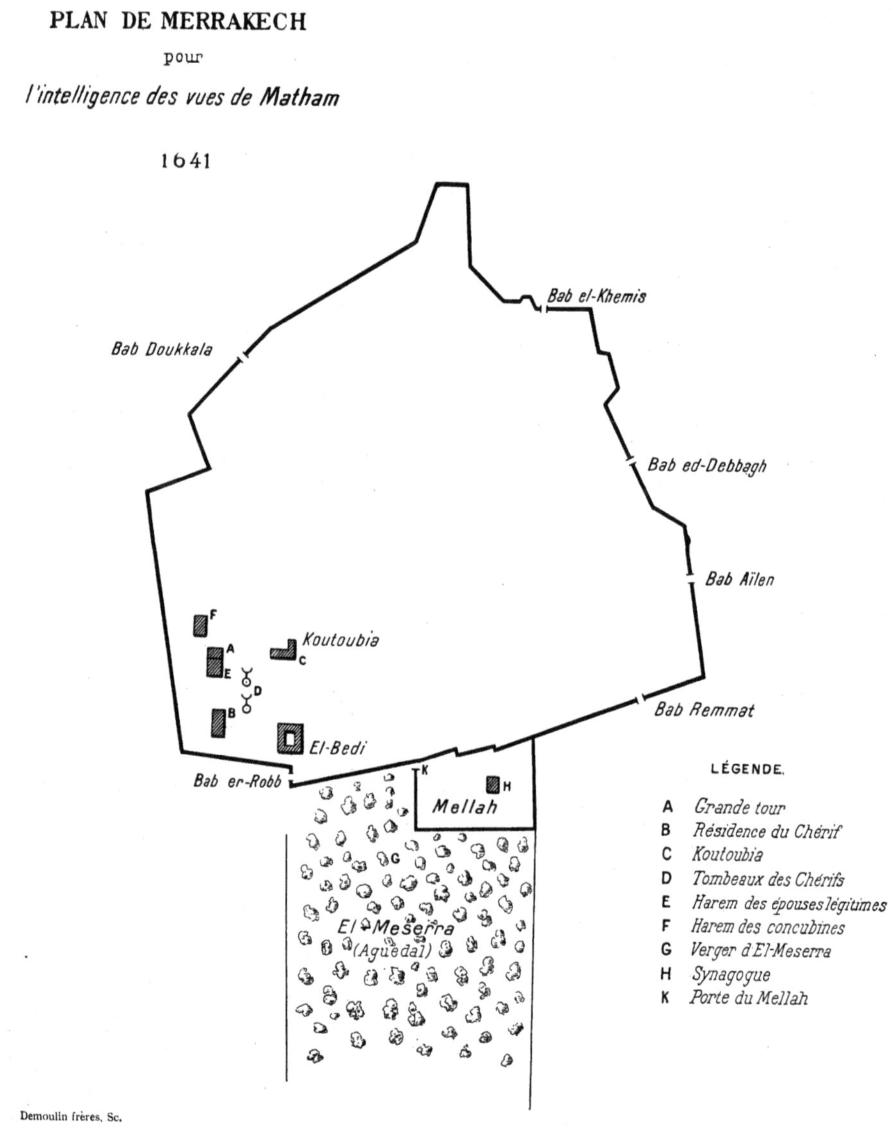

Figure 1.3. Map by Adriaen Matham, 1641. From *Les sources inédites de l'histoire du Maroc,* première série, *Archives et bibliothèques des Pays-Bas,* ed. Henry de Castries (Paris: E. Leroux, 1906–1923), vol. 4.

Figure 1.4. City ramparts. Postcard, Combier Imp. Macon. Private collection of the author.

was known as al-Matamir and contained fifty houses, while the larger, with two hundred houses, was called al-Salha. Etymological clues may place the first near an underground granary (*maṭāmīr*), while the second was probably located in the southeast portion of the *mellah* near the Jinan al-ʿAfiya gardens, which were known in the Almoravid period as *al-Ṣāliha.*[117]

Mellah *and Medina*

To understand the *mellah*'s place within the city as a whole during its formative years, it may be useful to compare Marrakesh to Fez, Morocco's oldest city, with a well-established Jewish community that, in the Saʿdi period, was still larger than that of Marrakesh. In both cities the *mellah* abutted the Kasbah, assuring the close "vertical" relationship with the sultan discussed earlier. In Fez, however, Kasbah and *mellah* were physically separated from the medina by many miles. Jews in the northern city paid for the sultan's protection through their isolation in *Fās jadīd,* "new Fez," a location that placed them in the crossfire of anti-dynastic struggles of the sixteenth and seventeenth centuries.[118] The Marrakesh *mellah,* on the other hand, had relatively easy access to the medina from its northeastern perimeter via the Kasbah. As will become apparent, the physical proximity of the two areas proved a significant determinant of Jewish-Muslim relations in Marrakesh. This important difference between the northern and southern *mellahs* was perceptible by outsiders from as early as 1596, as we see in an anonymous Portuguese description comparing the "*extra-muros*" activities of Jewish women in the two cities:

Figure 1.5. Aerial photograph of the *mellah*. Section de photographie aérienne, Escadrille 554, Reconnaissance du 7 novembre 1917. Archives des Services Municipaux de Marrakech.

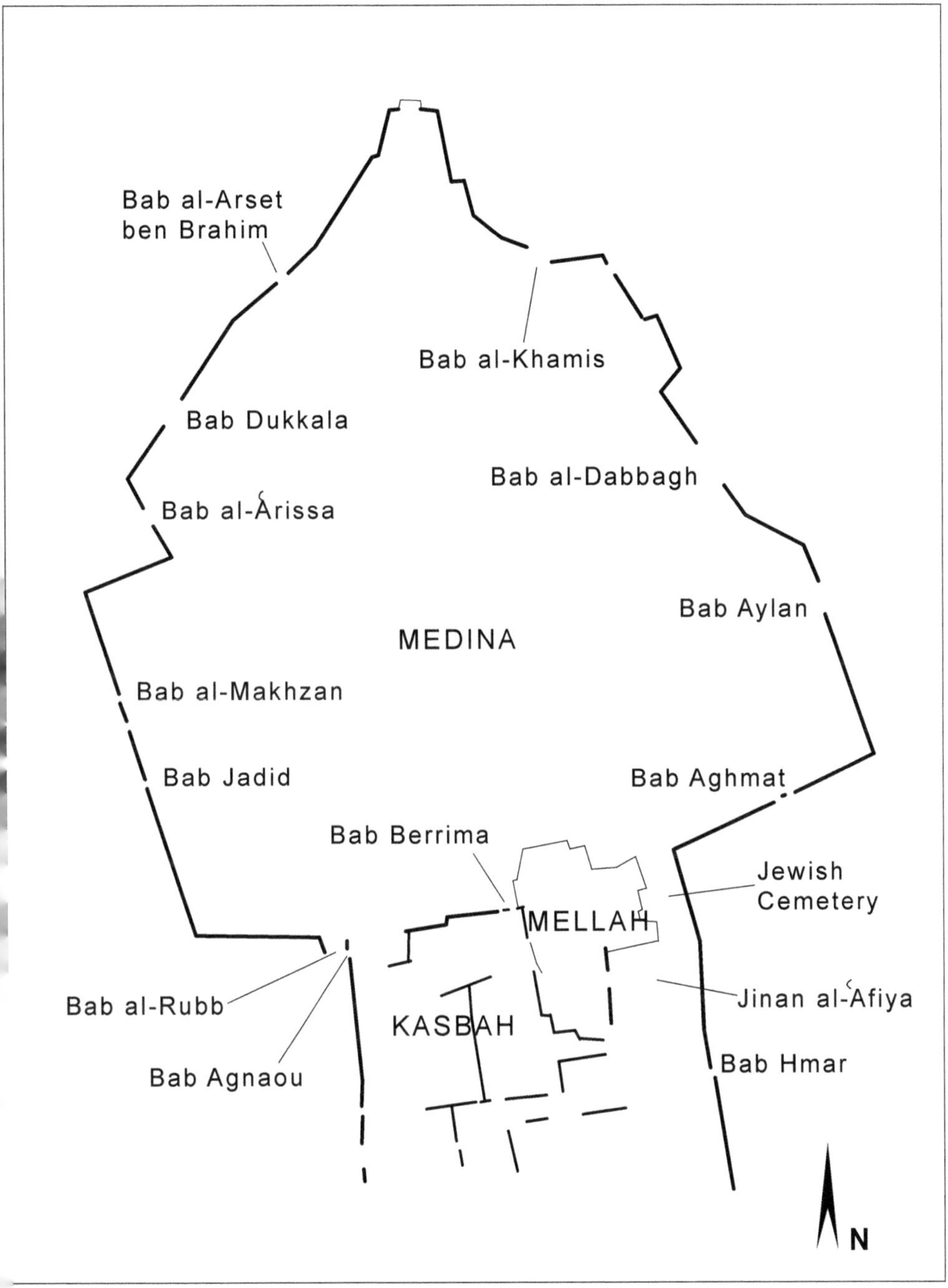

Figure 1.6. Gates of Marrakesh.

> The [Moroccan] Jewish women are pretty, cunning, and well brought up; they are always preening. They like Christians and are very generous with them, yet they will poison a man without a second thought. This is what happened in Fez where they have killed many such men, some gentlemen and some not. Jewish women in Marrakesh lack this perversity.[119]

Orientalist fantasies aside, we might nonetheless examine the subjectivity of the writer, himself a Christian, asking in particular what made him feel excluded from the attentions of Jewish women (though safer for it) in Marrakesh, but not in Fez. Perhaps it has something to do with the fact that in the northern capital, the *mellah*'s distance from the medina led outsiders to think it was accessible, whereas the mutuality of *mellah* and medina in Marrakesh left little room for Christian paramours to operate, despite the fact that Marrakesh was by far the more cosmopolitan city at the end of the sixteenth century and had a greater share of Christian residents, many of whom, as we have seen, lived inside the *mellah* itself.

Inhabited Space

It is difficult to know how Marrakesh Jewry responded to their mellahization. But from the example of similar population transfers,[120] we can assume that the move itself must have been traumatic. In at least one case, that of the Jewish widow, mellahization was actively resisted. Yet despite whatever hardships were endured by the Jews in the course of their relocation, the new *mellah* almost immediately became sanctified as protected Jewish space. The one gate that gave way to the medina, which could have easily been repudiated as an emblem of imprisonment, instead came to be treated as an object of reverence by the *mellah*'s inhabitants, as we see in this description from the early twentieth century:

> If one stops for a moment in front of this gate, one sees a curious thing: All who pass, children, beggars, peddlers driving their donkeys loaded with merchandise, old women, hunched-over men, all approach this dusty wall and press their lips against it with as much fervor as if they were kissing the holy Torah.[121]

Such behavior derives from a story told by Marrakesh Jewry about how the heroic Murdukhai b. ʿAttar once saved the *mellah*. One day not long after the creation of the *mellah*, a band of tribesmen "armed to the teeth" invaded the city. Ben ʿAttar happened to be just inside when they arrived at the *mellah*'s main gate, intent on pillaging. Hearing the ruckus on the other side, Ben ʿAttar fervently prayed for divine intervention. Suddenly, a flaming barrier appeared, blocking all entry to the *mellah*. The would-be invaders retreated, vanquished and impotent.[122]

The spiritual sense of the *mellah* at this early stage can be traced directly to the figure of Ben ʿAttar. He was made a saint upon his death, and his tomb

Figure 1.7. *Bāb al-millāḥ* (the *mellah*'s main gate). Photograph by the author.

became a popular pilgrimage site, the oldest in the Jewish cemetery. His "*baraka*" (charisma or beneficence of divine origin) was extended to the *mellah*'s gate through the burial of one of his relics in it, which may have been his *talith* (Heb., prayer shawl), a piece of parchment with a prayer written on it, a vial of oil used to light the lamp of his synagogue, or the stick the rabbi had held up which had miraculously ignited to save the *mellah.*[123] Jews thereafter attributed their escape from marauders and even from natural disaster[124] to the *mellah*'s sanctity and especially the *baraka* of its gate. (As an extra precaution, however, the main gate was locked at night and all day on Saturday so "that [the Jews] may trade peaceably, and keep their Sabbath and other festivals."[125] As we have seen, the sultan's soldiers stood guard.)

Our knowledge of how space was organized and used by the Jews in the early *mellah* is almost entirely speculative. In addition to walls, neighborhoods, a gate, and a cemetery, we can conjecture the existence of other buildings, structures, and places in the *mellah,* as well as add some detail to those noted above, by identifying some of the principal spheres of Jewish activity in the Saʿdi era and their corresponding spatial requirements.

The center of domestic life was the home, and there were more than three thousand homes in the early *mellah,* according to Marmol.[126] It is possible that a Sephardic aesthetic prevailed inside some of them, judging from Mocquet's comment that the Jews, unlike the Muslims, "have beds like us."[127] Public bread ovens, slaughterhouses, markets, and baths were also obligatory features of the domestic life of the early *mellah.*

The religious and scholarly life of the *mellah* was naturally located in the synagogue, which, alongside or overlapping the home, is among the most important institutions in Judaism. According to Marmol, synagogues were numerous from the earliest days of the new Jewish quarter,[128] an observation seconded by Francisco del Puerto later.[129] Legendre, however, specifically notes the existence of only two synagogues,[130] and Matham's engraving shows only one, a square building topped by a large dome (see figure 1.2). This discrepancy may stem from the fact that synagogues in Morocco were not necessarily visible to the passer-by. The vast majority were not separate edifices, as in Europe, but rooms in private homes, typically belonging to prominent families who could afford to sacrifice the space and whose name the synagogue would often carry. In the Saʿdi era, a special synagogue existed for the *megorashim,* who sought to maintain their religious traditions in Marrakesh. Though most synagogues in Morocco eventually incorporated some Sephardic practices, the Sephardic rite never came to dominate Jewish practice in Marrakesh as it did elsewhere in Morocco.[131] The synagogue fulfilled many functions beyond the obvious one of prayer. It probably housed, or at least was near to, a ritual bath complex (Heb. *mikvah*), rudimentary offices for the rabbinical court and possibly the *shaykh al-yahūd,* and schools. The latter would have included a *ṣlā* for children as well as some space where more advanced study or rabbinical training could take place, the seeds for Marrakesh's illustrious *yeshivot* (rabbinical academies), which would eventually serve all southern Morocco.

Whatever educational infrastructure actually existed, intellectual creativity was clearly nurtured in the early *mellah.* Although only a small handful of families dominated the rabbinical corps (including the Pintos and Azoulays), the general level of education during the Saʿdi period appears to have been quite high. According to the Fez chronicler, of 5,600 Jews killed in a bout of plague, "all were learned in the Law."[132] Hebrew books were ordered from Europe to satisfy the *mellah*'s educational needs during this period,[133] and the *mellah*'s reputation for learning was good enough to attract one of the outstanding Talmudists of the time, Jacob Sasportas. (Originally from Oran, Sasportas spent time in both Fez and Marrakesh during the early stages of his career before retiring in Amsterdam.) The *mellah* also produced several competent scholars of its own. The best-known is Moses Pallache, a member of the illustrious Pallache family and nephew of royal agent and diplomat Samuel Pallache, Moses was noteworthy for combining the service to the state typical of his family with serious scholarly pursuits, particularly oration.[134]

For those individuals whose proclivities tended more toward commerce than learning, Marrakesh provided more than ample opportunity. Under the Saʿdis the economy grew as quickly as the city itself. The most important trade entrepôt for southern Morocco, Marrakesh was considered "a merchant's paradise" in the sixteenth century,[135] a reputation it owed mostly to the trans-Saharan trade. Once the major routes had been conquered for Morocco by Mawlay al-Mansur (1578–1603), as many as thirty gold-laden mules arrived in Marrakesh each day.[136] The involvement of Marrakesh's Jewish merchants in long-distance trade is attested to by several sources, including Leo, who tells us that "they pass also by way of traffic even to Timbuktu."[137] At the other end of the caravan routes, on the coasts, the Jews' investments were overseen by their coreligionists who dominated the export trade in Safi, Morocco's largest commercial port of the period. Marrakesh's Jews traded in most commodities and even held exclusive rights over some markets, including sugar, a sultanic monopoly that was farmed out almost exclusively to the local Jewish merchants.[138] This arrangement did not escape the notice of foreign merchants:

> In this country are manie Jewes inhabiting, in whose hands consisteth the most parte of the trafique of the country being the onely merchauntes of sugers, mulasses, and other ritche merchandize which the same yieldeth; for the which they paye great sums of money to the King.[139]

Europe's hearty appetite for Moroccan sugar meant that the contract to oversee its sales could be quite lucrative, depending on the sultan's requirements. In England, sugar accounted for 93 percent of all imports from Morocco, and by 1589 royal consumption alone amounted to eighteen thousand pounds annually. (Queen Elizabeth herself would accept only Moroccan refined sugar for her household.[140]) Even more striking is al-Ifrani's testimony that the marble imported from Italy to build the Badiʾ Palace was paid for in equal weights ("*wazzanan bi-wazzan*") of sugar.[141] This is confirmed by Montaigne's *Journal de voyage,* which tells of artisans near Pisa carving fifty marble columns of great height for delivery to the "*King of Fez in Barbary.*"[142]

Because of its geographic location and its status as a royal city, Marrakesh was also a central market for the trade in European captives.[143] We know that Jews took part in this trade from the rescue books studied by Ellen Friedman, in which they are frequently listed as owners of Christian slaves.[144] Jews were also active in the ransoming process, even to the extent that it appeared to some observers to have been their exclusive prerogative.[145] Other sources make clear that in fact both Jews and Muslims were deeply involved in the exchange of captives in Marrakesh, from which they traveled as far as Taroudant to make purchases.[146]

In addition to commercial activities, Jews were also skilled craftsmen, particularly in metalwork, a vocation they came to dominate in Marrakesh as elsewhere in Morocco. Their work received high praise from Marmol: "The majority of these Jews are smiths who make beautiful silver headdresses and other ornaments for horses, with decorative spurs and stirrups."[147] Commercial and artisanal activities would have been expressed spatially in the *mellah* by edifices including a *sūq,* a *qaysārīya* (covered market), workshops, and ateliers. Storehouses and *funduqs* would have also been necessary. An additional venue to be noted is the taverns kept by Jews,[148] where no doubt the famous (or infamous, as the case may be) *maḥīya* (eau-de-vie) was in great demand. Unfortunately, the economic activities of Jews involved in the Marrakesh (and Moroccan) economy are too diffuse, and our sources too limited, to be fixed very firmly in space during the Saʿdi period.

The *mellah*'s origins and evolution are ultimately inextricable from those of the Saʿdis, the dynasty responsible for single-handedly transforming the city from "a phantom capital, a moribund city of nostalgia"[149] into one of the largest and most glorious capitals in all sixteenth-century Africa, and themselves into *Marrākshīs* par excellence in the process. The creation of the *mellah* played an integral part in both of these transformations. As such, it was intertwined with all the exigencies of sharifian rule in Marrakesh: tumultuous relations with Europe and locally resident Europeans, particularly the Iberians; the struggle for legitimacy against the prevailing image of *Fāsī* orthodoxy; the creation of a royal capital worthy of the title.

Though locally manifest, the origins of the *mellah* are also connected to many of the broader historical themes of the sixteenth-century Mediterranean world. A general rise in population, the expulsion of Jews and Muslims from Spain, and the gradual institutionalization of the walled Jewish quarter all are implicit in its creation. Once in existence, moreover, the *mellah* continued to reverberate with the defining events of the period. Epidemics, famines, and earthquakes did not stop at its gate despite whatever *baraka* it may have had, nor were the opportunities of the trans-Saharan trade or the early mercantilist exchanges with Europe foregone by the *mellah*'s capable merchants. The Jews of Marrakesh not only withstood the difficulties of relocation, they managed to begin investing their new quarter with special meaning. Firmly grounded in space and endowed with significance by its early history, the *mellah* gave Marrakesh Jewry a distinctive locus—indeed, a home—from which they would interact with the rest of the city, region, and country, as well as the larger Mediterranean, European, and Jewish worlds, for the next four centuries.

2

Counting Jews in Marrakesh

The Maghreb is teeming with inhabitants.
Only God can count them all.
Ibn Khaldun, *The Muqaddimah*

THE *MELLAH* IN THE AGE OF MAWLAY HASSAN

Although the ʿAlawis never replicated the close ties of their Saʿdi predecessors to Marrakesh, the southern capital was in no way abandoned by the new dynasty. With the creation of a third royal capital at Meknes in 1672 some of the country's political focus naturally shifted northward, but this was largely offset by the emergence of a strong ʿAlawi tradition whereby the "crown prince" served as the sultan's representative (*khalīfa*) in Marrakesh prior to assuming power himself, which ensured continued royal concern with the south. Like his father before him, Mawlay Hassan (r. 1873–1894) had been *khalīfa* in Marrakesh, and whatever attachment he had developed to the city and its inhabitants during that time seems not to have diminished upon his becoming sultan. Under Mawlay Hassan, the status of royal capital was shared almost equally between north and south. He spent 34 percent of his rule (not including expeditions [*ḥarakāt*, sing. *ḥaraka*]) in Marrakesh—where he was first proclaimed sultan—and 43 percent in Fez, with periods of residency in the south lasting as long as 502 days at a stretch.[1] It was under Mawlay Hassan that the Marrakesh *mellah* underwent the first major structural changes to its physical environment since the time of its creation.

Although Jews of Marrakesh would have to wait for the reign of Mawlay

ʿAbd al-Hafidh (r. 1908–1913) before exerting any real influence in Moroccan politics, their relationship to Mawlay Hassan was nonetheless close.[2] The sultan's attitude toward his Jewish subjects generally can be seen in the Makhzan's letter to "The Elders of the Jewish Communities Dwelling in Europe" in response to congratulations it received from the Anglo-Jewish Association on the occasion of Mawlay Hassan's ascent to the throne in 1873:

> With regard to your brethren in the happy domains of our Lord, He . . . has placed them under His shadow; our Prophet . . . recommended that these subjects and tax-paying peoples should be protected, and our Lord . . . will also respect with due consideration the honored edict issued to the Jews by our Lord . . . and our Lord will continue to put it in force; and will extend them, if it please God, justice and benevolence, not permitting that injustice should be done unto them, and that there should be no hindrance in their obtaining justice either in the towns or the countryside.[3]

The Jews' close vertical relation to the ʿAlawi rulers is amply demonstrated by their regular presence in the royal compound. During at least the period 1860–1892, a Jew served as the sultan's head chef.[4] It was customary for Jewish women to be invited to the royal harem to visit and receive gifts during the feast of Mulūd.[5] On one such occasion, the following message was transmitted to the visitors from the sultan:

> Never has a ruler of Morocco shown such compassion for his non-Muslim subjects as His Majesty Mawlay Hassan, imbued as it is with the religious principle that it is only through the protection of the chief of state of the weak Jews of his country that his throne can be secure and his rule powerful.[6]

Similar festivities surrounded the wedding of Mawlay Hassan's son, when two elaborate picnics were held for local Jews in the palace gardens.[7]

As stable as the sultan's relationship to Moroccan Jewry may have appeared on the surface, it was still susceptible to the increasingly precarious position of the Makhzan itself. The fall of Algeria in 1830, Morocco's defeat to French forces at Isly in 1844, and the Spanish occupation of Tetuan in 1860 placed all aspects of Moroccan sovereignty under the very real threat of conquest. Even in the Hawz, where new agricultural technologies had been introduced and the area opened to modernization, Mawlay Hassan's efforts at furthering his father's internal reforms did little to slow European penetration. Indeed it was during his reign that the French began their massive seizure of agricultural land in the Marrakesh region. Between 1880 and 1914 the territory cultivated directly or indirectly by Europeans in the Hawz grew from negligible amounts to ten thousand hectares.[8] More and deeper reforms were required to offset such trends, and their cost, compounded by war indemnities and interest on foreign loans, put an enormous strain on the *bayt al-māl* (royal treasury). Mawlay Hassan had to marshal all the country's remaining resources in order to pay for the restructuring that might stave off direct European control for a few more decades. The Jews, from the point of view of the Makhzan, were one such resource. As part of a strategy to exploit them more fully, the Makhzan undertook an unprecedented administrative act. In the autumn of 1890, it carried out Morocco's first modern census, the subject of which was the Marrakesh *mellah*.[9] Here in the most marginal quarter (at least in the popular imagination) of the country's most isolated capital, Mawlay Hassan would carry out one of his most dramatic efforts at *niẓām* (literally "order"), the massive program of administrative, educational, military, financial, and diplomatic reforms that was undertaken by rulers throughout the Middle East and North Africa in an effort to modernize their countries quickly enough to repel, or at least limit, colonial encroachment.

The significance of the 1890 census of the Marrakesh *mellah* can be demonstrated on a number of levels. First, it is surprising that such a text even *could* exist, let alone actually did, given that scholars have long assumed that the Makhzan possessed only minimal understanding of modern administrative practices prior to the establishment of the French Protectorate. What efforts at administrative innovation the Makhzan did pursue during this period were largely concentrated on managing Morocco's spiraling debt to foreign powers and limiting the influence of European merchants, diplomats, and their representatives on the coasts. The Jewish communities of the interior of the country did not figure prominently in either of these areas of concern. The carrying out of the census was not remarked upon by any of the contemporary sources, and probably went unnoticed by everyone except those immediately concerned, i.e., the Jews being counted and the municipal authorities counting them. Just two years after the census had been completed an otherwise relatively well-informed newspaper introduced an article on the Jewish population of Morocco with the statement that "Morocco is an absolutely non-statistical country."[10] A few years later, a letter from the French legation at Tangier to the minister of foreign affairs in Paris reported, "no official statistics exist for Moroccan Jewry."[11] The 1890 census clearly disproves this. Not only does it show that Moroccans had significant understanding of European-style municipal procedures prior to the establishment of the French Protectorate in 1912, it also offers a concrete example of just how such practices were adapted to meet the particular needs and concerns of the Makhzan in relation to the country's Jews. Just what these needs and concerns were in Marrakesh, and how they were made to fit into emerging conceptualizations of *niẓām*, is the focus of the current chapter.

DISCIPLINING SPACE: THE IDEOLOGICAL FOUNDATIONS OF THE 1890 CENSUS OF THE *MELLAH* OF MARRAKESH

Where did the Makhzan get the idea to count people, a practice alien to both Jewish and Muslim traditions? More to the point, what might counting have meant in the context of pre-colonial Morocco? Censuses are typically carried out for the dual purposes of assessing soldiery and taxes.[12] This was roughly the role of the *defter* (cadastral survey) within the classical Ottoman system of the fifteenth and sixteenth centuries, with which the Moroccans may have been familiar.[13] Another possible influence was the Egyptian census of 1846. (It is doubtful, however, that the Moroccan government was aware of the Montefiore census of Alexandria in 1840 and others carried out under his auspices in Palestine, precisely because they focused exclusively on the Jews.) Certain aspects of the 1890 census of the Marrakesh *mellah* are also reminiscent of a European administrative orientation. The use of the home as a standard unit for counting, absent in the land-based *defter* but present here, first emerged in medieval Europe as the extremely varied domestic units of antiquity gave way to the more commensurate (and hence comparable) "households" of the seventh and eighth centuries.[14] Moreover, the more contemporary principles of positivism—the quest of nineteenth-century European intellectual society to collect, quantify, and categorize—are apparent in the document's organization. Yet the census is ultimately best understood in terms of its own unique form and function.

The census begins with a simple one-paragraph introduction outlining its motivation and implementation:

> The complaint reached the mighty *sharīf* [concerning] the *dhimmīs* of the happy city of Marrakesh, that the living spaces in the *mellah* have become crowded [literally, "narrowed": *ḍāqa*]. So the sultan ordered that the crowded houses be counted. This [task] was put into the hands of the well-educated *faqīh* and vizier Fadul Gharnit, who ordered it done by his scribe, ʿAbd al-Kabir b. Hashim al-Kittani, who proceeded hence as mentioned with Pasha qāʾid Ahmad Umalik's police officer, namely, the servant ʿAbdallah b. ʿUmar al-Shiazmi, who noted it in the statement below. It was done on 6 Rabīʿ II in the year 1308 [19 November 1890].[15]

The *mellah* is then divided into four distinct quarters. The first quarter surrounds the central storehouse (*al-funduq al-wusṭā*). The second is in the area of the great mosque (*al-jāmiʿ al-kabīr*), which presumably was located alongside the western wall of the *mellah*, adjacent to the Kasbah and its mosque. The third quarter lies in the vicinity of the saint (*walī*) Yusuf al-Mlih. The fourth quarter begins at *"Derb al-Maqnin,"* suggesting either that a legal body, perhaps the *bayt dīn*, was located nearby, or, more likely, that a prominent Jewish figure of the 1830s by that name had resided in the area.[16] Proceeding quarter by quarter, each house is given a number, its owner is named, and its immediate neighbor is noted. Within each house the rooms are then counted, with information given on the size or shape of each, and on where it lies in relation either to the previously counted room (across from, following, or to the left or right of) or to the house's general layout (in the corner, above the door, etc.). Finally, the inhabitants of each room are identified. The head of the room is named, and the rest of its occupants are enumerated according to their relationship to him or, occasionally, her. In addition to the immediate family (husband and wife or wives,[17] their children, his and/or her parents), other relationships indicated are grandparents, aunts and uncles, and sisters- and brothers-in-law and their parents, spouses, siblings, and children. We are specifically told that children (*al-ṣaghār*) are not included in the census, though offspring who are past puberty (masc. *bāligh,* fem. *bāligha*), teenagers (masc. *muhāriq,* fem. *muhāriqa*), and men (*rajul,* pl. *rijāl*) are counted. Two other categories are "*ghāʾib,*" those absent at the time of the census takers' visit but still considered to "belong" to a particular room, and the somewhat enigmatic "*ayyim.*" In most dictionaries, this term is defined as "a widow or widower."[18] However, it also has the connotation of a non-virgin adult female without a spouse, which would include widows as well as divorcées or otherwise unmarried adult women.[19] This broader definition opens the door to the possibility, and, judging from complementary sources, even probability, that some of these women were slaves or prostitutes. Most of the women who fall into this category have no demonstrable familial ties to the other occupants of the rooms in which they live, and many live alone in a room (the only category of people to do so in the census) or grouped together with other *ayyims*. Although Jews in Morocco were officially forbidden to own slaves, there is evidence that they did so in other Moroccan towns, such as Essaouira.[20] If the *ayyims* of the census were indeed slaves, it would conform to Haim Zafrani's observation that the slaves owned by Jews in southern Morocco were almost always women, and were highly integrated into the domestic life of the Jewish home.[21] The question of whether they were prostitutes will be taken up in the coming chapter. For now, suffice it to note that a large number of women fall into this category. Out of a total of 2857 women counted by the census, 309 are *ayyims*.[22]

The first house treated by the census is described as follows:

> The house known as that of Masʿud Bardukh in the neighborhood of Ibn Shimʿun b. Shaʿshuʿ. In room one to the left of the entrance is Ibrahim al-Dayan with his wife, and his brother with his wife. In room two opposite it is Salam b. Shimas with his two wives, and his brother with his wife. In room three following facing the entryway is Salam Buwida with his wife, and his brother with his wife. In room four opposite it under the archway is Shmuwil b. al-Ghazal with his wife, and his brother-in-law with his wife, and his sister-in-law with her husband and her sister with her husband, and his two teenage sisters. In room five in the opposite corner is Mushi Buqashish with his wife and his sister-in-law. In room six in the middle opposite it is Mayr Buqashish with his wife, and his son with his wife, and his brother-in-law with his wife. In room seven in the corner after it is Yaʿish b. Khalifa with his wife, and his son with his wife, and his brother-in-law with his wife. In the small room eight, the first to the right of the entryway going upstairs, is Hanina b. al-Shuwaykh and his mother and his wife and her mother. In

> the small room nine after it is Ibrahim Ashddu with his wife and her mother and his mother. In room ten in the corner archway is Dawid al-Shawi with his wife, and his son with his wife and her mother. In the smaller room eleven, the first on the right ascending to the upstairs, is Ishaq al-Qalʿawi with his wife and his brother-in-law. In room twelve opposite it is Dawid b. ʿAttar with his wife and his brother and his mother.[23]

Directly to the right of the paragraph-long account lies its classification: house number 1, with 12 rooms and 58 inhabitants. Thus the census has rendered this first house—and in due course all 210 of the houses in the *mellah,* with their total of 1272 rooms and 5032 inhabitants—legible, a first step in the production of the statistical knowledge that was such an integral component of creating *niẓām,* a "new order," throughout the Middle East.[24]

Yet even when it is thus neatly summarized on paper, one cannot help but be struck by the fact that Masʿud Bardukh's home must have been anything but orderly, given the number of people living in it.[25] As his house illustrates, population increases became the greatest challenge facing the *mellah* in the centuries following its creation. While Marrakesh as a whole retained its characteristic feeling of spaciousness over the course of the nineteenth century, the area within the *mellah*'s walls had grown desperately overpopulated. Crowding and its ill effects had become apparent to visitors to the Jewish quarter in the 1860s,[26] and only intensified over the course of Mawlay Hassan's reign.[27] By 1900, as many as fifteen thousand people lived in an area originally designated to accommodate only a few thousand. The extreme density of the *mellah*[28] caused it to be experienced on a visceral level above all others. José Bénech, the director of the Marrakesh branch of the Banque commerciale du Maroc during the 1930s and the main observer of Jewish life in the city under the French Protectorate, compared passing through the *mellah*'s main gate to descending into the Paris metro, with the attendant sensation of "suddenly breathing a more polluted air due to the abnormal density of the population."[29] Even A.I.U. teachers, whose stated mission was to "regenerate" Jews in just such places, complained bitterly when sent to Marrakesh, and at least one requested extra pay to compensate for the hardship of his assignment.[30]

The phenomenon of overcrowding is central to the *mellah*'s modern history, and will be taken up again in subsequent chapters. For now, however, it will be examined primarily in relation to the census, in particular as a mechanism for providing the Makhzan with a much-needed increase in its revenues. That is, with houses like Bardukh's bursting at the seams, the Makhzan could be certain of the Jews' cooperation (and indeed their initiative) in enlarging the *mellah,* a project that was carried out in conjunction with the census and gave the sultan several new properties on which to collect rent. The Makhzan was further able to capitalize on overcrowding in the *mellah* because any increase in the *mellah*'s population as determined by the census sanctioned a corresponding increase in the *jizya* paid by the Jews, which was, after all, a poll tax. Beyond its fiscal implications, the census's findings also raise the larger question of Jewish demographics in southern Morocco. How many Jews lived in Marrakesh at the end of the nineteenth century? What was the actual composition of this community? How well do common theories about Jewish population movements in Morocco fit their specific historical experience? The 1890 census sits at the juncture of these two important themes: fiscal matters—rent, property ownership, and taxes—and Jewish demographic patterns, and therefore will be key in finding answers to these questions.

THE EXPANDING *MELLAH*

Appropriately, it was at the walls of the *mellah,* the functional boundary of "official" Jewish space in Marrakesh, that the effects of overcrowding first became apparent. Some sections of the walls were of course quite ancient, dating back to the Almohad and Almoravid eras. Even those parts built under the Saʿdis were still several centuries old. And though the walls were quite thick, they were made of earth beaten with lime (*ṭābīya*), a material not known for its durability. Already described by Ali Bey as "half ruined" at the beginning of the nineteenth century,[31] the *mellah*'s walls proved an easy target for thieves, who in an 1884 incident bored holes through them in order to enter and rob *mellah* homes.[32] (That houses were built all the way to the exterior walls in the first place is one more indication of overcrowding.) The walls were again at issue just a few years later, when Pasha Umalik complained that multistory houses in the western quadrants of the *mellah* gave Jews a direct view into the palace. The increased height of some buildings in the *mellah* may have been the result of a special dispensation granted Jews by the sultan two years earlier to compensate for the catastrophic collapse of a bakery, allowing them to undertake repairs in the *mellah* without first acquiring permission from the proper authorities.[33] Umalik proposed cutting the offending houses down a story, but this solution was rejected by the sultan in favor of increasing the height of the walls.[34] The Jews criticized the pasha, with whom relations were already tense, for not applying the same restrictions to medina homes:

> The question asked by every Jew resident here is, "If the Shereefian command is according to law, why has it been confined to the Jewish buildings, while so many houses belonging to the Moors in the Kasbah and Madeenah are built so high as to afford a view even to the interior of the Palace, which is the case with the house of the Báshá himself."[35]

Contrary to official *dhimma* regulations restricting the height of Jewish homes and synagogues, buildings in the Marrakesh *mellah* frequently exceeded one story.[36]

Population increases are likely to have been behind other spatial changes in the late nineteenth-century *mellah* as well. The main *funduq* was renovated in December of 1879,[37] and a new *qaysārīya* was commissioned by Yeshouʿa Corcos and Yahya b. Sussan, the *mellah*'s two wealthiest residents, in 1891.[38] The building of a new covered market indicates that the *mellah*'s economy had grown along with its density, although not all individuals had profited to the same degree as Corcos and Ben Sussan. Indeed, class stratification became increasingly apparent in the *mellah* as the century drew to an end. In an 1894 British consular report, the wealthy notables of the *mellah* were accused of asserting their authority over poorer Jews by extortion, paying a particularly unpopular pasha of the period, Muhammad Wida, to threaten them.[39] The gap between the *tujjār al-sulṭān,* the sultan's elite corps of merchants (see below), and the peddlers and small shopowners had grown especially wide.[40] Even Umalik, not usually one to plead for leniency for the Jews who fell under his jurisdiction, urged the sultan not to punish Jews caught illegally selling tobacco too severely, as they were "not members of the rich *tujjār* but poor and abounding with doubt."[41] Financial resources largely determined who could escape the city during periods of epidemic, famine, or siege,[42] and also played an important role in resistance to the education and vocational training of girls, one of the more controversial cornerstones of the A.I.U.'s program. Contrary to what one might expect, such resistance was not articulated only in terms of Tradition vs. Modernity, but also in terms of class: the education of girls was relegated to the irrelevant status of a luxury.[43] Unlike the boys, the majority of female students paid their own tuition, suggesting that they came from the very richest families.[44] In 1915, for example, the school's best student was one Rachel Abenhaïm, the daughter of the chief rabbi, who happened also to be one of the richest men in the *mellah*.[45] A decade later, inquiries were made about sending this same student abroad to continue her studies.[46] Apparently, if the daughter of the chief rabbi could afford to pursue a modern education, then she went ahead and did so, at least in this case. Attendance at the girls' school quickly became a class marker in itself: When told that the silk dresses, family jewels, and hats from Tangier that they wore to class were not appropriate school attire, the female students resisted, asking how else people would know that they went to the Alliance school.[47]

Class stratification is also implicit in the most significant spatial change undergone by the nineteenth-century *mellah,* its enlargement. According to several different accounts, sometime prior to 1888 the sultan granted Marrakesh Jewry a portion of the Jinan al-ʿAfiya, the royal gardens bordering the *mellah* to the southeast, for the construction of new homes.[48] But in a pattern repeated elsewhere in Morocco, the proposed expansion was temporarily blocked by a group of *mellah* landlords who did not want to see the rents they collected decrease because of an increased supply of housing.[49] For the same reason, Jewish landlords in Essaouira had tried to block the expansion of that city's *mellah* by bribing the municipal authorities.[50] When it became clear that their efforts would fail, they switched tactics and instead used the sultan's grant to expand their own properties, for which they then charged exorbitant rents. This resulted, ironically, in a public appeal from "87 of the deserving poor" and their advocates to halt all construction in the Essaouira *mellah*.[51] Similar events also took place in Casablanca, where plans for building a new *mellah* were stalled by the refusal of the local Jewish notables to pay a "fee" demanded by the local governor to process the necessary paperwork. Thus only flimsy straw huts were allowed on the designated property, and in 1889 120 of these burned to the ground.[52] Back in Marrakesh, a second initiative to expand the *mellah* met with better results. On 8 November 1890 the *Times of Morocco* reported that a "petition was handed to the Sultan on the day of his entry to Marrakesh, by the Jews there, and he kindly granted them a piece of ground close to their *Mellah*, sufficient for building about 300 rooms."[53] Mawlay Hassan himself was said to have visited the proposed site the following April, where he had an encouraging meeting with the *shaykh al-yahūd*,[54] and in June came notice that construction had finally begun.[55] Yet from this point onward, the timetable for expansion becomes somewhat muddled in the European sources. For instance, though Miège endorses the dating of the *Times*,[56] in mid-1892 the newspaper itself speaks only of a *promise* of expansion extended to a delegation of Marrakesh Jews by the sultan.[57] Still later, in a report on "the Jewries of Marocco," *Times of Morocco* editor Budgett Meakin reiterated the story of the voracious landlords, saying that it took place "some years ago," but made no mention of more recent developments.[58] The schedule of the *mellah*'s enlargement can be clarified, however, with the help of the census and other Arabic source materials.

Mawlay Hassan was resident in Marrakesh when the census was completed in November 1890.[59] According to the biographer al-Marrakushi, the royal capital had in fact been definitively transferred (*istawaṭana*) to Marrakesh just a few years earlier, in 1305 AH (19 September 1887–6 September 1888), whereupon a series of urban projects was immediately begun.[60] Mawlay Hassan's plans for the city included the transformation of the Dar al-Bayda᾽ (the summer residence of a previous sultan) into a palace for his harem, and the restoration of the *qubba* (dome) on the grounds of the imperial palace near Bab al-Ra᾽is. (According to al-Nasiri, the work done on the *qubba* set the royal treasury back a hundred thousand *mithqāls*.[61]) Consistent with these projects, though not explicitly mentioned by al-Marrakushi, is the expansion of the Jewish quarter. Initial work on the *mellah* probably began during the period of Mawlay Hassan's residency in Marrakesh that most closely coincides with the carrying out of the census, that is, sometime between 19 October 1890 and 14 June 1891,[62] and was completed within a few years of his death in 1894. This timetable is supported by an assortment of royal registers (*kanānīsh*). Among the most compelling are 1) a letter of 23 Rabīʿ I

1309/27 October 1891 in which the sultan orders the Marrakesh *muḥtasib* (market provost) to compensate the owner of a plot of land in the Jinan al-ʿAfiya that has been "attached" to the *mellah*,[63] and 2) a detailed report calculating the costs of tearing down (*hadama*) and rebuilding the *mellah*'s walls, including expenditures for labor and specific materials.[64] The latter is consistent with the Makhzan's proposal of March 1891 to share the costs of expansion with the Jews: "The expenses of building the walls will be defrayed by the Sultan, and the houses by the Jews, with their own money, restoring them to the Sultan in case they leave town or in case of their death."[65]

The question of who paid for the *mellah*'s enlargement brings us back to our original concern with the fiscal bases of the census. We have just seen that the expansion was planned as a joint venture between the sultan and the Jews. While overcrowding explains why the Jews (excluding perhaps some landlords) participated in the project, what accounts for the Makhzan's willingness to cede valuable land to the *mellah*? Although European pressure on the sultan to alleviate the living conditions of Moroccan Jews had been steadily mounting since Montefiore's visit,[66] the Makhzan's decision to enlarge the Marrakesh *mellah*, I would argue, was taken neither as a concession to the European agenda nor as the result of any sympathy of its own for the Jews' situation. Rather, the decision grew directly out of the practical need for funds. A brief discussion of how property ownership worked in Marrakesh during this period clarifies this point.

The three relevant categories of land tenure in Morocco in the years under study are 1) Makhzan property (*amlāk al-makhzan*), that which is owned by the sultan and administered by the *amīn al-mustafād* (official in charge of revenues) in each city; 2) *aḥbās* (sing. *ḥubus*, Fr. *habous*, also known as *awqāf*, sing. *waqf*, elsewhere in the Islamic world), inalienable pious endowments whose proceeds support a public institution; and 3) freehold or private property (*mulk*). According to the census, the Marrakesh *mellah* contained none of the first type of property and only six houses of the second type.[67] The vast majority of the *mellah*'s houses were thus privately owned, mostly by Jews.[68] With ten houses to his name, the major Jewish property owner in the *mellah* was Yeshouʿa Corcos.[69] Jews could not own property in the city outside of the *mellah*, however, and I have found no indication that this law was transgressed in Marrakesh,[70] though many stores and workshops were rented by Jews in the medina.[71] Jews from Marrakesh also owned property in the surrounding countryside (see chapter 5).

Interestingly, Muslims owned almost 10 percent of the property in the *mellah*, or twenty of the 210 houses counted. The *mellah*'s single largest property owner, with eleven houses, was a Moroccan Muslim by the name of Bubeker Ghanjaoui, about whom I shall have more to say in the next chapter. The other Muslim landlords in the *mellah* were Muhammad al-Filali (one house), Salim al-Shawi (one house), Muhammad al-Ghazaʾil (one house), and Fatih al-Sahrawi (five houses). With a firm prohibition against their being present in the *mellah* after dark, it seems impossible that any Muslims actually lived in these houses, hence they can all be assumed to be rental properties.[72]

Individual rooms rather than houses were the basic family dwelling,[73] a division that the layout of the traditional courtyard house in Marrakesh made possible. In Jewish-owned houses, the owner of the house usually lived with his family in one of the rooms and rented out the rest, while in Muslim-owned houses all the rooms were rented out. It is significant that the rents for these rooms were on the rise during the period in question. For example, in 1901 a room in a *mellah* house cost 5 francs per month,[74] while in 1912 the price was 6–7 francs,[75] and in 1913 it had increased to 10 francs.[76] Tenants were never lacking, thanks to the combined pressures of population growth, the fixed number of houses, and the prohibition against Jews' living elsewhere in the city. To be a *mellah* landlord was obviously a profitable endeavor. But until the *mellah*'s enlargement, it was a market from which the Makhzan had, uncharacteristically, derived little benefit. (Investment in private property was seen by many in Marrakesh to be a good way of evading the Makhzan's rapacity.[77]) With available terrain just adjacent to the *mellah* and the assurance of the cooperation of prominent Jews in the *mellah,* the time was ripe for the Makhzan to insert itself more aggressively into this lucrative business.

The enlargement of the *mellah* southward, toward the Jinan al-ʿAfiya, and also to the northwest, into "a vague terrain . . . divided between different notables" henceforth known as *millāḥ al-jadīd* (the new *mellah*), clearly accomplished the Makhzan's goals.[78] Rents collected from the new houses owned by the Makhzan soon appeared in the royal revenues,[79] and both the Makhzan and private landlords were quick to capitalize on their investment by raising rents as high as the market could bear without "frightening the inhabitants."[80] (It would not have taken much of an increase to "frighten" the inhabitants of Behira, as the new area was called, for it quickly became the *mellah*'s poorest neighborhood.[81]) By 1905, Eugene Aubin was able to remark that houses in Morocco's *mellahs* were "often the property of the Makhzan,"[82] which was certainly not the case when the census was taken. That the Makhzan's motivation for expanding the *mellah* was ultimately economic was fully understood by the main investors on the Jewish side. When a local *amīn* interfered in the transfer of the land intended for the new buildings, the two men asked the sultan to intervene, reminding him that the sooner they could begin construction, the sooner the *bayt al-māl* (treasury) would start to collect rent.[83]

With rents from the new properties regularly replenishing the *bayt al-māl,* the Makhzan had succeeded in using overcrowding in the *mellah* to its own fiscal advantage. This was the first way in which the quantification of overcrowding via the census was used to the Makhzan's benefit. Let us now turn to the second.

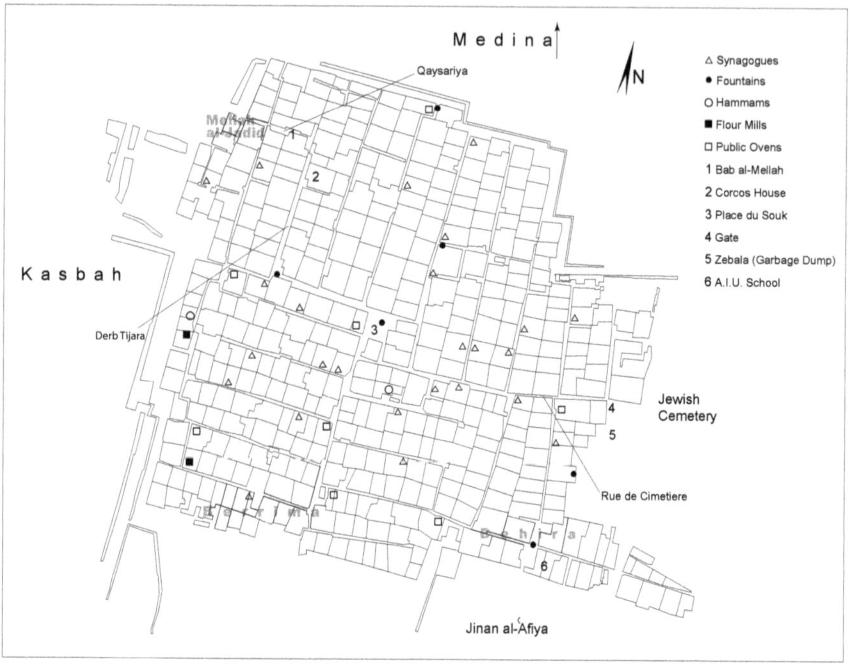

Figure 2.1. Map of the Marrakesh *mellah*.

THE *JIZYA* AND THE CENSUS

As the Moroccan historian Mohammed Kenbib has pointed out, one of the greatest challenges to understanding the history of Jewish-Muslim relations in Morocco is paying sufficient attention to the "discord between canonical dogmas and stipulations and the suppleness of social practice."[84] In no area is this more apparent than in the payment of the *jizya,* the religiously sanctioned poll tax paid by the *ahl al-dhimma* living under Islamic rule. Officially, the *jizya* was supposed to be levied on each male adult and paid by him in person once per year.[85] This is how the process is described in *Jewish Missionary Intelligence* in 1894:

> In the latter place [Marrakesh], the Governor, as well as the "Cadi" (judge), pitch their tents at the Mellah gate, accompanied by secretaries, a dozen soldiers, and the Sheik of the Jews. They send for the Jews, who are inscribed on the list of contribution, four at a time. The rule is, that a Jew cannot send his tax by a friend, clerk, or servant, but must come himself, even if he is ill! Then, when his name is called out, he takes off his shoes, uncovers his head, enters the tent, and crouching before the Governor, puts down his contribution, besides 25 per cent. extra, for the Governor and the Cadi's perquisites. He then receives three blows, more or less hard, on the head, from a soldier, with the palm of his hand . . . He then kisses the hands

> of all the Arabs who are there, and retires, saying, "May God prolong the life of our Sultan, and give him victory over his enemies!"[86]

In regular practice, however, things often worked a bit differently. In Tangier, for example, Susan Miller has found that the individual's role in the *jizya* was largely supplanted by a handful of the town's wealthiest Jews, who both came up with the required sum and personally delivered it to the pasha in a demonstration less of their humility in front of the Muslim authorities than of their authority within the Jewish community.[87] Discrepancies in the realm of *jizya* payment were common in Marrakesh as well. As in Tangier, it was typically not the individual but the richest members of the communal council (Heb. *ma'amad*) of Marrakesh who supervised the collection of the *jizya* and paid it from their own pockets when the communal coffers were bare. The tendency to limit responsibility for the *jizya* to an elite was, if anything, even more exaggerated in Marrakesh than elsewhere, because of the autocratic domination of the community by the *shaykh al-yahūd*. The career of Yeshouʿa Corcos, said to embody "the whole council in himself,"[88] is the best example of this tendency, but already in the late seventeenth century the *shaykh*'s ultimate responsibility for payment of the *jizya* was established fact in Marrakesh.[89] Theory and practice diverged in the regularity of *jizya* enforcement as well. Not only was the *jizya* paid haphazardly in Marrakesh throughout the nineteenth century, but unorthodox arrangements were sometimes made to replace it with other methods of maximizing Makhzan revenues, as observed by William Lemprière:

> Those [Jews] of Morocco [Marrakesh] were excused by Sidi Mahomet [Muhammad b. ʿAbdullah, r. 1757–1790] from this tax, upon condition of their taking off his hands, certain articles of merchandize, of which they were to dispose in the best manner they could, paying him five times their original value; by which they become far greater sufferers than if they had submitted to the annual tax.[90]

At other times Jews paid the *jizya* piecemeal, maintaining ongoing accounts with the Makhzan. For example, the *jizya* due in 1282 (27 May 1865–15 May 1866) was only partly paid during that year, with the remainder paid in the month of Ramaḍān 1283 (7 January 1867–5 February 1867).[91] Under Mawlay Hassan, such lapses were allowed to stretch even longer, often following the ebb and flow of the sultan's attention to Marrakesh and its *mellah*. In the summer of 1887, for example, not long after the Jews had been fêted for the prince's wedding, Mawlay Hassan forgave the *jizya* for seven years and also excused a debt of grain owed him by the Jews left over from an earlier famine. Apparently, the sultan's act of largesse followed the Jews' presenting him with "a translation in Arabic of the usual prayer for royalty . . . adopted by the Jewish community from time immemorial."[92] But with the high cost of reform weighing heavily on the *bayt al-māl*, the ready cash of the *jizya* (valued at 1,000,000 *mithqāls* in 1884[93]) could not long be forfeited in favor of pleasantries.

Since the *jizya* was theoretically a poll tax regardless of who actually paid it in the end, the Makhzan had an obvious interest in determining whether any growth had taken place in the *mellah*'s population. This alone was sufficient cause for carrying out a census, and indeed more stringent enforcement of the *jizya* is observable in the years directly following its execution. In October of 1891, eighteen years of back taxes were paid by the Jews of Marrakesh.[94] A year later, the *jizya* again arrived on schedule, this time including payment for the years 1293 (28 January 1876–15 January 1877) and 1308 (17 August 1890–6 August 1891) in addition to taxes due for the current year.[95] In the interregnum period following Mawlay Hassan's death, calls for the payment of back taxes owed by the Jews became commonplace.[96]

Finally, the 1890 census as a mechanism for promoting *niẓām* may have been connected not only to the expansion of the Marrakesh *mellah* but also to the expansion, and creation, of other *mellahs* in Morocco. That is, a detailed understanding of Morocco's largest *mellah,* such as the one provided by the census, allowed the Makhzan to generate a model for standardizing Jewish space. As is true for other areas of reform as well (most dramatically in the military), uniformity was to become a hallmark of the "new order" throughout the Arab-Islamic world.[97] And indeed, the ʿAlawis were major practitioners of mellahization, seeing to it that few towns lacked a clearly defined Jewish quarter. The ʿAlawis were in fact responsible for the creation of *all* Morocco's *mellahs* except for those in Fez and Marrakesh. Mawlay Ismaʾil (r. 1672–1727) installed the Jewish community of his new capital, Meknes, in a *mellah* in 1679, but it is Mawlay Sulayman (r. 1793–1822) whose name is most closely associated with the institution. In a spate of activity in 1807, he had *mellahs* built in four different cities: Rabat, Salé, Tetuan, and Essaouira. Unlike the earlier examples (Fez, Marrakesh, and Meknes), however, the intention behind these nineteenth-century *mellahs* was less to concretize dynastic authority in the royal capitals than to respond to the growing European presence in Morocco's coastal cities. Because Jews often served as the hosts, interpreters, and agents of such foreigners, it was hoped that separate Jewish quarters would help deflect the influence of Europeans away from the Muslim population. At the same time, newly instituted *mellahs* could enable the Makhzan to reestablish some control over the Jewish population of the coasts, which, especially because of the influence of the protégé system and the A.I.U., was quickly slipping out of its hands.

Two of the few Jewish communities to remain unsegregated in the late nineteenth century happened to be closely tied to the Marrakesh *mellah.* The first was in Safi, the principal port through which Hawz goods and produce were exported, and European wares destined for Marrakesh's Thursday market (*Sūq al-Khamīs*) were imported.[98] Jewish agents oversaw this trade on both ends. The second was in Demnat, which lay a hundred kilometers or so to the east of Marrakesh in the Atlas Mountains. It was home to one of Marrakesh's largest satellite Jewish communities. It was precisely while the major spatial changes to the *mellah* of Marrakesh were being planned and enacted that the prospect of mellahization reached these two towns as well. In 1886 it was reported that the Jews of Safi had been granted land for a *mellah,* though they hesitated to avail themselves of it for fear that it would become mandatory for all Jews to live within its walls.[99] The next year the news came that "the Jews of Demnat were granted a site for a new Mellah outside the town by the Sultan, when he passed through Demnat recently."[100] Although Safi's Jews succeeded in resisting segregation, in Demnat a *mellah* was created in 1894, just after the Marrakesh census had been completed and the Makhzan had been made aware of what the spatial requirements of a *mellah* might be. In Demnat, at least, some small-scale conformity was achieved from the perspective of the Makhzan.

The 1890 census of the Marrakesh *mellah* illustrates both the Makhzan's assimilation of the highest ideological principles of *niẓām*—enumeration, organization, and standardization—and also its ability to put this new knowledge to immediate, practical use. It was not imposed from the outside, as were similar attempts to administratively "capture" other areas of the Middle East, but was adopted by Moroccans for their own purposes, and was consistent with well-established patterns of Makhzan-Jewish interactions. Thus it is remarkable not only for what it reveals about Moroccan understandings of modernism in the late nineteenth century, but also for constituting an extremely rare example of reform not necessarily intended for European consumption.

MELLAH DEMOGRAPHICS

Another reason why the census is so valuable is that it produces the only population figures for the nineteenth-century Marrakesh *mellah* that were methodically determined. It thus obliges one to explain the huge gap between its findings and population estimates made by European visitors to Marrakesh during the same period. While it may be tempting to attribute such discrepancies—which can be in the thousands—to a lack of rigor on the part of the Europeans, on further investigation it becomes apparent that the gap is itself the key to unlocking hitherto unrecognized aspects of Jewish demographic behavior in southern Morocco, which in turn challenge common assumptions about the population movements of Moroccan Jews during the nineteenth century.

JEAN-LOUIS MIÈGE, URBANIZATION, AND THE "EMPTYING OUT" OF THE INTERIOR *MELLAHS*

By far the most influential source for population movements in pre-colonial Morocco is Jean-Louis Miège's five-volume *Le Maroc et l'Europe.* As the title suggests, Miège's approach is based on his observations of how Morocco was subsumed into a world economy through the penetration of European capitalism. According to Miège, a burgeoning Jewish bourgeoisie in the coastal cities lent this process its greatest momentum. Miège's model has a strong demographic element to it, which consists of two main parts. The first is urbanization. Miège argues that rapid economic growth combined with population increases allowed for the development of Morocco's first "real" cities between the years 1830 and 1867. Although this development varied according to place and time, on average it amounted to a 50 percent increase of the Moroccan urban population during a thirty-year period beginning around 1830.[101] Given the overarching claim of supreme European agency in *Le Maroc et l'Europe,* it should come as no surprise that the significance of urbanization is, in Miège's view, geographically limited to the coasts: "Of these changes, that affecting the coastal cities is, without contest, the most obvious and the most significant for the future."[102] The transformation of small fishing villages like Casablanca and abandoned presidios like Mazagan into major port cities, where European manufactured goods could be traded for Moroccan raw materials or bought with local currency, was of course dramatic. But the transformations that took place in the inland cities, and especially Marrakesh, also merit some attention. Yet, according to Miège, these are not even "real" cities at all: "In this country lacking in cities and where for a long time there were no real cities other than capitals or religious centers, the development of the commercial economy gave birth to new cities or infused mediocre villages with new blood."[103] Capitals like Fez, Meknes, and Marrakesh may have retained their traditional royal or *ḥadarīya* (civilized) status, but their economic vitality is understood by Miège as having been forfeited to the coasts. He acknowledges no urbanization *per se* of the interior, recognizing only an "amplification" of the long-established pattern of Berber influx from the surrounding countryside.[104]

The second element of Miège's demographic model separates out a specific Jewish pattern of migration from the interior to the coasts. Around 1850, he tells us, the inland *mellahs*, including, apparently, that of Marrakesh, began "emptying out."[105] The reason for this migration is understood as economic: the Jews abandoned their hometowns to take part in the development of cities like Essaouira, Mazagan, Safi, and eventually Casablanca, and with any luck to be hired by one of the big European firms there. Their knowledge of foreign languages and access to extensive networks of other Jewish merchants in Europe and elsewhere were invaluable to the migrants' success, as well as to the success of the economies of the new cities themselves. For Miège, this movement of Jews away from the interior is "one of the most important phenomena in the evolution of modern Morocco."[106]

How well do Miège's suppositions hold up to the actual demographic experience of Marrakesh Jewry? Was there indeed an "emptying out" of the Marrakesh *mellah* in favor of the coastal cities during the last half of the nineteenth century? Similarly, did Jewish and Muslim populations among *Marrākshīs* truly follow separate trajectories during this period, with Berbers immigrating to the city and Jews emigrating from it? One might also consider what effect the relatively late opening of the A.I.U. in Marrakesh, in the winter of 1900–1901, had on Jewish demographics in southern Morocco. In particular, what might have motivated Jewish migration to and from Marrakesh in the absence of the Alliance's Westernizing influence?

The first thing to recognize is that Marrakesh as a whole experienced population growth every bit as dramatic as that of the coastal cities, whether or not Miège recognized this growth as an aspect of urbanization.[107] Moreover, the sources clearly indicate that this increase included not only Miège's "Berbers,"[108] but many Jews as well. According to Ali Bey's observations, at the beginning of the century Marrakesh had a Jewish population of two thousand, a figure that increased to five thousand by the 1830s[109] and perhaps to six thousand by mid-century.[110] The most dramatic increases, however, occurred during the last quarter of the nineteenth century. Ironically, this is precisely the period that Miège identifies with the emptying of the interior *mellahs*.[111] Between 1875 and 1900 the Jewish population of Marrakesh doubled in size, from seven or eight thousand[112] to fourteen or fifteen thousand,[113] leading Aubin to remark during his 1902 stay in the city that "the *mellah* of Marrakesh . . . is the most important in Morocco."[114] This is not the portrait of a community in the midst of decline. The A.I.U. recognized this; it is difficult to imagine it undertaking the costly and logistically difficult founding of a school in Marrakesh if the demographic future of its Jewish community had been at all in question.

The growth in the *mellah*'s population in the nineteenth century can be traced to a number of factors. The practice of polygamy and marrying young[115] ensured a high birth rate among the Jews of Marrakesh. This was counterbalanced, however, by frequent epidemics of cholera, smallpox, and typhus. In the summer of 1888 alone, 1600 people died from smallpox in the Marrakesh *mellah,*[116] while in 1899, according to Aubin, 2500 children in Marrakesh died in a smallpox epidemic that began in the *mellah.*[117] In the twentieth century, the toll taken by disease would be dramatically reduced as the health and hygiene of the *mellah* improved under the auspices of the A.I.U. and the Protectorate administration. With the help of European doctors like Françoise Legey[118] and Emile Mauchamp,[119] modern hospitals and *maternelles* were opened to serve the residents of Marrakesh, and young Jewish women received training in European-style midwifery. But already in the preceding century there was some foreshadowing of the improvements to come. The European doctors who had begun to appear in Marrakesh in the nineteenth century were typically confined to the *mellah,* and thus treated many Jewish patients. Western-style medicine was practiced in Marrakesh by William Lemprière, surgeon of the Gibraltar garrison, in 1789, John Buffa, who treated the sultan himself in 1805, the Englishman

Table 2.1. Jewish Population Estimates for Marrakesh

Year	*Population (# of individuals, unless otherwise noted)*	*Source*
1540s	3,000+ houses	Luis del Marmol Carvajal, p. 59
1540s	2,000+	Diego de Torres, p. 46
1607	4,000+	Jean Mocquet, p. 400
1636	6,000	Francisco de San Juan del Puerto, p. 79
1763	4000	Pierre Flamand 1950, p. 371
1804	2,000	Ali Bey al-Abassi, p. 166
1810	2,000 families	James Gray Jackson, p. 115
1836	5,000	John Davidson, p. 39
1860	5,000	James Richardson, p. 150
1862	3,000–4,000	Joaquin Gatell (Miège 1989, 3:23 n.3)
1868	6,000	Paul Lambert, pp. 440–441
1875	7,000–8,000	*Bulletin de l'A.I.U.* 51
1876	8,000–10,000	Joseph Halevy (A.I.U. France IX.A.67–73)
1878	6,000	Manuel Pablo Castellanos, p. 18
1878	7,000–8,000	(Col.) Adoph von Conring, p. 152
1882	8,000	French diplomatic mission (Miège 1968, p. 86)
1888	600 families	Charles de Foucauld, p. 401
1889	10,000	Joseph Thomson, p. 350
1891	5,032	D.A.R., Al-tartīb al-ʿāmm
1900	14,000–15,000	*Bulletin de l'A.I.U.* 25, p. 95
9/16/1901	14,000–15,000	*Bulletin de l'A.I.U.* 26, p. 76
1904	7,000	Pierre Flamand 1950
1905	14,000	Nissim Falcon, (A.I.U. Ecoles XXVI.E.398–416)
1905	15,700	Albert Cousin & Daniel Saurin, p. 374
1906	14,000	Eugene Aubin, p. 286
1909	14,000	Nissim Falcon (A.I.U. Ecoles XXVI.E.396–416)
1912	12,000	Alfred Goldenberg (A.I.U. Ecoles XXVI.E.398–416)
1918	17,000	Maurice de Périgny, p. 137
1920	11,000	Pierre Flamand 1950, p. 371
1920	20,000	Jerome Tharaud and Jean Tharaud, p. 127
1926	12,718	*Encyclopedia of Islam,* s.v. "Marrākush"
1927	18,000	Nahum Slouschz, p. 440
1930	40,000	Pascalle Saisset, p. 146
c. 1930	21,000	Pierre Flamand 1950, p. 371

Year	*Population (# of individuals, unless otherwise noted)*	*Source*
1936	25,000	Goldenberg (A.I.U. Ecoles XXVI.E.398–416)
+1936	25,646	*Encyclopedia of Islam,* s.v. "Marrākush"
1937	25,000	A.I.U. Comités Locaux et Communautés II.B.9–13
1939	15,000	Paul Valence, p. 10
1939	13,000	George Orwell, p. 389
1948	15,700	Louis Voinot, p. 10
1949	18,310	Pierre Flamand 1950, 371
1951	16,459	Census de Services municipaux, in Pierre Flamand 1959, p. 267
1960	10,007	*Encyclopaedia Judaica,* s.v. "Marrakesh"
1965	3000	Rosenbloom, p. 210
1980	1820	Josette Sicsic, p. 67
1996	410–420	Jacky Kadoch, interview
2004	300	Jacky Kadoch, interview

John Davidson in 1836, Montefiore's companion Thomas Hodgkin in 1863–1864, and the German Dr. Schmidl in 1899. And from at least 1902, a German Jewish doctor named Holzmann resided in Marrakesh.[120] The Southern Morocco Mission and its medical clinic, founded in Marrakesh in 1891, had a more consistent impact on the local Jews' health.[121] The trend toward better hygiene and Western medicine may have brought a decrease in mortality rates, which in turn would have contributed to a population increase among the Jews.

But even if it is possible to show that Marrakesh experienced a rise rather than a drop in its Jewish population during the nineteenth century, the fact that Miège's claims are based on valid textual evidence must still be reckoned with. The first source he cites is the report of the French consul in Essaouira, Auguste Beaumier, in which the importance of Jewish immigration from Marrakesh to Essaouira is underlined. The second source Miège cites is more specific, and thus even more difficult to reconcile with what we know about population increases among Marrakesh Jewry. This is the report of Joseph Halévy, the A.I.U.'s first representative to visit Marrakesh. During his visit of 1876, Halévy remarked that rental prices in the *mellah* had dropped significantly as a result of the departure of many Jews from the city:

> Most [Jews], fleeing mistreatment by the authorities, are establishing themselves in the coastal towns where the presence of European agents shields them from persecution. The rest, for whom unknowable suffering has heightened the imagination, have left to the Holy Land to dedicate themselves to acts of devotion.[122]

The assertion that there was a decrease in the *mellah*'s population is altogether more striking when the census is reintroduced into the discussion. According to its calculations, the population of the *mellah* in 1890 was 5,032,[123] as little as a third of the figure of 10–15,000 found in the European sources for the same period. To what is such a dramatic discrepancy to be attributed? Were European estimates during the nineteenth century consistently inflated not by tens, nor even hundreds, but by thousands? Before dismissing the European sources out of hand, it may be worth taking a look at the report of a second A.I.U. representative who visited Marrakesh. Abraham Ribbi, the director of the Alliance school in Tangier, came to Marrakesh in 1897. Rather than seeing the veritable ghost town depicted by Halévy, Ribbi reports that "the activity that prevails in the *mellah* is intense." He further notes that the *mellah* is still extremely overcrowded despite its expansion in recent years:

> The houses in the *mellah* number approximately 600. Of this number, around a hundred are inhabited by a single family, comprising an average of ten or so people. The rest of the houses contain 8 or 10 families, thus comprising 60 or so people per house. If we assume an average of 25 people per house, we effectively arrive at a total of 14–15,000 people, which is, in effect, the approximate Jewish population living in the *mellah* of Marrakesh.[124]

Whereas his predecessor had all but closed the door on Marrakesh by recommending that emigration from the city should be encouraged,[125] Ribbi, in contrast, felt that Marrakesh Jewry was vital, growing, and warranted the immediate founding of a school.

The key to understanding the discrepancy between the findings of the census and what we know to have been a steady increase in the Jewish population of Marrakesh, and thus also between the reports of Halévy and Ribbi, is to compare the methods of counting employed by each. It can be recalled from the previous section that one of the main concerns of the census was the problem of overcrowding in the *mellah*. We know this not only from the fiscal benefits that the Makhzan derived from an increase in the Jewish population, but also from the methods employed by the census. The census looked for the number of people in a house, i.e., proof that the "living spaces" had become "narrow." For this reason it counted residents exclusively: those physically located within the rooms of a *mellah* home at the time of the census takers' visit. The requirement of residency helps explain why women were counted, including teenage girls and widows, whose relevance for the Makhzan had mostly to do with the space they took up (the *jizya* was levied only on men). On the other hand, the methods used by European visitors were not only less rigorous than those of the census, but, more importantly, were not based on residence within a house. Even Ribbi, whose approach may at first appear similar to that of the census, was in reality merely extrapolating from what he took to be an average number of inhabitants per house. Rather, European estimates were in all likelihood based on the number of Jews seen in the streets of Marrakesh, or on information supplied by the community itself.[126] Both calculations can be explained by an investigation into some of the broader demographic trends in Marrakesh at the time.

THE FLOATING POPULATION OF MARRAKESH

As the only major city between Fez and Timbuktu, Marrakesh supplied provisions not only to the people of the surrounding Hawz, but also to those of the Atlas, the Dadès, the Draʿ, and the Sus. To many observers, the southern capital was less a city than one big *sūq:* "A commercial center in constant contact with Fez, this is not a city of intellectuals nor is it a city that one loves; it is a city where one sells, where one lives, to which one goes and from which one returns."[127] As a result of its bustling economic life, Marrakesh historically attracted a large number of temporary residents, known as a floating population, since such individuals have no fixed residence in the city. In 1926, for example, this population was estimated to be between twenty and twenty-five thousand, the equivalent of one-sixth of the permanent population of Marrakesh at the time.[128] In the nineteenth century, for reasons soon to be discussed, there were times when Marrakesh's floating population was in fact equal to the permanent one. Jews have never been explicitly connected to this phenomenon, despite the fact that Marrakesh held many of the same attractions for Jewish migrants as it did for Muslims. Commerce, the *maḥalla* (the seasonal residency of the sultan and his entourage), and pilgrimage all stimulated significant influxes of both Jews and Muslims into Marrakesh. In addition, there were also a few categories of exclusively Jewish migration into Marrakesh. The existence of a Jewish floating population in Marrakesh, one that by its very nature was only minimally integrated into the domestic life of the *mellah,* fills the gap between the calculations of the census, based on occupation of a fixed space, and the European sources while at the same time adding new depth to the developing profile of the Marrakesh *mellah.*

"FLOATING" MERCHANTS

Despite a dismal prognosis in the early 1800s,[129] the Marrakesh economy quickly revived as the century unfolded. In long-distance trade, Marrakesh benefited both from an increase in the total volume of trans-Saharan exchanges and from the emergence of a Moroccan market for European manufactured goods, for which it served as southern Morocco's main center for redistribution. Nor had any vitality been lost in local trade: regional products like almonds, apricot kernels, wax, olives, oil, and animal hides were exchanged in great volume in Marrakesh's many markets. Moroccan Jews were deeply involved in most aspects of the city's commercial life. For present purposes, however, the focus will be on those Jewish merchants who, like their Muslim counterparts, came to Marrakesh from other parts of the country to take part in the great game of "*shirā' wa bayaʿ*" (buying and selling) that was so deeply woven into the urban fabric, and hence contributed to a floating Jewish population.

Especially in the period when the sultan's permission was required before foreigners could venture inland, it was common for European firms to employ Jews from the coastal areas as their agents (*nuwwāb*, sing. *nā'ib*) to do their bidding in the interior. The Moroccan archives contain many letters from these agents, written to the pasha of Marrakesh or other authorities, requesting safe passage from the coast as well as the official's good offices once the agent arrived. Sometimes agents even requested that their employer's extra-territorial status on the coast be extended to them during their stay.[130] Jewish merchants from the interior of the country were also present in Marrakesh. Those from Fez were a prominent enough feature in the *mellah* to support their own synagogue, the *Ṣlāt al-Fāssiyīn*. The *mellah*'s brisk trade in tobacco from Ketama suggests that Jews from that region likewise had occasion to travel south to Marrakesh.[131] The vast majority of itinerant traders, however, came to Marrakesh from the immediately surrounding countryside. As the *Times of Morocco* reminds us, "Being close to the Atlas, very many Soosis, and mountaineers, both Berbers and Jews are to be met in the streets, in their strangely marked clothes."[132] Jews from Intifa, Asni, and Aït Adrar were especially frequent visitors to Marrakesh, where they bought tobacco, textiles, tea, sugar, and coffee, items not easily found in the small *sūq*s of the interior.

THE *MAḤALLA*

The most dramatic increases in Marrakesh's population came with the arrival, usually in winter, of the sultan and his entourage, an event known in Arabic as the *maḥalla*.[133] Since at least the Saʿdi period, the *maḥalla* had been a key institution within the Moroccan political system. It had great symbolic as well as actual power; the movement of the sultan and his entourage between the royal capitals and into the countryside did much to compensate for Morocco's weak centralization. When the *maḥalla* came to the south, the region's taxes were collected, allegiances sworn, and disputes resolved, preventing any southern discontent from festering into dissidence.

Mawlay Hassan was a great believer in the *maḥalla*, undertaking nineteen such sojourns during his reign. Indeed he died while on a campaign to the Tadla region, of an illness he had contracted during an earlier expedition to the Tafilalt.[134] When Mawlay Hassan's *maḥalla* came to Marrakesh, its harem, soldiery, functionaries, and administrators could easily double the city's normal population.[135] Among the entourage were many Jews. Mawlay Hassan was known for bringing his favorite Jewish embroiderers, jewelers, and tailors with him to Marrakesh from Fez.[136] Other Jews came to Marrakesh independently during the *maḥalla,* attracted by the opportunities it presented. Not least compelling was the need to provision so many people, who in the course of their stay would consume "much tea, much sugar, many cakes, and many candles."[137] As a special precaution against shortages, a rule was enforced that no grain be exported from the south during the sultan's stay in Marrakesh.[138] All of this portended a significant economic boom for local Jews, as we see in an A.I.U. director's laments over the *maḥalla*'s departure:

> The presence of the Sharifian court and the Moroccan army in our city, in their capacity as consumers, brought the Jews considerable support. This clientele is now missing; business has fallen into a state of stagnancy, and merchants, tailors, jewelers, etc. are forced into unemployment.[139]

If tailors were among those who suffered the most from the *maḥalla*'s absence, it makes sense that they were among those that benefited most from the sultan's stay in Marrakesh, where it was customary to "repair the uniforms not only of soldiers, but also of servants, employees, maids, and slaves of all types."[140] We can assume that a good deal of this labor fell to Jews, both local and migrant, as several Jewish tailors were under exclusive contract to the court, and even accompanied it on expeditions from Marrakesh into the countryside.[141] Halévy reported, "In passing through the bazaar in the Arab quarter, I saw long lines of young Jewish girls, head and feet uncovered, at work sewing military uniforms for which they received only ten to fifteen *centimes* per day."[142] Wages aside, the effort required by these seamstresses must have been enormous when we recall that the army comprised as many as ten thousand men, making it the single largest contingent of the royal entourage.

That the overall quickening of the city's economic pace during the *maḥalla* was a magnet for out-of-towners is also indexed by the fact that the fee paid for the right to collect entry taxes at the door to the *mellah* (an indicator of goods brought into the *mellah* from outside the city) diminished significantly in the years that the sultan stayed away. In 1884, a year when the *maḥalla* did not come to Marrakesh, the highest bid for the right to collect taxes at the gate of the *mellah* was 25,000 *riyāl*s, 5000 *riyāl*s less than for the previous year. When the local *amīn*s were asked to account for the decrease in revenues, they explained,

> It comes to the sharifian knowledge that the Makhzan has great influence in the situation, and that its presence here encourages buying and selling and consumption in all commodities and other things, and when the sultan and his entourage go elsewhere the situation is the contrary.[143]

The *maḥalla*'s stay also attracted traveling Jewish musicians to Marrakesh, who entertained at the many celebrations that took place in honor of the sultan.[144]

The arrival of the *maḥalla* in Marrakesh also heralded the imminent appearance of the region's *tujjār al-sulṭān,*[145] the elite coterie of royal merchants responsible for conducting Morocco's international trade. Many of the *tujjār* were Jews from Essaouira. At regular intervals they came to the court to offer the sultan the customary *hadīya* (gift) in exchange for special dispensations. A few details about this process can be gleaned from the account by the English traveler James Richardson:

> When the Emperor resides in the South, he receives visits from the merchants of Mogador [Essaouira]. These visits are imperative on the merchants, if they are his imperial debtors, or even if they wish to maintain a friendly feeling with his government. Upon an average, the visits of deputations of merchants, take place every three or four years; more frequently they cannot well be, because they cost the merchants immense sums in presents, each often giving to the value of three or four thousand dollars. In return, they receive additional and prolonged credits. The number of Imperial merchants is about twenty, three of whom are Englishmen, Messrs. Willshire, Elton, and Robertson, Most of the rest are Barbary Jews. But the Emperor must have some European merchants connected with these Jews to maintain the commercial relations of his country with Europe.[146]

Leaders of Jewish communities in the tribal areas were likewise summoned to Marrakesh to give the *hadīya* to the sultan during his stay in Marrakesh, no doubt accompanied by entourages of their own.[147]

PILGRIMAGE

Pilgrims to the tombs of holy figures constitute a final category of Marrakesh's inter-communal floating population. Although this subject will be treated more completely in chapter 5, it should briefly be noted in the current context that Jewish pilgrims accounted for a large segment of the floating population in Marrakesh. Prior to visiting any of the region's other saints, Jews on *ziyāras* (literally visits; pilgrimages) were first expected to pay their respects to Hananiya Ha-Cohen, whose tomb is located in the Jewish cemetery adjacent to the *mellah.* While local Jews visited his grave regularly, often on Saturday nights—one woman recalled how she and her friends left the cemetery "as if leaving the cinema after a film"[148]—those who came on more structured visits from elsewhere in Morocco stayed for a full seven days. They lit candles, prayed, sang, and, especially in the case of the sick, waited for saintly intervention. As one pilgrim remembered, "the entire world gathered together at the tomb of Rabbi Hananiya."[149]

In addition to the reasons for temporary migration to Marrakesh shared by both Jewish and Muslim Moroccans, including commerce, the sultan's *maḥalla,* and pilgrimage, it was suggested earlier that some population

Figure 2.2. Jewish cemetery of Marrakesh. Photograph © Architecture Visual Resources Library, University of California, Berkeley. Lifchez Collection.

influxes had a uniquely Jewish character. These migrations, which comprised scholars, refugees, and Palestinian envoys, were likewise of a temporary nature, yet they made special claims on the *mellah* that the former categories of migrants did not. In this sense they are more closely aligned with trends in European or world Jewish history, though still closely informed by the Moroccan, and even more so the Marrakesh, environment.

In a pattern recognizable the world over, young Jewish men in Morocco traveled from communities where higher education was unavailable to the nearest center of Jewish communal life to pursue rabbinical studies.[150] Although Marrakesh never became known as a center of Jewish intellectual creativity (except perhaps for a brief interlude in the sixteenth century), it nonetheless served the necessary function of training young rabbis. The utility of its schools rather than their excellence was duly recognized by Nahum Slouschz, a Jewish traveler and Hebraicist well acquainted with the yeshivas of Europe: "The Talmud is taught in a Yeshibah under the renowned Rabbi Azar, but there are very few true scholars in Morocco, although there are gathered here the Jewish youths from all parts of the Atlas for instruction in the Law."[151] Since Marrakesh had the only advanced *yeshivot* in the south, scholars sometimes had to travel long distances to pursue their studies. For instance, the "traveling rabbi" Mordukhai Abisrour, best known for having served as guide and interpreter for the French explorer Charles de Foucauld, came

Figure 2.3. Grave in the Jewish Cemetery of Marrakesh. Photograph © Architecture Visual Resources Library, University of California, Berkeley. Lifchez Collection.

from Akka to Marrakesh to study prior to establishing himself in Timbuktu to participate in the trans-Saharan trade.[152] Several other young men came from the pre-Saharan regions of the Aït ʿAtta.[153] These scholars rarely became permanent residents of the *mellah*. Usually they remained in Marrakesh only as long as their studies lasted and then went back to their home villages. Even while they were studying in Marrakesh, their presence was sporadic. They often preferred to travel long distances back to their home villages to celebrate the major Jewish holidays with their families rather than remain in the capital.[154]

Refugees constitute a second group of specifically Jewish migrants. As the country's largest Jewish community, the Jews of the Marrakesh *mellah* had a special responsibility to take in their coreligionists during times of danger. Thus when pillaging broke out in Demnat or Tamarzit, it was to Marrakesh that Jews from these places fled.[155] Along similar lines, famine, drought, and epidemics also caused massive influxes of refugees into Marrakesh, as seen in the following report by Bubeker Ghanjaoui:

> The drought has given rise to very high prices and famine, and no one can leave his house on account of the number of beggars. People are selling their houses and property, but without profit, and if one wishes to give alms, it is impossible as an enormous number of persons immediately fall on him, and if it were not for the imported flour &c., every one would have died. No one, rich or poor, can go to the grain market. The whole city is

filled with bad characters, strangers and Bedouins from all quarters, and firing occurs always all through the night by the guards placed at the doors of houses, shops, and fondaks.[156]

The *mellah* was placed under enormous strain by the expectation that it would provide succor for all Jews in need. The summer of 1905, when failed harvests and rising prices wreaked havoc throughout the south, was an especially difficult period:

> The famine has fully set in. The last hope has evaporated: the harvests were worse than mediocre and the price of wheat continues to rise. The communal treasury is powerless in the face of such generalized distress. The *ma'amad*, which met a few days ago, has assigned each notable (there are between 30–40) a quantity of bread that he shall distribute each week. A loaf of bread is given to each family regardless of the number of members it contains. The roads are infested with bandits who rob the caravans; the camel seller sells his animals so as not to have to feed them. All communication with the coastal towns has become difficult and Marrakesh remains abandoned. To make matters worse, Marrakesh must feed all the unfortunates who have left their towns near the city and in the Sus and Draʿ.[157]

Inevitably, each new famine, draught, or epidemic in the countryside resulted in an appeal from the local A.I.U. teachers for emergency funds to aid the refugees.

Finally, a small but regular number of Jews came to Marrakesh from Palestine. Contact between Moroccan Jewry and the Jewish communities of Safed, Jerusalem, Hebron, and Tiberias was traditionally maintained through the sending of alms[158] and the exchange of visitors. For now, we will consider just one half of that exchange, namely the envoys who came from Palestine to Marrakesh, who had the special status of *shaliakh* (Heb., pl. *shalikhim*). The most famous *shaliakh* to visit Morocco was Elisha Ashkenazi, the father of Nathan of Gaza, who did much to popularize Shabbatai Tsvi's messianic message in seventeenth-century Morocco before dying in Meknes.[159] Most *shalikhim*, however, came to Morocco with the more modest goal of collecting alms for their communities back home:

> The *chalihim* are ordinary mendicants who come to beg on their own account, or, more often, collectors sent to get together funds for certain communities in Judaea. The latter are sure of the best reception in the Mellahs, all of whose budgets contain, each year, special sums set apart for them. It is by no means rarc for one of these licensed collectors to obtain as much as 1000 douros in a single trip, and their personal gains amount to 35 per cent of their takings.[160]

Marrakesh was a requisite stop on the *shalikhim*'s routes. The region's satellite Jewish communities were also important destinations, judging from the many requests sent to the Makhzan for letters of introduction to the regional *qā'ids* whose territories the envoys planned to traverse.[161]

COUNTING THE FLOATING JEWISH POPULATION

Because the requirement of residency (again, defined by physical presence in a room within a *mellah* house) is what distinguishes the census's findings from the population estimates of foreign visitors, it is necessary to try to figure out as much as we can about where these various migrants stayed in Marrakesh to determine into which group they fell—residents or floaters—and thus whether they were accounted for in the census or not.

Of all the migrants who made up Marrakesh's Jewish floating population, only two groups are likely to have been lodged in *mellah* houses. Because status (religious more than economic) appears to have played the greatest role in deciding whether a migrant would be taken into a Jewish home or left to his or her own devices, the *shalikhim,* who carried with them the aura of the Holy Land, were typically lodged with the same generosity with which they were given alms, leading Aubin to comment that "in Morocco Jewish hospitality is willingly displayed only to the Rabbis from Palestine."[162] Similarly, the young men who came to Marrakesh to pursue rabbinical studies were housed with the wealthier families of the *mellah,* for whom such acts of hospitality were considered a *mitsvah* (Heb., pious deed).[163] This honor often fell to the *shaykh al-yahūd:*

> It is he who procures for distinguished travelers and delegates (*shalikhim*) from the Holy Land hospitality and means of existence that often exceeds the resources of the community. Our brothers in Marrakesh, so sober, so careful with their money, become prodigious to the point of excess toward the strangers they receive under their roofs.[164]

The *mellah*'s less prestigious Jewish visitors did not fare quite so well. While merchants, at least the wealthier ones or those with partners or family members in Marrakesh, could presumably secure lodgings without too much difficulty, refugees, peddlers, and those without money or connections were faced with a much harder task in what was already an overcrowded environment. Especially in times of crisis, Marrakesh swarmed with beggars in search of relief. During the drought of 1905–1906, we are told that "Every street is filled with wretches in all states of starvation."[165] That some of these "wretches" were undoubtedly Jews is apparent from a similar crisis that occurred two years earlier, when the A.I.U. director in Marrakesh was forced to appeal to Paris for extra funds to help house the Jews who flooded into Marrakesh during a period of severe unrest in the countryside.[166] Moreover, even if the Jews of the *mellah* wanted to take in refugees, they were sometimes forbidden to do so by the local authorities. In one instance a group of

Jewish families expelled from the village of Asni roamed around the outskirts of Marrakesh for weeks in a state of near starvation because the pasha of Marrakesh would not allow any of the local Jewish communities to open their doors to the refugees. Only European protégés dared ignore the pasha's command, including Jacob Hazan, a *mellah* notable with French protection, who took in fifteen of the Jews from Asni.[167]

Many members of Marrakesh's Jewish floating population inevitably ended up camping in the cemetery, whose spaciousness lay in stark contrast to the overcrowded *mellah*. Some were pilgrims who slept in the cemetery for weeks at a time to be closer to the saints they believed could heal their illnesses.[168] Others were refugees from the countryside. Even in calmer times, a semi-permanent group of marginal characters (including "a mad Muslim") set up camp there.[169] The same phenomenon occurs today.[170] Despite the fact that the adjacent *mellah* is now nearly devoid of Jews, at least one Jewish young man, obviously mentally ill, continues to pass his days smoking cigarettes among the gravestones.

The homeless contingent of the Jewish floating population was not counted in the census because it did not fulfill the Makhzan's criteria of residency. Even the Jewish migrants who were housed in *mellah* homes, the *shalikhim* and scholars, may have been omitted from the census as well, as can be deduced from the fact that the census includes at most only five single males without direct familial ties to other residents of the same room or house. Thus despite their probable omission from the census and the related difficulty of determining where, aside from the cemetery, such migrants slept, a significant floating population of Jews, comprising merchants, members and followers of the *maḥalla,* pilgrims, scholars, refugees, exiles, and Palestinian envoys, was a constant presence in Marrakesh. This population not only fills the gap between the census's calculations and those of other sources, but also had a very real impact on the demographic and social history of the *mellah,* as well as on perceptions of overcrowding.

PATTERNS OF EMIGRATION

Yet neither the presence of a floating population of Jews in Marrakesh nor a steady increase in the *mellah*'s overall numbers precludes a simultaneous emigration from the *mellah* of the sort Miège suggests. The population influx into Marrakesh identified above does not negate the possibility that Jews also emigrated from Marrakesh to the coasts, perhaps even so many as to threaten plans for the enlargement of Essaouira's *mellah:* "As fast as the new buildings are erected and occupied, the places vacated in the old town will be filled up by strangers from Marocco [Marrakesh] and the neighbouring provinces."[171]

But how important was this flight to the coast within the context of the other population movements taking place at the time? Did the opportunities provided by Morocco's entry into a world economy constitute, as Miège implies, the main cause of Jewish emigration from Marrakesh, or were other destinations and motivations significant as well? Though there is insufficient statistical information to answer this question in quantitative terms, the major trends in Jewish emigration from Marrakesh can nonetheless be identified, just as patterns of immigration to the city have been.

Some Jews left their native *mellah* to acquire protégé status. As Beaumier points out, several *Marrākshīs* traveled to Essaouira for this purpose.[172] But Morocco's coastal cities were neither the only, nor even the most convenient, place for Jews from southern Morocco to acquire foreign protection of one type or another. Jews from Marrakesh traveled as far away as Egypt to obtain British protection through the chief rabbi of Cairo,[173] but the most common destination was Algeria. The reasons for this were simple: not only had Algeria been under direct French control since 1830, but the Crèmieux decree of 1870, which granted French naturalization to Algerian Jews, could be stretched to cover Moroccan Jews without too much difficulty. One *Marrākshī* Jew who went to Algeria to take advantage of the decree was Mardochée Asseraf. He made immediate use of his new status: on his way back to Marrakesh he was robbed, and he appealed to the French minister of justice for compensation.[174] Algeria was also a destination for Jewish refugees from Marrakesh,[175] and, according to one report, for Jewish men who had converted to Islam in Morocco and wished to return to Judaism.[176]

Emigration to Algeria raises an interesting point about Jewish demographic patterns in Marrakesh, one that is not explicitly recognized by Miège's model. Namely, the fact that women and children were typically left behind by men attempting to acquire foreign protection or return to Judaism suggests that such migrations were probably conceived of as temporary, or, as they have been termed elsewhere, "circular."[177] The Makhzan itself clearly recognized the dynamic of circular migration and used it to ensure the Jews' return. As a letter from the French minister of justice in Algeria complains,

> We learn from this information that foreigners who have emigrated from their country [Morocco] to practice their professions with greater freedom and protection than [exists] in the Empire of Morocco have had to leave behind their wives and children who are held by the authorities.[178]

The expectation that the men would return is likewise reconfirmed by the 1890 census of the Marrakesh *mellah,* which not only registers a significant disparity between the numbers of men and women (2030 men vs. 2857 women) but, as can be recalled, also includes a special category for those "absent" (*ghā'ib*). Fully forty-seven spouses of the married women counted by the census in fall into this category.[179] The temporary nature of Jewish emigration from Marrakesh ought to be kept in mind when determining how much the supposed "emptying out" of the Marrakesh *mellah* contributed to overall urban growth on the coasts.

It is perhaps ironic that the two forms of departure that had the greatest impact on life in the *mellah* did not involve emigration at all. The first was death from disease. The second was conversion from Judaism: the option of abandoning the Jewish community without ever leaving Marrakesh at all. Although conversion from Judaism in nineteenth-century Morocco did not have a significant impact on demographic figures, its spatial and social significance in Marrakesh nonetheless makes it a useful means for examining the *mellah*-medina relationship (see chapter 4).

Daniel Noin, in lamenting the paucity of primary sources relevant to the study of Moroccan demography, has remarked, "it is not impossible that Arabic language archives, which are far from being organized and inventoried, contain some surprises."[180] The 1890 census of the *mellah* of Marrakesh, one such "surprise," has served as the basis for the current inquiry into Jewish demographic patterns in Marrakesh. This unique document provides a microcosmic view of a multidimensional space from a variety of perspectives, ranging from the smallest room in a house in the corner of the *mellah* to the larger crossroads at which Morocco found itself at the moment of the census's execution. With the help of the census, the logic of the Makhzan's relationship to the *mellah* at a specific moment in its renewal has been illuminated as never before. Following from the Saʿdi understanding of the *mellah* in ideological terms (as a political asset in the rivalry with Fez), Mawlay Hassan, operating under the new imperatives of *niẓām*, recognized its more practical possibilities: the *mellah* was a fiscal resource to be exploited to the fullest. The rent from newly constructed Makhzan properties and the reinstatement of the *jizya* after a long period of irregularity would help offset the high price of keeping Morocco independent for a few more years.

The census has also allowed for the drawing of a demographic portrait of the *mellah* to test some of the prevailing theories about Moroccan population movements in the nineteenth century. As we have seen, urbanization was as significant a phenomenon in Marrakesh as it was on the coasts, and Jews were an integral part of this process rather than part of a separate, specifically Jewish pattern of emigration to the coasts. The Marrakesh *mellah* experienced a rise in its population in the nineteenth century, not a decline.

Finally, it has illuminated emigration patterns. Some Jews left Marrakesh to pursue economic opportunities in Morocco's Europeanizing coastal cities, though other reasons and other places, particularly Algeria, were equally if not more powerful and attractive. In most of these cases, temporary migration seems to have been the rule. In addition to physical emigration from Marrakesh, conversion and death by disease also diminished the population of the *mellah,* though these factors were not significant enough to reverse the overall increase in the Jewish population of Marrakesh in the nineteenth century.

3
Muslims and Jewish Space

Dubbed *Marrakech la Rouge* in French and *al-Ḥamrā'* in Arabic for its red ochre visage, Marrakesh was surely an Orientalist's dream city. As the winter home of the sultan, it bore the all-important title of "royal capital," for which reason it was also a city to which foreigners had only restricted access, its inaccessibility reinforced by the impressive walls that surrounded it. Built by the Almoravid sultan ʿAli b. Yusuf, they formed a hexagon almost six miles around, twenty feet tall, and five feet thick.[1] But the remoteness of Marrakesh and its late Westernization only served to increase the city's mysterious allure for European observers. Then there were its markets, bursting with all the "exotic" exports of Africa. Tropical and desert fruits, animal hides, and Morocco's finest crafts filled the many *sūqs* of the medina, and three times a week the wool market was transformed into an auction block, where slaves were paraded and sold to the highest bidder. Finally, the Jmaʿ al-Fna provided in abundance the snake charmers, acrobats, musicians, storytellers, magicians, and healers that were quickly becoming the stuff of legend in Europe. Astute observers were also careful to note the city's classical tripartite plan: the Kasbah for the ruling class, the medina for the Muslim masses, and the *mellah* for the Jews. Such efforts at segregation were apparent even in non-residential areas. In addition to its cemetery, the *mellah* maintained its own prison, which was used by the guard of the main gate (as well as the

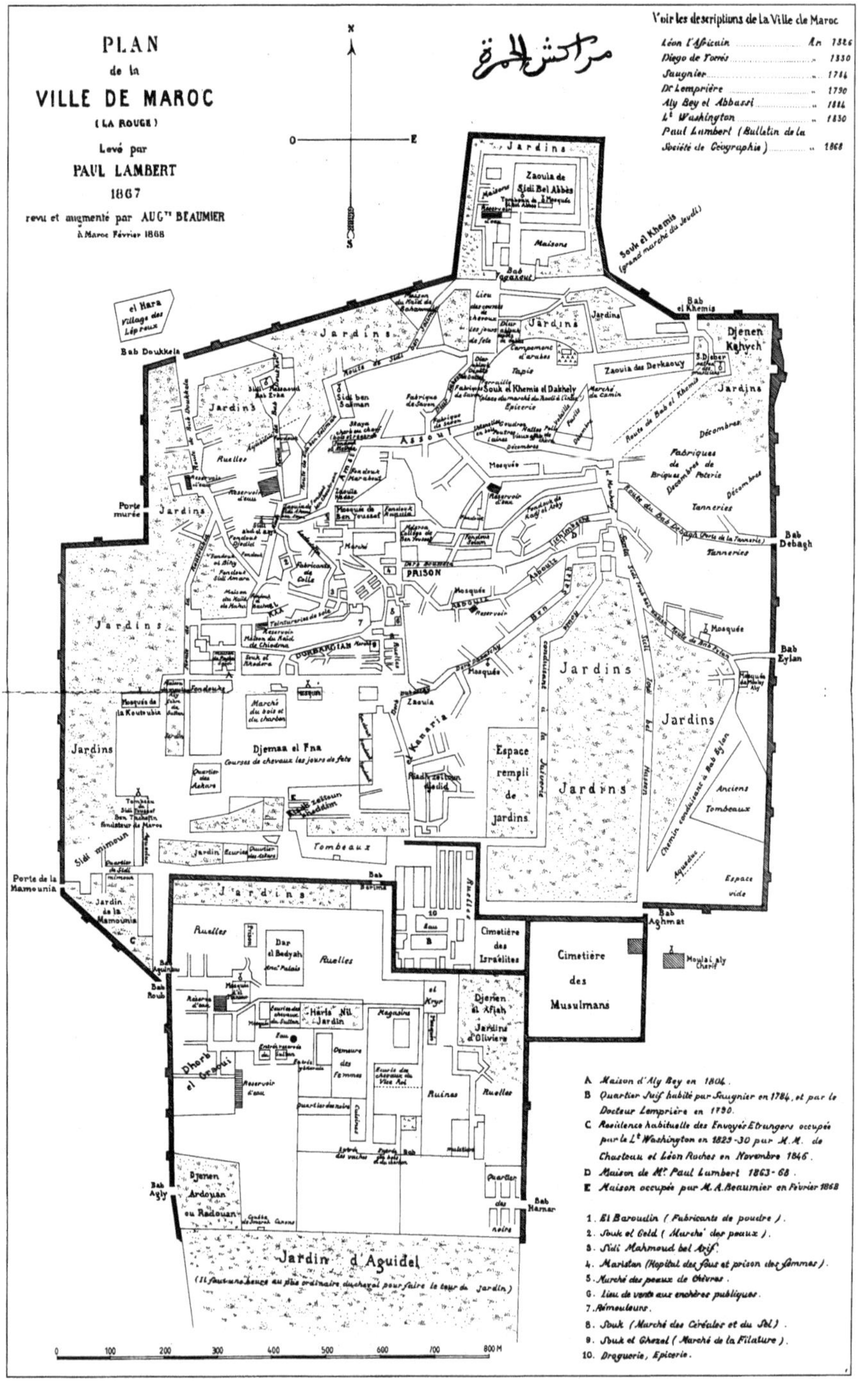

Figure 3.1. Map of Marrakesh by Paul Lambert, 1867. From Said Mouline, *Repères de la mémoire: Marrakech* (Rabat: Royaume du Maroc, Ministere de l'habitat, 1993).

shaykh al-yahūd) to punish Jews for minor infractions.[2] Segregation was also the rule in the medina prison, where the city's more serious criminals were kept, and where several rooms were set aside for Jews.[3] A special prison for female offenders, known by the Persian term *māristān,* stood adjacent to the medina prison and did double duty as an insane asylum. It also had Jewish inmates, though it is unclear whether or not they were kept apart from Muslims.[4] Segregation was the rule even outside the city proper: As confirmed by Ali Bey,[5] Lambert,[6] and Erckmann,[7] the leper colony (*ḥāra*) beyond Bab Dukkala, established several centuries earlier by the Saʿdis, continued to function in the pre-Protectorate period and contained a separate section for Jewish sufferers, complete with its own synagogue.

As indicated by the above, boundaries between Jews and Muslims and the hierarchies of space they implied were certainly the ideal in Marrakesh, both for the Orientalist observer and for the Moroccan authorities (not to mention for Jews themselves, for whom self-segregation has long been an important element in communal life[8]). But to what extent were they also a reality? Separate institutions surely helped shape the ways in which relations between the communities were conducted, but did they ever succeed in fully isolating Jews from Muslims in Marrakesh, or vice versa? Moreover, what does the answer to this question hold for our understanding of the role of Jewish space within Moroccan society; or, conversely, the role of Muslim space within the lives and imaginations of Jews? By carefully examining the points of intersection between the populations of the *mellah* and the medina in this chapter and the next, we can discover the extent to which "ethnic quarters" actually functioned as inter-communal space.

The Muslim presence in the *mellah* was hugely significant not only because of the number of individuals involved,[9] but also because of what their presence meant. Like the Jewish presence in Muslim space, it was primarily motivated by economic concerns. The *muḥtasib,* in defending his right to intervene in the economic affairs of the *mellah,* put it this way: "The commerce and crafts of the *mellah* are linked to the medina because they are all markets."[10] Of the many goods that passed through Marrakesh, Jewish merchants dealt mainly in oil, sulfur, almonds, apricot kernels, cotton, barley, and wax. Hence such products were often made available for purchase in the Jewish quarter first, after which they were resold in other parts of the city. Muslim shoppers were naturally attracted to these goods, and hence were especially visible in the *mellah* on Friday mornings when the main *mellah sūq* was particularly well-stocked for the coming Jewish Sabbath. Because kosher meat was acceptable for consumption under Maliki law, many Muslims patronized the Jewish butchers in the *mellah,* though this probably had less to do with a taste for kosher food than with sporadically cheaper prices for meat. (In the late nineteenth century, butchers in the *mellah* were repeatedly chastised by the authorities for illegally slaughtering cows during

Figure 3.2. Jewish merchants. Postcard, P. Grébert. Private collection of the author.

periods of enforced livestock replenishment following drought and bad harvests, thus lowering prices.[11])

Muslims came to the Jewish quarter not only to buy, but also to sell their own goods and services. Muslim water sellers and porters were a common sight in the *mellah,* as were Muslim beggars. Additionally, many Muslims oversaw real estate holdings in the *mellah.* As indicated by the 1890 census, nearly 10 percent of the houses in the Jewish quarter were owned by Muslims.[12] Since these were presumably rental properties, Muslim landlords doubtless came to the *mellah* periodically to collect rents and inspect their investments. The creation of an Alliance Israélite Universelle school in Marrakesh in the winter of 1900–1901 added yet another dimension to Muslim usage of the *mellah,* as the school employed several Muslim guards and other helpers. A very limited number of Muslim students also attended the school from the time of its opening.[13] The A.I.U. considered hiring a Muslim professor of Arabic in 1910, though it is not clear whether he ever took up the position.[14]

To a somewhat lesser extent, Muslims also used Jewish space for religious purposes. At least one of the saints buried in the Jewish cemetery, Hananiya Ha-Cohen, was venerated by Muslims as well as by Jews.[15] Originally marked by a tree and a simple edifice (a large mausoleum has recently been built at the site), his tomb is believed to date from the mid-seventeenth century. According to local folklore, the Jewish cemetery was also the site for a ritual meant to help Muslim women find spouses:

> If a Moorish maiden does not get married quickly she is taken seven times running to the Jewish cemetery; all her clothes are taken off her, and she is washed all over with graveyard water, after which her thighs and pelvis are fumigated with the evil fumes produced by burning the bristles of a hedgehog, horn from the hoof of an ass, gum arabic, and sulphur. An old sack full of holes which formerly served for carrying about earth from the graves is then drawn down over her head and shoulders, and she is made to step out of it, after which it is thrown away. The mischief made by the evil eye which prevented her from getting married is then left behind in the Jewish cemetery.[16]

Muslims went a step further, and assimilated not just Jewish space but the Jews themselves, or material objects associated with them, into popular religious practices. Cloth torn from a Jew's cap[17] and ashes from a Jew's oven[18] were sought after as occult items in the medina. More valuable still were a Jew's bodily excretions. One of the many uses of a Jew's urine, for example, was as an ingredient in a lethal couscous.[19]

That sites of Jewish-Muslim commercial and cultural exchange existed both inside and outside the *mellah* does not in itself contradict the idea that the larger framework for social relations in Marrakesh was determined by Islam as a religion, even when these exchanges took place in a quarter that was the exclusive residence of Jews. What did pose a real challenge to attempts to order the cityscape along confessional lines, however, was that Muslims also came to the *mellah* to pursue activities that Islam considered illicit and immoral, such as drinking alcohol, gambling, smoking, mingling with Europeans, and gaining both visual and sexual access to women's bodies. The *mellah,* in short, was where a Muslim (or a Jew, for that matter) was free to act in ways that would risk the severe reprobation of the *umma* (Muslim community) if they were indulged in outside the Jewish quarter. Such behavior by Muslims in Jewish space further belies the *mellah*'s isolation from the rest of the city, bolstering its inhabitants' claim to a common *Marrākshī* identity. At the same time, the special nature of these interactions loosens the linkage between Islam as a religion and the disposition of space more generally, leaving room for a more nuanced understanding of the role of Jewish quarters in Moroccan urban history.

THE *MELLAH* AS LIMINAL SPACE

> *Le mellah est considéré comme un quartier infamant.*
> Captain Jules Erckmann, 1885[20]

Like Shanghai or Las Vegas, contemporary Marrakesh is a city rarely noted for its high moral character. Its breathtaking beauty only barely offsets its reputation, at least among non-*Marrākshī*s, for pickpockets, "fake guides," and drug addicts. Despite its popularity as a center for countercultural activities in the 1960s, this reputation is not entirely new; indeed Marrakesh was considered unseemly, or at least something less than totally orthodox, from the very time of the city's founding in the eleventh century. With neither the cultural legacy of al-Andalus nor the Idrisid ties to original Arabian Islam that its northern rival, Fez, could lay claim to, Marrakesh instead looked southward, to the land of its founders and greatest rulers: the Sanhaja Almoravids, the "blue men," so called for the blue veils that the men (and not the women) wore, who first anointed the hot, empty Hawz plain as a new center of Berber Islam and filled it with gardens and palaces. They were followed by the Masmuda Almohads, who tore down the Almoravid city only to build it up again as a testament to their own doctrine of *tawḥīd* (unity). Then came the Saʿdis from the Sus, who fashioned the city into a true royal capital with strong links to the Sudan. Marrakesh clearly belonged to the Atlas Mountains and the continent beyond, where Islam was slow to be absorbed into the local culture and then only with significant compromise. As Gaston Deverdun has remarked, "Whereas Fassis [people from Fez] are admired for their formality and strictness, *Marrākshīs* enjoy the somewhat dubious reputation of a '*gaîté fort libre.*'"[21] If the southern capital's tenuous ties to orthodoxy were not enough of a hindrance to even living a good Muslim life, let alone somehow imprinting that life onto the urban fabric, the attractions of the *mellah* made it all but impossible.

The concept of liminality was originally defined by the anthropologist Victor Turner to explain ephemeral, transitory passages between social roles.[22] It can be usefully adapted here to space, specifically the space of the Moroccan *mellah.* In Turner's view, liminality is a temporary state of being that is typically resolved through the completion of rituals by the person experiencing it, who then rejoins society with a new status. In this way liminality is clearly distinct from "outsiderhood," the condition of being permanently outside the structure of the dominant social system. Putting aside the unlikely prospect of conversion en masse by Moroccan Jews (which would theoretically resolve the ambiguity of their situation), the liminality of the Marrakesh *mellah* is altogether more fixed in both time and place. Nonetheless, Jewish space still seems "betwixt and between," particularly from a Muslim perspective. This quality derives not only from the collective experience of being *Marrākshī* but not Muslim, but also, and more to the point here, from the ways in which this particular type of difference became inscribed in the space of the *mellah* itself.

When the *mellah* was created in the mid-sixteenth century, it was considered one of the city's most attractive quarters, "the fairest place and quietist lodging in all the citie" according to a representative of the Barbary Trade Company.[23] Its spaciousness more than anything else lent the Jewish quarter its attractiveness, an attribute shared by Marrakesh as a whole. As seen previously, only three to four thousand people lived within its walls during the Saʿdi period. By the turn of the twentieth century, however, an area made

Figure 3.3. Street in the Marrakesh *mellah*. Postcard, Lévy et Neurdein Réunis. Private collection of the author.

significantly smaller by flood damage and land expropriations accommodated approximately five times that many people. Overcrowding in the *mellah* only exacerbated what were already dismal conditions due to an extreme climate—summer temperatures in Marrakesh reach well into the triple digits Fahrenheit—and poor sanitation. The *mellah* lacked any system of drainage; household waste was simply tossed into the street, where it accumulated so high as to raise the street level as much as a meter above the thresholds of the houses.[24] This garbage included human waste. According to Levy, homes in the *mellah* contained toilets but they were infrequently used. Instead, adults accomplished their "*besoins naturels*" in the courtyard, and children used the streets.[25] Muslims dumped their garbage at the *mellah*'s entrance when no more suitable place could be found,[26] and few visitors to the *mellah* failed to notice the main *zabāla* (rubbish heap) that towered above the perimeter wall, marking the division between the Jews' living quarters and their cemetery. Estimated to be ten meters high,[27] it was apparently broad enough for Muslims to ride their horses on top of to get a good view of the city and deep enough for the rabbis to bury a woman in it as punishment for having had sexual relations with a gentile. As the missionary Zerbib remarked, you could always tell when you were in the *mellah* by the stench.[28]

Given these conditions, it is not surprising to learn that cholera and other epidemics often began in the *mellah* before making their way through the rest of Marrakesh, or jumping directly to the *mellahs* of other Moroccan cities via infected Jewish travelers.[29] (Trachoma and other dust-borne eye diseases were likewise more common in the *mellah* than in other parts of the city.) Snakes and scorpions were another serious menace, and their images were sketched throughout the *mellah* as a prophylactic. Jews also filled trenches with water along the inside of courtyard walls to drown such vermin before they could reach their victims. The expansion of the *mellah* in 1890 eased the crowding somewhat, but it did little to ameliorate the chronic ills that had already taken root in the *mellah* and helped establish its poor reputation among its neighbors (not to mention among hygiene-obsessed observers from industrialized Europe).

MAḤĪYA: THE WATER OF LIFE

Al-yahūd b'lā maḥīya b'hal l'sulṭān b'lā liḥīya.
[A Jew without *maḥīya* is like a sultan without a beard.]
Popular saying in southern Morocco[30]

Maḥīya, the strong brandy-like concoction made of figs, dates, grapes, or a mixture of them, was perhaps the most powerful of all the *mellah*'s illicit attractions. Strictly forbidden by Islamic law and thus absent (or at least better concealed) in other parts of the city, *maḥīya* was seemingly everywhere in the Jewish quarter. In keeping with their concerns about the correlation between alcohol, hygiene, and morality, French Jewish observers lambasted *maḥīya* as corrupting Moroccan Jewish living space both morally and physically:

> The *mellah* is poisoned by alcohol. Even women and children drink *maḥīya (eau-de-vie).* Sometimes poor devils come to the school begging for a glass of alcohol as if for a piece of bread. I saw a baby at its mother's breast swallow a spoonful of *eau-de-vie* that she had laughingly forced on him; the baby was already emaciated and marked by consumption. Youths between 10 and 15 years old make bets as to who can drink the most in the least amount of time. The flow of alcohol is tremendous.[31]

Maḥīya was provided to visiting foreign dignitaries and supplied to the parties Jews attended in the Kasbah. But mostly it was served by the glass at makeshift bars that stood in the passageway leading from the small eastern door of the *mellah* to the Jewish cemetery. These bars were operated by Jews and served a clientele of both Jews and Muslims.[32] In the Protectorate era, many of these bars migrated to a nearby building that had been granted to the A.I.U. for use as a school by the French Administration des domains. This caused the school's directors to become embroiled in a losing battle against the "*gens mal famés*" who gathered there to drink *maḥīya* and engage in other unsavory activities.[33]

Drunkenness was at the root of a multitude of disturbances in the *mellah.* Family squabbles escalated into violence when *maḥīya* was involved,[34] and Muslims often got into trouble in the *mellah* after drinking too much (including one who ate a number of potatoes without paying for them),[35] as did Jews visiting the medina.[36] After much *maḥīya* had been consumed at the Sabbath lunchtime meal, some local Jews, sufficiently emboldened to act on their misgivings about the A.I.U. and its Jewish *mission civilisatrice,* attacked the school itself. The A.I.U. director hired a special Saturday guard—a Muslim—to protect the building from attacks by inebriated Jews.[37] The Muslim guard at the *mellah*'s main gate was likewise charged with controlling alcohol consumption. He prevented *maḥīya* from being brought into the medina, and, with somewhat less success, discouraged soldiers visiting the *mellah* from imbibing.[38]

The consumption of alcohol in the *mellah* was associated with other vices, most notably smoking. The sale of tobacco and related items was in fact restricted to the *mellah* by the Makhzan during certain periods,[39] and the government's regulation of supply led to a flourishing black market involving both Jews and Muslims, again centered in the *mellah.*[40] Finally, gambling and card playing were other illicit activities that tended to go hand in hand with drinking and smoking in the *mellah.*[41]

SEXUAL VICE

As a corrective to the practice introduced by Max Weber of measuring the Middle Eastern city against the supposedly normative Western one, several scholars have attempted to distinguish characteristics held in common by cities across the Islamic world which could then form the basis of a supposedly more accurate model.[42] Gender segregation, as presented below by Janet Abu-Lughod, is frequently cited as one such common denominator that distinguished Muslim from Western, implicitly "Christian" cities:

> By encouraging gender segregation, Islam created a set of architectural and spatial imperatives that had only a limited range of solutions. What Islam required was some way of dividing functions and places on the basis of gender and then of creating a visual screen between them. This structuring of space was different from what would have prevailed had freer mixing of males and females been the pattern. Such spatial divisions were a functional supplement to alternative patterns of person-marking which were also used but often not fully satisfactory. Semiotics of space in the Islamic city gave warnings and helped persons perform their required duties while still observing avoidance norms.[43]

According to such a conceptualization, the *mellah,* whose inhabitants did not abide by Muslim regulations governing either the mixing of the sexes or "person-marking," particularly among women, is once again partitioned off from the history of Middle Eastern cities and relegated to exceptional status. But in Marrakesh, as throughout Morocco, Muslims were regularly confronted with Jewish women. This happened not only in the medina but also in the *mellah,* where weaker "avoidance norms" helped provide a setting in which sexual vice could and indeed did flourish, making its contribution to the *mellah*'s sense of liminality.

Evidence from the pre- and early Protectorate period suggests that Jewish women were highly visible throughout Marrakesh. According to a 1902 study of Jewish occupational patterns in Marrakesh by A.I.U. director Moïse Levy, over one-third of the wage-earning population of the *mellah,* or 1,935 individuals out of a total of 5,049, were women.[44] While the majority of these (1,030) were seamstresses, Jewish women also worked as maids, cooks, embroiderers, wool spinners, button makers, and water carriers. Women in fact outnumbered their male counterparts almost seven to one in the last occupation (see table 4.1), which is especially notable here in light of how visible they must have been, carrying jugs back and forth between the city's fountains and private houses all day. Women were also responsible for the most of the non-remunerative household labor, which likewise brought them into the public eye on occasion.

Outside their working lives, Jewish women appeared in public as members of search parties sent out to look for lost individuals, and as parties in legal disputes in both the Muslim courts and, later, the consular courts. Whatever their activity, the fact that Jewish women did not cover their faces made them doubly visible, as noted by many visitors to Marrakesh. Far from appearing modest (at least according to prevailing Muslim standards of "person-marking"), Jewish women wore clothing and ornaments that revealed their beauty to its best advantage to locals and foreigners alike. The pseudonymous Ali Bey Al-Abassi, a Spaniard, remarked, "Their rose and jasmin faces would charm Europeans; their delicate features are very expressive, and their eyes enchanting."[45] Thomas Hodgkin, Montefiore's travel companion, was likewise duly impressed by the "well-dressed ladies" gazing down on him from the upper floors of the Corcos home.[46] The London *Times* correspondent Walter Harris noted simply, "The Jewesses are sometimes pretty, and always vain."[47]

The relatively high visibility of Jewish women contributed to the *mellah*'s reputation for sexual vice, but it was not the only factor. For even when the fascination with indigenous women and "native" sexuality apparent in many European sources is taken into account,[48] the historical record still suggests that sexual impropriety was a basic part of life in the *mellah.* Adultery[49] and syphilis[50] were both chronic in the Jewish quarter; divorce was also extremely common. In the *bayt din* records of Marrakesh from the 1920s and 1930s, divorce certificates far outnumber marriage certificates, and the current notary of the Jewish community informs me that this has "always been the case" in Marrakesh. Women were not merely the passive victims in these proceedings, but often the instigators. As one observer put it, "the women change husbands like they change shirts."[51] The ultimate marker of sexual vice in the *mellah,* however, was prostitution.

The association of Moroccan Jews with prostitution is a persistent one. To a significant extent, it reflects anti-Jewish stereotyping,[52] yet like many such stereotypes it also contains certain elements of a real history. It derives in part from the restrictions on female visibility discussed above, to which might be added the fact that Jewish women, unlike their Muslim counterparts, posed for European painters and photographers,[53] and were also counted among the country's most famous dancers and singers (*shaykhāt*), a profession closely associated with prostitution in the Arab world. Such linkages were made altogether more explicit by European travelers who reported seeing Jewish prostitutes in nearly every part of the country, from Tangier in the north[54] to the tiny town of Demnat in the Atlas, where at one point four Jewish prostitutes lived "perpetually on the verge of expulsion."[55]

At the same time, prostitution has long been associated with the city of Marrakesh, and was indeed considered one of the southern capital's "principal industries."[56] Gaston Deverdun alluded to it: "Naturally hardworking and sober, *Marrākshīs* have always loved pleasure, and, despite the appearance of severe restriction of female life in the city, they avoid moral corruption only with great difficulty."[57]

Thus it is not altogether unexpected to find early and ample evidence of Jewish prostitution in Marrakesh. The first such mention appears in 1626–1627, in relation to the *mellah*'s impoverishment in the wake of a severe famine and epidemic.[58] Crisis appears to have been a catalyst in later periods as well, underlining the fact that prostitution was often provisional and informal. For example, the political and economic upheavals of 1905–1906 forced so many of the Jewish women of Marrakesh into prostitution that "the excommunications rain[ed] down on the young girls [and] women who sell their bodies."[59] The threat of excommunication or imprisonment did little to curtail such activity, however. Nor, one would imagine, did the apparent collusion of various local authorities, including at one point the *shaykh al-yahūd* himself.[60] The abandonment of women and children was probably also behind some cases of prostitution, as the wives of the "absent" men found themselves having to provide for themselves and their children in whatever ways they could.[61] Divorce may have also left some women in similar straits. In any event, by the beginning of the Protectorate period there were reportedly one thousand Jewish prostitutes in Marrakesh,[62] corresponding to over 15 percent of the adult female Jewish population.[63]

As for the spatial distribution of the trade, there is some indication that Jewish prostitutes worked in the medina, as did Muslim prostitutes.[64] However, the activities of Bubeker Ghanjaoui,[65] a Muslim entrepreneur in Marrakesh whose name has already come up in connection to the *mellah,* suggest that Jewish prostitution in the pre-Protectorate period was largely concentrated within the space of the *mellah* itself.

Ghanjaoui was a British protégé best known for his vast fortune, amassed through disreputable dealings. A "fixer" and "the greatest capitalist in Marrakesh,"[66] he primarily interested himself in contraband goods, moneylending (it was illegal for a Moroccan Muslim to lend money at interest, which Ghanjaoui most certainly did), and prostitution, all of which he carried out with varying degrees of cooperation by local Jews in Marrakesh. In one of many letters from the Makhzan concerning Ghanjaoui, in this case dealing with his disputed protégé status, the "support he receives from Jews and others with bad reputations" is invoked. Soon thereafter we read,

> It is rumored in Morocco in specific and general [terms] that Bubeker is the agent of the country of England to the presence of his sharifian Highness, and that he runs houses of ill repute in Marrakesh, and that he sells female and black slaves, and that he is among those that take interest in secret.[67]

For present purposes, the most significant accusation leveled against Ghanjaoui is the second, concerning the "houses of ill repute" ("*maḥallāt bi-marrākush mashghūla bi-mā lā yuʿnī*" [It is not inconceivable that the third complaint, trafficking in female slaves, was also related to prostitution]). On the basis of Ghanjaoui's close dealings with Jews,[68] combined with evidence from the 1890 census of the *mellah* of Marrakesh, it appears that many of these houses were in fact located in the *mellah* and housed Jewish prostitutes. Ghanjaoui owned eleven houses in the *mellah,* the largest holding by any individual, and equal only to the combined properties of all the members of the Corcos family. Moreover, compared to other houses in the *mellah,* the properties owned by Ghanjaoui not only contained a disproportionate number of women, they also contained a disproportionate number of "*ayyims*," the ambiguous category of non-virgin adult women without spouses. Of Ghanjaoui's eleven properties, only one lacked a woman in this category, while the remainder contained an average of 2.1. (The average number of *ayyims* per house in the rest of the *mellah* was 1.4.) One of his houses contained seven *ayyims* out of a total of twenty residents, sixteen of whom were women. Prostitution in one form or another may also explain one of the stranger pieces of evidence found in the census: a woman with two "husbands,"[69] living together in a house owned, perhaps not coincidentally, by Ghanjaoui.

Prostitution in Marrakesh was not limited to Jews, nor was it necessarily more prevalent in the Jewish quarter than in other parts of the city. Yet its association with the *mellah* provided a particularly dramatic and salacious fillip to a space that Muslims already regarded as suspect. This can be seen, for example, in the attempts of the municipal authorities to regulate access to the *mellah* by Muslim women. In 1893, a proposal to install a new door linking the *mellah* directly to the medina (rather than via the Kasbah) was rejected on the grounds that allowing Muslim women to enter the *mellah* unsupervised might call their reputations into question.[70] Moral concerns of a broader nature were also a priority for the teacher of Arabic who sought a position at the A.I.U. He attempted to negotiate a higher salary on the grounds that his character was sure to suffer if he worked in the *mellah.*[71]

"*AL-RŪMĪ*"

The presence of foreigners in the *mellah* was also a source of liminality. Foreigners, especially Europeans, were in fact so constant a feature of life in the Jewish quarter that it would not be inaccurate to say that the *mellah* functioned less as an exclusively Jewish space than as a more generally *non-Muslim* space. Indeed, the first European source to use the term "*mellah*" with regard to Marrakesh, in 1767, clearly emphasized the quarter's Christian aspect:

> The city is divided in two: the first part, which one calls the Mullah, is the place where Christians and Jews reside. The Spanish have a convent there consisting of seven or eight priests or monks. The other part, which one calls the Médine, is the place where the Moors live. It is much prettier than the Mullah.[72]

Though the Catholic church mentioned above had fallen into disuse by the late eighteenth century,[73] a "*Derb* Francisco" in the *mellah* attested to its memory over a hundred years later.[74] By the mid-nineteenth century, however, Protestant missionaries had effectively replaced the Catholics. Their targeting of local Jews (proselytizing among Muslims being strictly forbidden by the Moroccan sultan) was cited by the A.I.U. as a major impetus for opening a school in Marrakesh,[75] which itself would be construed as yet another foreign element by the local populace. European merchants and travelers were likewise restricted to the *mellah* during their visits to Marrakesh, a tradition dating from Saʿdi rule in the sixteenth century and carried over by the subsequent dynasty. The French explorers Paul Lambert and Louis Gentil and the Englishman Budgett Meakin are just a few of the more prominent Europeans who made the *mellah* their home while in Marrakesh during the period in question.

In theory, Christians living under Muslim rule shared with Jews the status of "People of the Book." That is, because they subscribed to a monotheistic religion that pre-dated Islam and was based on a revealed scripture, their existence and the practice of their faith was to be tolerated as long as they adhered to certain restrictions. As may be recalled, they held the status of *dhimma,* those "protected" under Islamic law. The Christians who resided in Marrakesh were not technically *dhimmīs*, as they had not been conquered by Islam but lived under Muslim rule temporarily and by choice. Yet their small number, combined with the fact that they generally behaved with respect toward the dominant religion, meant that they were nonetheless typically treated as such. They were often referred to by Moroccans collectively as *al-Rūmī,* literally "Romans," with negative connotations similar to those of the term "Franks" as used in the Middle East. With foreign powers increasingly encroaching on Morocco in the latter half of the nineteenth century, however, the image of the Europeans in Marrakesh was transformed from one of *dhimma* to one more closely resembling *dār al-ḥarb* (the abode of war), a concept that evolved in the early Islamic era to signify the external non-Muslim enemies of Islam (as opposed to the conquered non-Muslim minority living within territories under Muslim authority). Further capitalizing on anti-European sentiment were the followers of the Mauritanian rebel Ma al-ʿAynayn (and later his son El-Hiba), whose forays into Marrakesh during the first decade of the twentieth century typically culminated in verbal and physical attacks on Europeans.[76]

The deterioration of Christian-Muslim relations in Marrakesh can be traced to two principal changes that took place in Morocco during the pre-Protectorate period. First, the number of Europeans in the country as a whole increased significantly. Whereas only 248 Europeans resided in the country in 1832, by 1867 their number had grown more than sixfold, to 1,497.[77] This was a direct consequence of the dramatic expansion of trade between Europe and Morocco initiated by the 1856 treaty with England, to which other treaties favoring European commerce were quickly added. The pressure from foreign trade forced the sultan to open the interior of the country to non-Moroccans for the first time. In 1867 travel restrictions were officially eased and more Europeans began to visit Marrakesh, with a small number settling there on a permanent basis. Among the Germans, the employees of large manufacturers such as Mann, Krupps, and Mannesman were the first to establish offices in Marrakesh, soon followed by consular representatives. Missionary and philanthropic activities provided the English with their first foothold in the southern capital, which in due course likewise led to a more formal diplomatic presence. Finally, France sent one M. Maigret to Marrakesh in 1910 to serve as French consul, replacing a series of local Jews who had previously filled that post.

The second reason for the change in local attitudes toward Europeans in Marrakesh was a shift in behavior among the foreigners themselves. Whereas in earlier periods Europeans often learned Arabic, wore Moroccan clothing, and made a sincere effort to adapt to life in Marrakesh, their deference to local mores declined as their numbers grew.[78] Meanwhile, their protégés, many of them local Jews, did not hesitate to take advantage of their special status by committing a variety of abuses, knowing that they had fiscal and judicial immunity from the sultan's authority.[79]

This transformation of the European presence in Marrakesh had serious repercussions for the *mellah*. Not only was the Jewish quarter the part of the city where Europeans were most conspicuous, but even during their sporadic absences (and those who could flee Marrakesh during times of trouble almost always did), the foreign trappings and institutions that they left behind served as constant reminders of impending European domination:

> The consentaneous [*sic*] progress of Morocco in the universal movement of the age, is argued by the merchants from an increased use of chairs,

> knives, and forks. Some years ago, scarcely a knife and fork, or a chair was to be found in this part of Morocco [i.e., Marrakesh]. Now, almost every house in the Jewish quarter has them. The Jew of Barbary can use them with less scruple than the orthodox Tory Moor, who sets his face like flint against all changes, because his European brethren adopt them. Many innovations of this domestic sort are introduced from Europe into North Africa through the instrumentality of native Jews.[80]

(Enough of the local aesthetic remained, however, to make the mix appear less than harmonious, at least according to some observers: "European furniture, beds, tables, chaires [*sic*], chests of drawers, etc. look strangely out of place where they have been introduced, and they are seldom put to their intended use."[81]) The post office was another glaring symbol of European power in the *mellah*. In 1891, a privately owned postal route between Mazagan and Marrakesh was established by Isaac Brudo, the son of the French consular representative in Mazagan, "at his own risk and peril."[82] To accommodate the new route, a group of Jews in the Marrakesh *mellah* opened the city's first post office the following year. The sultan, it turns out, was planning a similar project at the same time. But the royal postal service that was finally established by *dahir* (royal edict) in November 1892 never succeeded in supplanting the private one, which was eventually purchased from Brudo in 1910 by the Administration des postes françaises au Maroc, with Jacob Hazan as its official "*Receveur des postes*" in Marrakesh. Thereafter the French post office (as well as an Italian one) continued to operate in the *mellah*, employing a mostly Jewish staff.

The provenance of such commodities and institutions did not escape the attention of the local Muslim population. As Europe increasingly came to represent the enemy of Moroccan independence, the negative implications of the *mellah*'s association with things European were compounded. When the introduction of a new coinage in early 1904 sparked riots among a combination of merchants and tribesmen in Marrakesh, an angry mob set off to "eat" the *mellah* (as the Arabic idiom has it). When they found their way blocked, they settled instead for vandalizing the Christian cemetery, where they dug up the head of a European woman and paraded it through town on a pole.[83] A similar association was made during the El-Hiba revolt of 1912, when the followers of the Saharan rebel El-Hiba forced their way into *mellah* homes, where they smashed only the European furniture and glass, before moving on to the A.I.U. to destroy the "*ṣāḥib al-nāṣarā*" (friend of the Nazarenes, i.e., of the Christians).[84] Finally, the most famous instance of anticolonial rioting in Marrakesh was sparked, it may be recalled, by the telegraph equipment spotted on the roof of the French doctor Emile Mauchamp's residence in the medina, which, it was thought, had been placed there to establish a connection to another antenna that had been similarly installed on the roof of the A.I.U. school in the *mellah* (but which may have been nothing more than a pole on which to string a clothesline).[85]

Although the European presence in the *mellah* contributed to its perception as liminal space among Muslims, it should be noted that the association was not nearly so clear nor so readily accepted within the Jewish community itself. Moroccan Jews certainly welcomed the interest that foreign powers and European Jewish organizations had begun to take in them, as their myriad appeals to the A.I.U., the Anglo-Jewish Association, and various European consulates attest. Yet a very different set of circumstances prevailed on the local level, where relations between Jews and resident Europeans were extremely tense and sometimes openly violent.

While the animosity between Jews and Europeans in Marrakesh was mutual, it had significantly different sources. European attitudes toward Moroccan Jews were largely informed by the major political theories of the time, including imperialism and racial anti-Semitism. The travel accounts left by European merchants, explorers, scientists, and members of the colonial administration who visited Marrakesh were often riddled with anti-Semitic tropes. One particularly virulent passage describes a "cringing Jew" who "hugs his dirt as he hugs his gold." Elsewhere in the same work, in a section entitled "The Truth about the Jews," the author refers to his subject as "maggots and parasites."[86] The two ideologies, imperialism and anti-Semitism, were often joined, as can be seen in the following impassioned defense of Moroccan Jewish identity by a local employee of the A.I.U., written to the French chief of municipal services for Marrakesh:

> I conclude that I am innocent. Not entirely, my commandant, as I have two great faults: I am Jewish! And I am Moroccan, Moroccan! That is to say, without protection and consequently without rights, but nonetheless with obligations . . . Is Marrakesh not part of the Protectorate? And, as such, are not its Jews French protégés? Even [as a] Moroccan, am I not a man like you? Do you ignore the fact that like you I have my honor and dignity to defend? But apparently it is only my Jewishness that you attack. You speak with disdain of my person, my little pants and my little jacket, though you know well that the clothes do not make the man, and that I wear my clothes—me, a Jew!—with as much dignity as you wear your military stripes.[87]

Ideological biases, together with foreign competition for markets that local Jewish merchants were used to dominating, caused similar friction, as we see in the following remarks by the director of the Alliance school in Marrakesh in 1907:

> For all time, the Israelite was the country's only trafficker, the only intermediary between Barbary and civilization. Only he could traverse the country without too much danger, thanks to the flexibility of his character and

> his knowledge of the language and ways; he could go anywhere, including the areas of greatest *siba* [revolt] of the most ferocious caïds. No one was threatened by him. He visited the souks, bought cereals, animals, etc., sold sugar, tea, cottons . . . What advantage has the newly installed European in this country brought him? Has he ameliorated his moral situation? Quite the contrary. The European has only fomented jealousy; he has always scorned him as a pariah. The greatest commercial center in Morocco, Casablanca, is well known to be a hotbed of anti-Semitism, and the French consul himself is hardly tender toward our coreligionists. In other towns, the movement is less visible, because the Europeans there are less numerous and the Jews can still be useful. The Jews understand this perfectly.[88]

These circumstances naturally left Jews on the defensive, as the A.I.U. employee's expostulation shows. But when Jewish-European tensions erupted into actual violence, Jews were occasionally perpetrators as well as victims. The European consular records abound with reports of both types of incidents. In one case, a local Jew was charged with the robbery and assault of a Maltese subject,[89] while in another, a group of Italian musicians murdered a Jew in a scuffle over smoking on the Jewish Sabbath. To the utter amusement of the denizens of the medina, the Jews responded by going on a rampage in the *mellah* and threatening to kill all the Christians. An eyewitness to the events, a European resident of the *mellah,* was forced to write his account behind locked doors while Jews threw stones at his house.[90] Whatever goodwill Jews might still have had for the Europeans residing in the *mellah* was surely destroyed by the French merchant who captured and hanged Jews, though "he bound them from the midriff, rather than the neck, as his purpose was to amuse himself rather than to kill them."[91] Such animosity persisted well into the Protectorate period, moreover. In the mid-1920s one "Mrs. Bruce" of England physically attacked a local Jewish woman, hitting her and calling her a "dirty Jew" who ought not to set foot out of the *mellah.* The case ended up in the consular courts.[92]

Not surprisingly, many instances of hostility between Europeans and Jews arose from the former's proselytizing activities. As mentioned previously, Marrakesh had known only Catholic missionaries prior to the nineteenth century. But by 1852, Protestant competitors had begun to gain access to the Moroccan interior.[93] The new missionaries were often individuals of Russian or Eastern European Jewish origin who had converted to Christianity and sought the same for their former coreligionists in Morocco, which made them that much more despised by local Jews.[94] As mentioned above, the targeting of the Jews by missionaries was sufficiently worrisome for the A.I.U. to cite it as one of their main reasons for opening a school in the southern capital.[95]

There were in fact two Protestant groups active among Marrakesh's Jews. The first was the Southern Morocco Mission, a Presbyterian organization based in Glasgow. In 1891, Cuthbert Nairn and his wife established a mission in its name in the Amesfah quarter of Marrakesh. Like many such organizations, the Southern Morocco Mission pursued its missionary work in conjunction with a medical clinic. As Nairn himself explained, "the sole object in opening it [the clinic] was to get into contact with the people and thereby obey the command to 'heal the sick, and preach the gospel.'"[96] Although statistics were not kept for the first few years of the clinic's operations, in the period 1899–1934 a total of 740,610 patients (including both Muslims and Jews) visited the clinic, a figure that does not include many individuals who came outside the regular hours of service.[97] When Aubin visited the *dār al-ṭabīb,* as the clinic was called in Arabic, it saw an average of fifty patients per day and employed seven Moroccan girls to supplement its permanent staff.[98]

Altogether more provocative was a second missionary organization, known as the London Society for the Conversion of the Jews. Though based in Essaouira, on at least one occasion its members were expelled by the Jewish community there and found their way to Marrakesh.[99] The comportment of J. B. Crighton Ginsburg, the Society's director, was no doubt at fault. Ginsburg—himself a Russian convert from Judaism—was openly hostile toward Moroccan Jews, accusing them of extortion, "filthy habits," and "eating up the Moors." The depth of his ill will toward the Jews of Essaouira surprised the English consul:

> It is somewhat curious to hear such an account as this from a man, who, one would imagine, must have gone up inclined to espouse the cause of the "chosen people"; at this distance it is difficult to accurately estimate whether his version is true, or whether the truth may lie half way between the newspaper accounts and his.[100]

The Society managed to incur the wrath of Morocco's usually supportive European residents. When informed of Ginsburg's plans to come to Marrakesh, the British consul Harry Maclean answered, "I am rather sorry as I hear he is a man that kicks up a dust wherever he goes which is a nuisance but I will do all I can to have nothing to do with him if he comes."[101] Even the Moroccan sultan, who normally turned a blind eye to European proselytizing as long as it was limited to the Jews, made his objections to Ginsburg known.[102]

Local Jews' relations with their European coreligionists were often no more harmonious than those with European Christians. Aside from the occasional Jewish traveler[103] and a Jerusalem-born, German-educated doctor,[104] the European Jews with whom the local Jewish community had the most contact were the teachers and directors of the A.I.U.[105] As noted earlier, the A.I.U. fought a continuous uphill battle to gain acceptance for its program. Resistance came from a number of sources. As elsewhere in Morocco, the rabbis were opposed to the schools' determinedly secular outlook, its limited Hebrew and Talmud instruction in favor of European languages and "modern" vocations, and the competition the A.I.U. schools posed to the rabbis' *ṣlās*, from which they earned already meager livelihoods. Holding prize ceremonies far from the *mellah* on Shabbat, when Jews were not supposed to travel, and articulating its intentions in terms of "conversion" did little to improve the A.I.U.'s image. It is worth noting that the chief rabbi in Marrakesh made his first visit to the school only in April 1904, several years after the school had opened.[106]

Resistance to the A.I.U. from "traditional" elements was common throughout Morocco, and was for the most part dealt with through compromise in curricular matters and increased sensitivity to religious issues.[107] In Marrakesh, however, the A.I.U. confronted an additional challenge, one that nearly did the school in: the not quite benign indifference of Yeshouʿa Corcos, the all-powerful *shaykh al-yahūd* of Marrakesh. Although his monetary contributions to the Alliance were consistently larger than those of his fellow Jews,[108] and he himself was a French protégé, his reluctance to abandon his strong patronage ties to the local Muslim authorities in favor of European allies made him highly untrustworthy in the eyes of the A.I.U. Corcos's relations with the first A.I.U. director in Marrakesh, Moïse Levy, were especially difficult, with the latter accusing Corcos of "selling out" his coreligionists: "jealous of his influence and wanting to hold on to total control, [Corcos] stops at nothing to belittle his coreligionists in the eyes of the local authorities instead of lending them his support as a French protégé." Levy went on to say,

> As for me, always outside the different parties, I maintain my best relations with all members of the community. But I think that my mission here must be more; thus it is my obligation, in the interest of protecting a number of unfortunates attending the Alliance, to indicate to you that we have in M. Corcos a powerful enemy, whom eventually I will probably have to fight.[109]

It did not take long for Levy's prediction was to come true. Corcos did indeed have several run-ins with the A.I.U., accusing it of Christianizing Jewish children and inculcating them with "irreligion."[110] His differences with the A.I.U. at one point threatened to divide the *mellah* into warring factions, with Corcos on one side and two other notables, Coriat and Turjman, on the other. The school's second director, Nessim Falcon, had correctly predicted in 1905, "the struggle will be rude."[111]

With the support of neither the rabbis nor the *shaykh al-yahūd*—the religious and political authorities of the *mellah,* respectively—the A.I.U. had limited prospects for success in Marrakesh. The masses mostly followed their leaders' cues, accepting the warm meals, donated clothing, and elevated social status of being associated with the A.I.U. without ever really giving themselves over to its larger program (at least in the eyes of its perpetually frus-

Figure 3.4. *Alliance Israélite Universelle* school in Marrakesh. Photograph courtesy A.I.U., Maroc XXX.E.384, Bibasse, 2 February 1928

trated directors and teachers), particularly when it came to paying their fees. Furthermore, the political unrest in the south during the early part of the twentieth century caused frequent closures, after which it was often difficult to re-register students in school. By 1911, a decade after the A.I.U. had established itself in Marrakesh, only 320 children attended two schools that together were meant to accommodate a thousand students.[112]

It is possible that the inherent contentiousness of European-Jewish relations in Marrakesh was one reason that local Jews were hesitant to ally themselves with the colonial powers. Not only was Europe slow to make the potential benefits of such an alliance felt by Jews in the interior of the country, but when its message finally arrived, the messengers themselves often became entangled in antagonistic relationships with the *mellah*'s residents. Anti-Jewish biases and missionary zeal in the case of gentiles, and a short-sighted vision of a Jewish *mission civilisatrice* in the case of the A.I.U., served to harden the *mellah*'s resistance to external efforts at Westernization. This was manifest, for instance, in issues of dress, which was an important indicator of the social and political climate for Jews in Morocco (see chapter 4). Whereas many coastal Jews had adopted European clothing by the late nineteenth century, Jews in Marrakesh at this time were still loath to trade in their caftans and kerchiefs. The Makhzan's decision in 1885 to oblige Jewish protégés to wear Western suits was met with an outcry. As one observer remarked,

"Their objection to forced adoption of European garb is apparently even stronger than the desire to retain their slippers."[113] The Jews also knew from experience that any amalgamation of themselves and the Europeans in their midst put them in danger, and thus urged the Europeans to evacuate in times of political uncertainty, as in the chaos following the murder of Mauchamp.[114]

However large it may have loomed in Jewish life, intra-*dhimma* wrangling was nonetheless all but lost on the local Muslim population. For them, the association between Jewish space and the intruding Europeans was a well-established fact, to the detriment of both the image of the *mellah* and eventually Jewish-Muslim relations as a whole.

The porousness of the Marrakesh *mellah* lay at the very heart of inter-communal relations. Every day (with the exception of the Sabbath and Jewish holidays), Jews left the *mellah* through its main gate to pursue a wide variety of activities in the medina or Kasbah. On their way, they passed Muslims entering the *mellah* for many of the same purposes, and also to engage in activities specific to Jewish space. Some of these latter activities not only had little to do with the practice of Islam but stood in direct contradiction to its teachings: drinking alcohol, gambling, smoking, engaging prostitutes, encountering Europeans. In short, the *mellah* harbored activities proscribed by Islam while still remaining an integral, organic part of the city as a whole.

4
Jews and Muslim Space

Clearly, Jews felt most at home in the *mellah,* where, even if they didn't always enjoy the total autonomy sometimes suggested, they nonetheless owned property, practiced their religion with minimal interference, maintained their own institutions, worked, and raised their families: activities, moreover, which they had been carrying out in that same space for several hundred years. Jews felt sufficiently secure to defend this "citadel of their independence"[1] against intruders, even using physical force when it seemed necessary. The *mellah*'s gate was locked from within, not from without. But once they ventured beyond the *mellah*'s walls, Jews' confidence quickly eroded and was replaced by an acute sense of vulnerability. Jews who found themselves in one of the city's Muslim quarters faced potential humiliation, sometimes in the form of insults, rocks, urine, or spit hurled their way. More often, however, a subtler means of abasement and control was at work in the medina: Muslim space was where a Jew became a *dhimmī.*

DHIMMA AND THE NEGOTIATION OF MUSLIM SPACE

Up to now, the abstract notion of *dhimma* has largely been passed over in favor of the rich record of inter-communal relations at our disposal. Inadequate as it may be for explaining how Jews actually lived among Muslims, particularly in a context as distant in time and place from the medieval Arabian ideal as modern Morocco, *dhimma* is nonetheless a recurring motif in the language and content of many Moroccan sources,[2] particularly those dealing with how Jews and Muslims interacted in areas of the city outside the *mellah.* One particular aspect of *dhimma,* its sumptuary laws, stands out as a consistent cause of Jewish ambivalence about the medina, and so warrants further investigation.

The Pact of ʿUmar states that non-Muslims living under Islamic rule are required to accept the following restrictions in their dress: "We shall not attempt to resemble Muslims in any way with regard to their dress, as for example, with the *qalansuwa* [conical cap], the turban, sandals, or parting the hair (in the Arab fashion) . . . We shall always adorn ourselves in the traditional fashion."[3] Although originally intended to prevent administrative mistakes, gradually such restrictions came to be read as signs of humiliation. Nowhere in the Muslim world, however, were they ever enforced for any great length of time.[4] In Morocco, for instance, where Jews were the only group subject to such restrictions, they were only reintroduced by Mawlay Sulayman in 1815 after having fallen into disuse.[5] Their application on the local level continued to vary widely, in Marrakesh as elsewhere. The following is a description of the dress of a Jewish woman in Marrakesh during the late eighteenth century, a time when sumptuary laws appear to have been little in force:

> The dress of the Jewish women consists of a fine linen shirt, with large and loose sleeves, which hang almost to the ground; over the shirt is worn a *Caftan,* a loose dress made of woolen cloth, or velvet, of any colour, reaching as low as the hips, and covering the whole of the body, except the neck and breast, which are left open, and the edges of the *Caftan* being embroidered with gold. In addition to these is the *geraldito,* or petticoats, made of fine green woolen cloth, the edges and corners of which have sometimes a gold ornament; this part of the dress is fastened by a broad sash of silk and gold, which surrounds the waist, and the ends of it are suffered to hang down behind, in an easy manner; when they go abroad, they cover the whole with the *haick,* the same used by the Moorish women. The unmarried Jewesses wear their hair plaited in different folds, and hanging down behind; and to this they have a very graceful and becoming method of putting a wreath of wrought silk round the head, and tying it behind with a bow. This dress sets off their features to great advantage, and distinguishes them from the married women, who cover their heads with a red silk handkerchief, which they tie behind, and over it place a silk sash, leaving the ends to hang loose on their backs. None of the Jewish women have stockings, but use red slippers, curiously embroidered with gold. They wear very large gold earrings at the lower part of the ears, and at the upper, three small ones set with pearls or special stones; their necks are loaded with beads, and their fingers with small gold or silver rings; round each wrist and ankle are fixed large and solid silver bracelets; and the rich have gold and silver chains suspended from the sash behind.[6]

The dress of Jewish men was not nearly so elaborate. It typically consisted of a dark blue or black *jallāba* with a black skullcap or kerchief covering the head. Jewish men from the Atlas Mountains could sometimes be distinguished by longer sidelocks (Heb. *payot*),[7] or by a blue headscarf with white dots.[8]

But it is what Jews wore on their feet (more generally, who could wear shoes of what kind where) that best indexes what was, despite the presence of walls and gates, a sometimes fluid boundary between Jewish and Muslim space, and that also serves as an uncanny indicator of the state of Jewish-Muslim relations at any given moment. At one end of the spectrum was the worst-case scenario, in which Jews were obliged by the municipal authorities to walk barefoot in all parts of the city, including inside the *mellah*. Broken glass or burning coals might be strewn along their paths to remind them of their lowly condition.[9] Only one source, Halévy, gives any indication that this rule was enforced in Marrakesh in the late nineteenth century, and even he is unclear. The published account of his visit to Marrakesh says that Jews went barefoot throughout Marrakesh, "even in the *mellah*." The original hand-written version of his report is slightly different, however. There one reads that the Jews were barefoot in "all other quarters of the city outside the *mellah*,"[10] though the phrase is crossed out. Halévy's lack of clarity in this matter suggests that it was probably more typical for Jews to be allowed to wear shoes, or more precisely slippers (*babūsh*s), within the confines of the *mellah*—the women red and the men yellow—but were required to remove them upon entering the medina or Kasbah. This was precisely the situation witnessed by the French doctor Lemprière in the late eighteenth century: "The Jews [of Marrakesh] have a market of their own, and as at Taroudant, when they enter the Moorish town, castle, or palace, they are always compelled to be barefooted."[11] The authorities reverted to these restrictions when they deemed that the Jews' behavior had become "too bold," often in conjunction with abuses in the protégé system, and conversely ignored them when Jews were particularly in favor. The pasha Umalik was especially vigilant in the matter of shoelessness. On at least two occasions, he summoned the *mellah*'s elders to his residence, where, among other reproaches, they were ordered to remove their slippers "in accordance with their ancient status of *dhimma*." Thus made visibly vulnerable, the Jews were then taunted all their way back to the *mellah*.[12] Even Jews with legitimate foreign protection, which normally gave them the right (and sometimes the obligation) to wear European shoes, were ordered to walk barefoot at least in the Kasbah.[13] The regional political situation was also a factor in the enforcement of this baseline. For example, among the Rehamna rebels' demands in return for calling off a planned siege of Marrakesh in 1907 was that the Jews be required to blacken their *babūsh*s when in the *mellah* and remove them altogether upon leaving it.[14] Similar calls were heard during the upheaval caused by El-Hiba's arrival in the southern capital in 1912, when Jews were again made to blacken their slippers and also to replace white vests with black ones.[15]

Such crackdowns inevitably led to foreign diplomatic pressure being exerted on behalf of the Jews, and much greater tolerance usually followed. This end of the spectrum is described in the following letter, sent by the French government to Mawlay ʿAbd al-ʿAziz on behalf of Marrakesh Jewry:

> The situation of the Israelites has improved in the last 4–5 days. I dare think that my entreaties to M. Régnault [the French minister in Tangier] and the promise he made me to send a note to Mawlay ʿAbd al-ʿAziz in support of the Jews had a positive result. One says, in effect, that a letter arrived from Fez to Mawlay Hafidh and that since then the inhabitants of the *mellah* can circulate in the medina in shoes and even mounted [on animals].[16]

In this case, however, the pendulum quickly swung back. In October of the following year, the intervention of the grand vizier Glaoui, prompted no doubt by his various business interests in the Marrakesh *mellah,* was required before the Jews would again enjoy such freedoms.[17]

As the above instances show, fluctuations in the enforcement of sumptuary laws were common during the last few years of Moroccan independence, when European encroachment and the resulting unrest regularly upset the municipal status quo in Marrakesh. But they were not limited to these years. In the 1880s, for example, a letter from a group of Marrakesh's Jews bemoaning Umalik's severity harkened back to earlier, better times: "The protégés circulate freely in Marrakesh, wearing their babouches, and no one notices or says a word. Even those who are not protégés are equally tolerated."[18] A lax climate was again apparent in 1902, judging from the following incident: a local Jew was arrested for riding a horse in the medina and wearing shoes. When asked if he was a protégé, as such behavior would suggest, he responded that he was protected "only by the Sultan and by God," an answer which earned him his immediate freedom.[19]

Between these two extremes, tolerance was negotiated inch by inch. In relatively clement times, Jews could wear slippers in most of the medina with certain exceptions, such as when passing in front of a mosque.[20] In 1880, in an indication that the Jews' status was on a downward slide, Umalik suddenly forbade them to wear shoes in parts of the medina where they had previously been allowed:

> We have just been banned from wearing our shoes in an area where we have always kept them on our feet. Recently, a Jew returning from the medina arrived at this area and wanted to put on his sandals. A soldier who noticed him threw a rock at his head and opened a large wound that gushed blood. He showed it to us all. We have become the bêtes noires of the Arabs, who hit us each time they see us in the medina.[21]

In even more trying times, parts of the *mellah* itself became subject to sumptuary restrictions. In 1910, as anti-French and anti-A.I.U. sentiment was at a peak, bare feet suddenly became required in the area of the *mellah*'s central fountain (indicating, incidentally, that this was an area frequented by Muslims).[22]

The manipulation of sumptuary regulations was a particularly clever form of abasement in that it caused great anxiety among Jews without actually inflicting serious harm. Dress was an important part of the processes, mechanisms, and conditions of coexistence. Jews were also ambivalent about the medina because of the threat it posed of conversion to Islam. Yet here, too, a surprising degree of flexibility on the part of the Makhzan helped to mitigate Jews' anxieties about Muslim space.

MUSLIM SPACE AND THE THREAT OF CONVERSION

Despite the concerted efforts of the Christian missionaries in Marrakesh, the dominant religion, Islam, was the more obvious choice for Jews abandoning Judaism. The Christian missionaries themselves jealously noted that a special quarter in the center of the medina, called "Harth-Soora" (Ḥarat al-Sūra), was set aside for such converts.[23] A powerful preoccupation with the prospect of Islamicization is likewise reflected in local Jewish folklore and hagiographies. Typically, the saints venerated by both Jews and Muslims were converts to Islam, though among Jews such conversions were almost always understood as forced or uncompleted.[24] In the few cases where conversion cannot be shown to have been other than voluntary, the Jewish oral tradition in Marrakesh is careful to point out the evil character of the convert and the retribution that awaits him or her. The corruption of the convert is then used to reconfirm the goodness of those who have remained Jews. The story of Rabbi Tahoné, recounted by an A.I.U. teacher in Marrakesh in 1929, is typical in this respect:

> It is not known exactly when Marrakesh was ruled by the Black Sultan (so named because of his skin color).[25] Having no children, he one day made a vow: "If God would give me a child, I would entrust him to the Jews to educate him and teach him Hebrew."
>
> His prayer was answered: that same year he had a son whom he entrusted to a great rabbi with instructions to educate him well.
>
> The sultan had an advisor who was a Jew converted to Islam; he sent him each day to the rabbi's house to get news of the child. The advisor always brought candies to the young prince. One day he went to the rabbi's house and found the child all alone. On the pretext of buying him some candy, he took the child. Arriving in a desolate area, the advisor cut off his head and threw his corpse into the Jewish cemetery. When the rabbi returned home, imagine his surprise to not find the child. He took to the streets of the city bemoaning his loss, eventually arriving at the cemetery, where he was stupefied by the sight of the child's corpse. Sobbing, he left to announce the death of the prince to all the Jews, and ordered them to fast. When the sultan learned of the disappearance of his only son, he flew into a fury. Be-

lieving that it was the Jews who took him away, he threatened them with extermination if they did not bring his son back to him.

During this period, there lived a rabbi named Moussa Tahoné. He lived alone and never left his house. With a white beard and a back bent with the weight of years, he devoted his time to praying to the Eternal. His wife brought him his food.

The day of the prince's death, he waited in vain for his wife. That evening, he sent her out to have a look around. She came back and told the rabbi all that had happened.

Rabbi Tahoné transported himself to the sultan's palace and from there to the cemetery where the Sultan saw the prince's corpse. Rabbi Tahoné hit the child with a stick he held in his hand which revived him immediately:

"Tell me quickly, who killed you?"

"Him," said the child, pointing out the advisor. And then he fell unconscious again.

The sultan asked the rabbi to resuscitate the child, but he responded:

"He who has died will never come back to life."

That very same day the advisor was executed.[26]

Despite their wide circulation, cautionary tales such as this one failed to put an end to Jewish apostasy in Marrakesh. Nonetheless, conversion was in many cases far from permanent. Forced conversion, cited by European Jewish organizations as a major problem in Morocco,[27] was, in reality, difficult to make stick. This was due in no small part to the sultan's willingness to reverse the harsh rulings of local authorities, as illustrated by the following incident: In early 1893 a Jew from the Marrakesh *mellah* decided to convert to Islam, and "presenting it in a favorable light to his wife and [their] baby daughter, beseeched them [to join him] as required by the *sharīʿa*."[28] The wife rejected his entreaties, however, and fled to the home of Yeshouʿa Corcos, who placed her and the child under his protection. Upon discovering that his wife had escaped, the husband sought the help of the pasha, Muhammad Wida, who in turn presented the case to the *khalīfa*. The latter decided in favor of the husband. To help persuade the wife to follow in her husband's footsteps, it was ruled that she would have to spend a month living in a Muslim home.[29] This ruling incited the "impoliteness" (doubtless a euphemism) of Corcos, who threatened to leave the country. His threat may be why the sentence was never carried out. Instead, the woman was released and Wida was severely chastised by the sultan for his behavior. Whether the sultan's intervention in this case was the result of Corcos's threat, or of subsequent pressure from European diplomats,[30] or of the pleas of a delegation of Jews from Marrakesh who went to the Tafilalt to complain directly to Mawlay Hassan about Wida's cruelty[31] is unknown. Whichever it was, Wida was admonished not to concern himself with the Jews anymore, and to refer all further issues regarding them directly to the rabbinical courts.

Conversion to Islam was further curtailed by the fact that, despite popular conceptions to the contrary, the act itself was not uncomplicated. To gain official recognition, an individual wishing to convert had to pass through administrative channels leading all the way to the sultan. In one such case, a notarized letter was sent to the sultan from the *ʿudūl* (notaries) of Marrakesh verifying that the recitation of the *shahāda*, or profession of faith, by a Jew wishing to become Muslim had been correctly made and officially witnessed. A physical description of the convert was also included, so as to avoid any confusion about his identity.[32] Even when correct procedure was followed, questionable circumstances could cause a conversion to be overturned by the Makhzan, especially once the A.I.U. was on hand to intervene. Such cases include that of a teenager who was mistreated by his parents and ran away to the pasha's residence, where he converted,[33] and also that of three women and two youths who converted during "difficult times," partly to obtain food and lodging but also to escape punishment by the rabbinical courts for an unnamed transgression.[34]

Fluctuations in the application of *dhimma* restrictions and flexibility in the area of conversion helped mitigate Jews' anxiety about Muslim space. These mechanisms for easing inter-communal tensions operated even in moments of extraordinary danger. For example, in all the major crises of the period, individual Jews found protectors in the medina. In an upheaval in 1891, for example, we are told that "the Jews who were in the medina during the chaos clung to those whom they trusted until they brought them back to the *mellah*, and nothing happened to them."[35] Jews were also taken in by their Muslim neighbors during the 1894 tribal attack on Marrakesh. According to the *muḥtasib*'s report of the events, some five hundred Jews, fearing the sacking of the *mellah*, jumped over the wall to spend the night in the medina, some at the *muḥtasib*'s house.[36] Finally, Jewish merchants hid in their *funduq*s in the medina during the revolt against the new coinage in 1904,[37] and one individual who had been injured in the melee sought refuge in a Muslim companion's home, where he stayed until calm was restored.[38]

Why was so much effort exerted to allay Jews' fears about Muslim space, and thus ensure that they would continue to frequent the medina? The answer lies in the same force that mitigated Jewish-gentile tensions nearly everywhere in Morocco during this period: Jews' contribution to the local, regional, and even national economy.

JEWS IN THE MARRAKESH ECONOMY

As European powers tightened their hold over Morocco's domestic and foreign trade in the latter half of the nineteenth century, many of the country's traditional economic centers began a slow demise. Once-thriving cities like Essaouira and Mazagan were increasingly bypassed in favor of port cities, such as Casablanca and Safi, that were more accessible to Europeans. Yet Marrakesh, still the south's largest center for redistribution ("the crossroads of the Moroccan world," as Miège has called it) mostly managed to avoid a similar fate. Until 1894, caravans from Timbuktu laden with gold, ostrich feathers, wax, and slaves continued to pass through Marrakesh on their way to the coastal towns.[39] Thereafter, Marrakesh's markets were filled with European goods, which in turn made their way further south. As was the case throughout its history, the southern capital owed its continued economic relevance not only to geographical factors, but also to the great industriousness of its Jewish community, as Halévy noted in 1876:

> Marrakesh remains one of the most active commercial and industrial centers of the realm. The Jews contribute a great deal to this activity, as more than 4000 of them subsist by their work, or rather the work that the Arab corporations permit them to exercise.[40]

Given the prominence of Jews in the Moroccan economy, discussions of the penetration of European capitalism into pre-colonial Morocco often single out the role played by the country's Jews in this process.[41] Yet Jews in Marrakesh—still the country's largest Jewish community at the time—were hardly the agents of modernity and Europeanization one might expect. As has been shown to be the case in the related subjects of dress and urbanization, the economic activities of Jews in Marrakesh during this period were rarely directed toward advancing Western-style capitalism.[42] Rather, as Levy's 1902 labor survey reveals, just a decade prior to the establishment of the French Protectorate the majority of Marrakesh's Jews continued to earn their livelihoods through manual labor and the production and sale of traditional crafts[43] (see table 4.1). The relatively slow adoption of Western modes of behavior by local Jews, including economic behavior, can again be linked to the durability of inter-communal spatial arrangements in Marrakesh. A brief survey of Jews' artisanal, commercial, and financial activities in the medina will help clarify the type and extent of Jewish economic activity in Muslim space during this period.

Crafts

Silver- and goldsmiths were considered the "aristocracy" of Marrakesh's Jewish artisans, a status derived not only from the relatively steady incomes and strong tradition of father-to-son succession that distinguished the profession, but also from the amazingly varied repertoires of its practitioners. Precious stones, coral, pearls, and Italian sequins were commonly worked into their creations, which included jewelry as well as such items as talismans, stirrups, tobacco cases, and Qur'an holders.[44] As can be surmised from the last item in particular, the jewelers had a significant Muslim clientele that included important *shaykh*s and tribal *qā'id*s.[45] A desire to accommodate this Muslim clientele perhaps helps explain why, in the course of the expansion of the *mellah* under Mawlay Hassan, Ba Ahmad relocated

Table 4.1. Occupations of Jews in Marrakesh, 1902

Occupation	*# of Practitioners*
seamstresses	1030
spinners (women)	300
button makers (men)	276
tailors	258
slipper embroiderers (women)	250
slipper embroiderers (men)	246
distillers/sellers of alcohol	227
goldsmiths	159
sugar and tea merchants	126
tobacco and matches merchants	124
water carriers (women)	100
sellers	92
silk braiders (men)	83
druggists	80
porters	80
commercial agents	79
sandal repairers	75
produce merchants	72
button makers (women)	66
tinsmiths	62
butchers	58
money changers	57
glass merchants	53
rabbis (calligraphers)	51
belt makers	51
brokers	48
spice merchants	43
woodworkers	37
rabbis (notaries)	35
stirrup makers	33
spinners (men)	32
silk braiders (women)	30
rabbis (teachers)	28
sandal makers	27
bronzesmiths	27
retail textile merchants	26
carpenters	26
steelsmiths	25
launderers	24
masons	24
charcoal merchants	23
braiders	23
mattress makers	23
leatherworkers	22
sewage workers	21

Table 4.1. (*continued*)

Occupation	*# of Practitioners*
grain merchants	20
painters (whitewashers)	19
brokers	18
garbagemen	18
saddle makers	17
candy merchants	16
slaughterers	16
billows makers	16
woodworkers	15
water carriers (men)	15
ovenkeepers	15
fishmongers	13
comb makers	13
commercial employees	12
flour merchants	12
fowl merchants	12
coral merchants	10
silver engravers	10
wallet makers	9
woodworkers	9
barbers	8
doughnut sellers	7
judges at rabbinical tribunal	7
public criers	7
blacksmiths	7
embroiderers (textile)	6
rabbis (judges)	5
tanners	5
dyers	4
slaughterhouse inspectors	2

Source: *Alliance Israélite Universelle* Ecoles XXVII.E.417–442, 10 February 1902, Moïse Levy.

the metalworkers, including the jewelers, in their own *sūq* just outside the *mellah*'s walls.[46]

As seen earlier in the context of the *maḥalla,* sewing and related tasks also brought Jews into Muslim space. According to the 1902 labor survey, seamstresses in fact accounted for the single largest occupational group among the Jews, numbering over a thousand. Their main clientele consisted of policemen and soldiers, whose uniforms they mended in an enclosed area between the medina and the *mellah.*[47] Seamstresses also worked in the medina proper, "sewing and mending for bachelors" in the *sūqs.*[48] Meanwhile, male tailors entered Muslim space by making house calls in the medina. One such

Figure 4.1. Medina market. Postcard, Combier Imp. Macon. Private collection of the author.

individual regularly delivered his best wares directly to the home of an important client named Mawlay Qadur.[49] It should be noted, however, that house calls were not always voluntary. Jewish tailors and others complained of being summoned to the homes of Marrakesh's notables to labor on some task, often through the night or on Saturdays (in violation of the Jewish Sabbath), for minimal pay.[50] Marrakesh's only slipper market was located in the medina, obliging the many Jews involved in this trade (as both fabricators and embroiderers) to leave the *mellah* in order to sell their wares. Thus it was a serious threat to their livelihoods when in early 1912 the *amīn* of the *babūsh* market, with the support of the pasha, suddenly sought to bar the *mellah*'s twenty-eight slipper-makers from the medina. To support the ban, a group of local Muslim notables produced an apparently fraudulent document declaring that Jews lacked permission to sell their *babūsh*s in the medina. The Jews, for whom the ban meant possible starvation,[51] eventually prevailed by citing their historical right to engage in commerce in the medina, which dated to before the reign of Mawlay Hassan.[52] Last but not least, mention should be made of Jews who took part in Marrakesh's informal economy. They included porters, peddlers, junkmen, and day laborers of all types, who, following any opportunity to make a day's wages, often sought work in the medina.

Commerce

Erckmann was perhaps exaggerating when he said that the commercial life of Marrakesh was almost entirely in the hands of the Jews.[53] Aubin may be closer to the truth in implying that, at least in terms of exchanges with the European commercial houses of the coasts, the Jewish merchants of Marrakesh were as well represented as their Muslim counterparts, if not more so, despite their smaller population overall.[54] The names of a few individuals stand out in records of commercial life during this period: Corcos, Rosillio, Turjman, Obadia, and Coriat. All were members of the *mellah*'s elite, connoting a certain degree of authority over their coreligionists as well as the responsibility of dealing with foreign powers, the A.I.U., and the Makhzan. In their business affairs, however, they were primarily oriented toward the Makhzan, which not only sponsored their trade but also sought their advice in resolving difficult economic matters.[55] Corcos, "the millionaire of the *mellah*,"[56] was by far the most powerful member of the group. His wealth came partly from his real-estate holdings. (Indeed, of the men mentioned above, only he and Rosillio owned property in the *mellah*. Rosillio and Corcos also shared a barley contract.[57]) Corcos was also the *shaykh al-yahūd* for much of the period under discussion, and his autocratic streak in this position extended to economic affairs as well, as when he obliged the Makhzan to grant him a monopoly over the rural wax market by forcing out another Jewish bidder from Tamlalet. Even more revealing is the fact that there were no local bidders for the contract, as "not one Jew of Marrakesh could enter this market out of fear of Corcos."[58]

Jewish merchants who, like Corcos, participated in the city's commercial exchanges had to make frequent forays into the medina. In the first place, the *mellah* was too crowded to provide space for storing goods brought in from the countryside. Hence, other than the "*funduq al-millāḥ*"[59] and a few smaller storage areas, the storehouses used by the Jews were located in the medina,[60] as were many of their commercial establishments (*comptoirs*).[61] (The commercial activities of the Jewish agents of the big trading houses on the coast were also conducted in the medina.[62]) Still, some goods, such as cotton, were first auctioned off in the *mellah* and then resold at higher prices in the medina:

> I find that cotton goods are cheaper here than in Gibraltar, I could not make this out until the other day a Jew told me that the merchants on the coast send the Jews here cotton goods that the merchants on the coast have no money or very little and do all their business by bills that when they get hard [pressed] on the coast the merchants send here to their agents to say I must have so many dollars in a named time and then the Jew sells by auction in the Jews town the cotton goods taking care to buy the goods amongst themselves and then sell it again to the Moores—all the Jew agents here are wealthy and I am told this is the way.[63]

Finally, it can be recalled that the tobacco trade also brought Jews into the medina, although the makeshift stalls they used were not authorized by the Muslim authorities.

Because of its great importance in Marrakesh, the slave trade is another aspect of commercial life worth mentioning in this context, though Jewish involvement in it, officially forbidden, is difficult to verify. The slave market in Marrakesh was the country's largest in the late nineteenth century, accounting for 75 percent of all urban sales of slaves in Morocco.[64] It was also the most resistant to European attempts to curtail the slave trade.[65] Twice a year, caravans departed from Timbuktu (where, incidentally, a small community of Moroccan Jewish merchants was established in the early 1860s[66]), usually passing through Tinduf and Tuwat on their way north. Upon the caravans' arrival in Marrakesh, local dealers auctioned the slaves in a special market in the medina on Wednesdays, Thursdays, and Fridays. James Richardson reports that as many as ten thousand slaves a year were sold in these auctions at mid-century,[67] though a more sober report by John Drummond Hay relates that two thousand slaves were brought into the country annually.[68] Even taking the lower estimate, the sheer volume of this trade suggests at least the potential for Jews' involvement, especially in light of Erckmann's comment that they played a dominant role in Marrakesh's commercial life. While Jews would have had difficulty participating in the public slave market, they would presumably have had access to the private auctions, away from the eyes of the authorities, where a large portion of these sales were conducted.[69] Slaves may also have changed hands in the course of Jews' extensive dealings with the previously mentioned Bubeker Ghanjaoui, who, in addition to being a *mellah* landlord, was also known as Marrakesh's largest slave dealer.[70] But this is only speculation, as I have found no evidence directly linking Jews to the slave trade in Marrakesh.

Finance

Finance is the last form of Jewish economic involvement in Muslim space to be investigated here. Because financial dealings were usually carried out in conjunction with the Muslim authorities, we can presume that the Jews' presence in the Kasbah or medina was at times required. Although the spatial dimension of Jews' financial activities is admittedly vague, this aspect of economic inter-communality is crucial to completing the picture of Jewish-Muslim relations in Marrakesh.

Marrakesh's Jews were intimately involved in all areas of finance. As in many places, Jews were moneylenders. Some were also debt collectors: Solomon Corcos, a native of Marrakesh, requested this job from the sultan in 1845,[71] while other Jews collected debts for European patrons. The latter included a French protégé named Nissim Isra'il al-Jiziri in 1865[72] and a man named Murdukh al-Inglizi, whose name indicates that he may have been an agent for the English, in 1866;[73] both of these men requested the good offices of the pasha while pursuing debtors in Marrakesh. The debts they were sent to collect were typically those of other Jews, though they occasionally received payments from the municipal government as well.[74] Jewish financiers, including Haim Corcos,[75] were also in the business of supplying "bail bonds" to both Jewish[76] and Muslim[77] prisoners. More often than not, these guarantees were paid in oil rather than money.[78] In one instance, however, a Jew's guarantee for a Muslim was deemed unacceptable for the reason that he was a *dhimmī*.[79]

Jews also worked as money changers, a risky venture during the period as counterfeit and adulterated coins were in wide circulation and one risked getting stuck with debased coinage or being accused of counterfeiting.[80] There was more than a little truth to the latter accusation. At least twice in this period, local Jews were caught bringing debased coins into Marrakesh, which contributed to serious inflation and near bankruptcy for the city's merchants, including other Jews, who were in fact the initiators of such complaints.[81] The involvement of Jews in counterfeiting is ironic, however, as another financial activity of Jews was the inspection of the coinage of the realm. (According to an early nineteenth-century source, Jews also did the minting themselves.[82]) One reason that Jews were chosen for this task was their familiarity with European weights and measures, a body of knowledge few Muslims possessed at the time. In 1884, four of the *mellah*'s most prominent businessmen, Masʿud Corcos, Mimun Ahayon, Haroun Ibris, and Makhluf Abrij, were added to a team of *umanāʾ* (sing. *amīn*) "to count and weigh money in grams and kilos, or to inspect it by biting." All four names (one man fell sick and was represented by his son) appear on the boxes of specie along with those of the *umanāʾ* and the totals.[83]

THE SANCTIFICATION OF MUSLIM SPACE BY JEWS

As the above activities show, the division between *mellah* and medina could be a bridge as much as a boundary, depending on the circumstances and mitigating factors. Economic exchanges may have formed the foundation of the bridge, but in no other area was the continuum between Jewish and Muslim space more seamless than when it came to investing the city with specific ritual and sacral sense. Jews in Marrakesh liberally attached religious meaning to sites throughout the city, in the *mellah* and the medina, and these religious sites sometimes overlapped those of Muslims. Indeed, the *mellah* itself is framed by its saints: Murdukhai b. ʿAttar at the Bab al-Mellah and Hananiya Ha-Cohen (and others) in the cemetery. Domestic space was especially sacralized.[84] In addition to the requisite mezuzah, nearly every *mellah* home also displayed a *khamsa* (a protective charm in the shape of a hand) to avert the evil eye. As noted previously, the threat posed by serpents and scorpions was met with complicated talismans, often including a sketch of the offending creature, as described below:

> Besides the paper containing a portion of the law, another is struck on the door-post of every room, on which is drawn the rude picture of a scor-

> pion. Above this, is an array of mystical words, in Hebrew characters, arranged on the principal of the ancient *abra-cadabra*. Below is a solemn imprecation. The Rabbi who prepares this precious document must, in order to make it effective, rigidly observe certain ceremonies. It must be written only on the first night of [the Hebrew month of] Sivan near Pentecost. It is necessary for him to immerse himself three times in a bath, and then he must cut his nails.[85]

The efficacy of one such amulet is verified by an observer, who tells of how "[a] large scorpion ran to the door of a room and then stopped suddenly, as if stupefied; it was, in fact, a case of no admittance."[86]

In addition to these permanent markings, *mellah* homes were also temporarily embellished to signal specific events. A rooster's head, a broom, broken glass, and some biscuits might be left on the doorstep of a house in which a baby had recently been born, in whom these items were thought to instill courage and strength.[87] A house in which someone was sick was identifiable by a brazier left burning through the night, as charcoal was thought to lure demons away from their human victim.[88] Domestic space was also the site for relics associated with saintly miracles. In the doorway of the house once inhabited by the rabbi Yusuf Pinto, a black stone dangling from a cord of twisted palm fiber was said to have been the head of a would-be robber who was turned to stone when his break-in interrupted the rabbi's prayers. Jews brought it offerings of money, candles, oil, and wheat.[89] Streets were likewise invested with supernatural power. One of the *mellah*'s main fountains was believed to be inhabited by a genie, to whom women brought myrtle branches and eggs when a family member was ill.[90] That these offerings took place at night indicates a high level of belief in the powers of this particular genie, as Jews in Marrakesh generally avoided leaving their homes after dark.[91] A less benevolent genie was thought to occupy another small passage. Wedding and funeral processions took special care to avoid this area, as this genie was believed to have once carried off a bride.[92]

Repositories of Jews' religious aspirations continued just beyond the *mellah*'s gate, with a tree in the goldsmiths' quarter said to have once been the staff of a holy man. Most of its visitors were "women threatened with baldness and . . . spinners discontented with their earnings at their trade."[93] They stuck hairs and bits of yarn in the tree's branches to be blown away by the wind along with the evil spells believed to be at the root of their misfortunes. A short distance away, in the southeast corner of the medina, Jews made pilgrimages to the tomb of Yusuf b. ʿAli, one of the famous "Seven Saints" of Marrakesh, discussed in chapter 5. Still further from the *mellah*, Jews collected water from the man-made spring located at Bab al-Khamis, one of the city's main gates in the far northeastern corner of the medina. This water was given to new mothers to drink in the belief that it would help them produce plentiful milk.[94] At the far north of the medina, Jews also visited a pond in the gardens of the tomb of Sidi Bel Abbas, the so-called patron saint of Marrakesh, where sufferers searching "for the cure of demoniacal possession, of fear, and of all nervous conditions" performed a series of complicated ablutions.[95] The synagogue in the leper colony at Bab Dukkala in the northwest part of the city has already been noted; Marrakesh Jewry maintained holy sites in the countryside outside Marrakesh as well, as will be discussed in the following chapter.

For Muslims, the *mellah* was a "*quartier infamant,*" the locus of all the city's vices. For Jews, the potential for humiliation associated with their status as *dhimma* combined with the threat of conversion gave an equally negative coloration to Muslim space. The two groups' mutual suspicion was greatly mitigated, however, by their mutual interest in fostering Jews' participation in the larger Marrakesh economy. Jews clearly recognized the value of their goods and services to the rest of the city, and did not hesitate to use access to the *mellah* as a bargaining chip in their relationship with the municipal authorities, as when Muslims were denied access to the talents of the *mellah*'s most important resident, Yeshouʿa Corcos, when Corcos threatened to leave Morocco in a dispute over a forced conversion, or when Jews "talked of closing the gates of the *mellah* and ceasing to do business" when a local Jewish woman was beaten by soldiers.[96]

Like the complex set of political expediencies that underpinned the initial creation of the *mellah* in the sixteenth century, how Marrakesh functioned during later periods was also determined largely by the messy realities of daily life, the material as well as the spiritual.

5
Hinterlands

In the summer of 1891, a group of men from the Ahmar tribe came to Marrakesh looking for trouble. According to their legends, there was a treasure buried somewhere in the Ahmar territories, but finding it would require the help of a Jewish child. Their preference was for one with red hair who was also nearsighted, as they believed that the blood of such a child, when spilled, would lead them to the hidden loot.[1] The logical place to look for a Jewish child was the *mellah,* where apparently they found one that fit the description. But their kidnapping attempts failed. The following is the Makhzan's version of the events:

> It came to our Sharifian knowledge that an Ahmar tribesman stole a child from the mellah, with the intention of bringing him home and slaughtering him in the belief that only the blood of the sons of the Jews will reveal the treasure's location. The Jews, who caught the man with the child hidden inside his clothing, took him to the servant Umalik and informed him of what had taken place. Umalik searched the man and found two magical papers [*siḥr*[2]] and so he sent him to prison.[3]

The story did not end there, however. Two days later, companions of the captured Ahmar man came to the *mellah* and tried to steal another Jewish boy. Once again their plans were foiled when the child, struggling beneath

Figure 5.1. Tribal divisions in the Marrakesh region. Based on Paul Pascon, *Le Haouz de Marrakesh,* 2 vols. (Rabat: Editions marocaines et internationals, 1977).

the burnoose worn by his captor, was detected by some passing Jews. With the help of the guardian of the *mellah*'s gate the Ahmar men were arrested and taken to see the pasha, Umalik. On the way to the Kasbah, one of the men pulled out a knife and injured seven people with it, but it was taken away from him before he could escape. Upon arriving at Bab Berrima the second of the two men suddenly fell to the ground and pretended to be dead. Leaving him there, the guard continued on his way to see the pasha with the first man in tow. But when they arrived at their destination, this prisoner suddenly pretended to be mute. Umalik searched him and found two more papers with magic writing on them, and so put him in jail as well. Back in the streets, Muslim passersby encountered the other Ahmar man pretending to be dead, and, assuming that the Jews had killed him, ran to the *mellah* to exact revenge for the apparent murder. The chaos that ensued was terrifying. According to the Makhzan report,

> The Muslims . . . went to the mellah and wanted to eat [destroy] it. [The mellah] was locked, and any Jews coming back from the medina were hit with [pieces of] iron and stones. Twenty men and three boys are missing. The pregnant women in the mellah miscarried and as for the women who were in the medina, it was not known what was done to them. Then the servant Umalik arrested seven Jews and the mellah remains locked.[4]

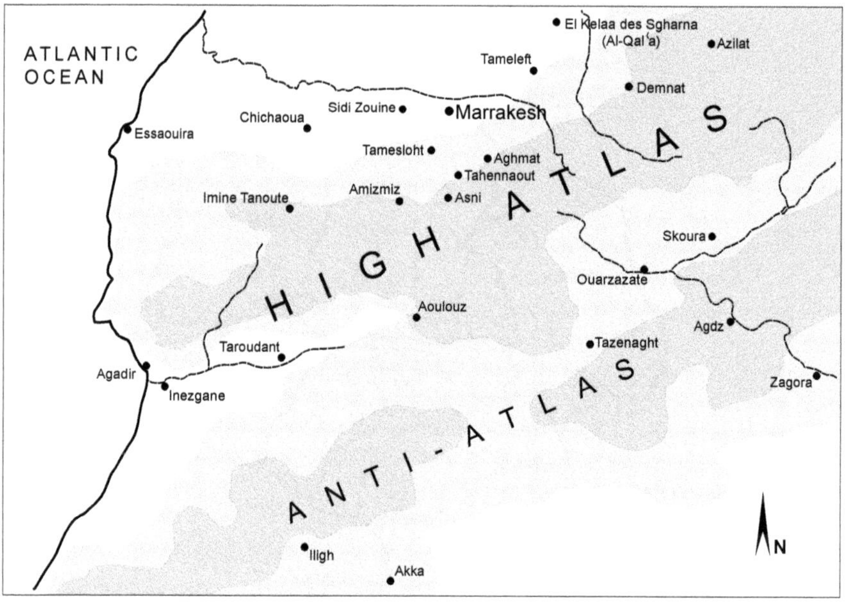

Figure 5.2. Map of the High Atlas mountain region.

The uproar eventually subsided, with the sultan issuing a stern warning to his son, the *khalīfa:*

> If what was reported about eating the mellah was correct, and [the mellah] wasn't defended, then it is a result of your coldness and neglect [and] not being resolute or attentive. The Jews paid the army to defend them and their belongings [so that] what shouldn't happen to them doesn't, and what was reported shouldn't happen to them.[5]

He further admonished the *khalīfa,* as well as the other municipal authorities, to expend every effort to find the missing Jews and arrest any wrongdoers.

While the above story can be understood on any number of levels, its relevance here is primarily as a means of addressing the city's relationship to its hinterland, specifically that of the *mellah*'s inhabitants to the tribal populations of the Hawz and Atlas. On the one hand, it reinforces some of the basic characteristics of Jewish-Muslim relations in Morocco: mutual ambivalence and (mis)perceptions, associations with magic, and the complex intermediary role played by the Makhzan and its representatives. Yet implicit in the Ahmar incident is also the unique set of challenges for Jewish-Muslim "commensality" that came into play only in matters involving the countryside, where Jews of the *mellah* were unable to count on a shared *Marrākshī* identity and urban ethos to guide them in their dealings with the rural Muslim population. By the same token, relations between Marrakesh's Jews and their coreligionists in the countryside likewise grew strained at times, as shared religious identity could only partly offset the differences separating urban and rural Jews. These inter- and intra-communal relationships played themselves out against a backdrop of advancing European colonialism, which, especially after the death of Mawlay Hassan in 1894, seriously undermined what was already a fragile balance between Marrakesh and its hinterland.

As the ongoing discourse on questions of urban-rural relations in the Arab-Islamic world has shown, what was once perceived as a solid boundary between city and countryside has begun to break down.[6] In the Moroccan context, the urban-rural continuum has been especially well documented in histories of Essaouira,[7] and also of the Sus and Sahara.[8] In the case of Marrakesh, Paul Pascon has similarly proven that the southern capital was anything but a "closed city of Islam," as was once suggested by Deverdun. Indeed, the linkages between Marrakesh and the surrounding countryside are so strong that it has sometimes been described as a city overwhelmed by its hinterland.[9] Marrakesh was given its start by the Atlas Mountains, whose water was brought down by *khaṭṭāras*[10] to irrigate the hot plains of the Hawz, and it was on the grain of the Misfiwa region that the city grew and thrived.[11] Economically, Marrakesh prospered by virtue of its access to the major trade routes of southern Morocco (including parts of present-day Algeria), a position it exploited equally well whether in trans-Saharan exchanges or in a precolonial mercantile economy. Even when it came to politics the countryside influenced almost all the major events of the period. In its own way, the *mellah* also contributed to the sense of continuity between Marrakesh and its hinterland. The various types of exchanges with the people of the countryside, its Arab and Berber tribes as well as its satellite Jewish communities, will be explored in the drawing of this last in a series of concentric circles.

The Mellah and its Satellites

In Europe, Jews were almost exclusively concentrated in cities and towns. Moroccan Jews, however, particularly those living in the south, were a significant presence in the smallest of rural villages and sometimes owned agricultural land that they farmed themselves.[12] Halévy "discovered" 53 such rural Jewish communities in the Marrakesh region alone (see table 5.1), while Flamand's list numbered 150, with 36 additional communities recognized as "dead."[13] Despite their (mutual) dependence, the lifestyles of rural and urban Jews differed in several important ways. First, there were few walled Jewish quarters in the countryside. Where formal *mellahs* did exist, they were significantly newer than that of Marrakesh; for example, that of Demnat was created in 1894. Rural and urban Jews' relationships to the Muslim authority were also not the same. Though the rural Jewish communities technically fell under the administrative sway of the pasha of the Kasbah of Marrakesh, in practice they followed the local custom of seeking out the protection of a local patron, often

Table 5.1. Satellite Jewish Communities of the Marrakesh Region in 1876

Regions	*Villages*	*Number of Jewish families*
Orika	Akhliz	50
3 villages	Anrar	20
	Elghzi	30
Mesfiwa	Aït Taguent	50
6 villages	Tabia	20
	Aït el s'ghir	19
	Debra	30
	Tamazirt	20
	Equin Esmaïn	29
Gheghaya	Tasloumt	25
5 villages	Tahennaout	20
	Akraïç	15
	Aghitghour	30
	Aïn Nafad	35
Glaoua	Zaouit Si Rahl	100
9 villages	Tesemsit	16
	Tirzel	10
	Aït Rhalt	15
	Aït Mansour	10
	Thoudrin	25
	Zarkesen	20
	Tagmout	15
	Tabia	10
Tigana	Elarba	30
3 villages	Tahsent	25
	Younir	unknown
Ouarzazat 4 villages	names unknown	population unknown
Chkoura 4 villages	names unknown	population unknown
Other localities	Demnat	150
19 villages	Ahmedna	30
	Aït Tidil	20
	Guizdama	unknown
	Tifnout	unknown
	Elkala (Qalʿa)	150
	Tamlelt	30
	Disra	20
	Netifa	100
	Aït Taleb	unknown
	Bezrou	150
	Tasbibt	150

Regions	*Villages*	*Number of Jewish families*
	Amizmiz	50
	Tizguin	40
	Asif el mal	30
	Tadla	50
	Draoua	unknown
	Tafilalt	unknown
	Ctaoua	unknown

Source: *Alliance Israélite Universelle*, France IX.A.67–73. 8 August 1876, Joseph Halévy.

referred to as a "friend" (*ṣāḥib*) or "lord" (*sayid*). This protection was given in exchange for payment or services, as attested by Leo Africanus in the sixteenth century and again by Aubin in the early twentieth: "There is no tribal Kaïd who does not have at the neighboring village a Jew whom he calls his *chkara* [pocketbook], who performs the various functions of banker, commissioner, and agent."[14] This "protection" was especially important, indeed essential, for Jews living in tribal regions over which the Makhzan's authority did not effectively extend, including at various times both Misfiwa and Rehamna.

Given their differences, friction between urban and rural Jews was not uncommon. Marrakesh and Demnat were involved in an especially heated rivalry, which caught the attention of Nahum Slouschz:

> Demnatis are very proud of their town which, they believe, is one hundred years older than the city of Morocco or Marrakesh. Their arrogance and lack of manners have moved the people of Marrakesh to compose a Hebrew satire, ridiculing their pretensions. What the Hara of Jerba is to the Jews of Tunis, the Mellah of Demnat is to those of Marrakesh.[15]

It is perhaps to this "Hebrew satire" that Flamand is referring when he quotes the following saying, reputed to be popular in the south when he visited: "When an Arab cries, it is because he was cheated by a Jew. When a Jew from Marrakesh cries, it is because he was cheated by a Jew from Demnat."[16] The Jews of Demnat claimed not only a longer history than their cousins in Marrakesh, but also greater erudition. Slouschz continues, "There are several rabbis in Demnat, fair Talmudists, who believe themselves the superiors of the rabbis of Marrakesh."[17]

This rivalry occasionally went beyond mere braggadocio, however, as when a group of three Jews from Marrakesh were accused of falsely testifying against a rabbi from Demnat in an effort to ingratiate themselves with the local governor:

> The three Jews Ibaddan Ederi, Mimon Bensibo and Mordejay Benkesso, who are friends of the kaid had declared in Morocco that nothing had been

> robbed from [me] at the gates of Demnat, whereas they are not eye-witnesses, and know nothing, but that they made that declaration merely to injure [me], and with the view of pleasing the kaid Gileni [Jilani].[18]

Accusations of theft were also exchanged between urban and rural Jews.[19] In 1865 the Makhzan intervened when "the *dhimmī* Yosh," a merchant from Marrakesh, stole seven donkeys from the Jews of Idawzdik.[20] On another occasion, one of the young men who had come from an Atlas village to study in Marrakesh was charged with serving as a fence for jewels stolen from a *mellah* home.[21] That in both of these cases the accused was said to have acted with a Muslim accomplice suggests that the amorphous "group feeling"[22] among Moroccan Jews sometimes took a back seat to more tangible interests, particularly when the Jews came from different communities. Along these same lines, a *Sefer Torah* that was stolen from Demnat in 1894 and ended up in the *sūq* of Marrakesh was surely intended for a local Jewish buyer, who was at least presumed to have little compunction about acquiring such an object in this way.[23]

Whatever differences may have separated the two groups, the Marrakesh *mellah* nonetheless provided several crucial services to its satellites. In addition to offering educational opportunities unavailable in the countryside, the *mellah,* with its larger pool of candidates, was also a source of spouses for the surrounding communities, who were bound by strict religious requirements to marry within their own faith. For a rural Jew, marriage to a *Marrākshī* was a mark of high status, as indicated by the celebrations surrounding the engagement of the richest Jewish man from Asni to a woman from the Marrakesh *mellah.*[24] As discussed previously, another of the *mellah*'s responsibilities was to provide refuge for victims of epidemics or abuse. If the intervention was timely enough, however, the *mellah* could save rural Jews from having to flee from their homes in the first place. With a location that allowed for direct access to the Makhzan, and, from late 1900, to the representatives of the A.I.U., the *mellah* was able on a number of occasions to do precisely this. When the village of Tamesluht was attacked by tribes in 1889,[25] and when a cruel new governor took office in Taroudant in 1908,[26] pleas for help were quickly dispatched to Marrakesh and the situation was resolved. A rural *shaykh al-yahūd* might himself be the cause of such appeals, as in 1914 when the Jews of Asni begged the pasha of Marrakesh via members of the Marrakesh Jewish community to remove their *shaykh,* whom he had originally appointed.[27]

The Jewish communities of the countryside have been referred to repeatedly here as "satellites," yet it should be made clear that their dealings with Jews of the Marrakesh *mellah* did not always take place in, nor even always concern, the city itself. In fact, many significant exchanges between the two groups took place in the countryside, where Jews from Marrakesh ventured for a variety of reasons, though the most important were pilgrimage and commerce. It is to these two activities that we now turn.

Saint Veneration among Jews in the Marrakesh Region

The religious meaning of saint veneration and pilgrimage in Morocco and its complex position within both Orthodox Islam and normative Judaism has received extensive attention from scholars elsewhere, so will not be dealt with in great detail here.[28] As a historical phenomenon that served to bind rural and urban Jews in the Marrakesh region together, however, it does merit some attention. Known as *Ṣaddīqs* (Heb. *Tsaddik*), the saints venerated by Marrakesh's Jews did not typically inherit their holiness, at least insofar as inheritance implies a sharifian lineage or descent from a marabout (*murābiṭ*).[29] (A few Moroccan Jewish families nonetheless managed to produce several generations of saintly figures. Most famous among these are the Abuhatzeras, originally from the Tafilalt, who count Baba Salé and R. Yaʿqub among their most prestigious members.) Marrakesh's Jewish saints typically gained their status through heroic acts, often ones that involved their serving as conduits for divine intervention to protect their communities. Murdukhai b. ʿAttar, who repulsed an attack on the *mellah* with a wall of fire, clearly fits into this category, as do several others. The tombs of such saints (and they were almost always dead, as opposed to their Muslim counterparts, who could be living carriers of *baraka*) were especially reputed for their healing powers. Indeed, so many sick people visited the Jewish cemetery of Marrakesh that an A.I.U. teacher cautioned visitors against touching the small commemorative stones placed upon the saints' tombs, warning that those who did so were "sure to catch a sickness."[30] The cross-veneration of saints, an important mechanism in Jewish-Muslim relations throughout Morocco,[31] naturally occurred in Marrakesh as well, though, here as elsewhere, considerable debate surrounded the "true" identity of such individuals (itself a reminder of how deeply interwoven Jewish and Muslim lives were in Morocco). The ambiguous origins of Yusuf b. ʿAli, one of the "Seven Saints" of Marrakesh, provides some insight into this problem.

In Muslim hagiography, Sidi Yusuf is a Job-like character, a twelfth-century leper renowned for his great patience and forbearance.[32] A saint by the same name, also born in Marrakesh, figures in the Jewish oral tradition as well. His story is recounted below by one of the teachers of the A.I.U. girls' school:

> "No one is a prophet in his own land," yet Yossif ben Ali was born in Marrakesh and grew up in his native city. He was endowed with a marvelous voice, and his reputation quickly spread beyond the walls of the *mellah* in which he lived. He was a Jew much admired for his piety.
>
> One night, the sultan Mawlay Hassan was strolling in the streets of the mellah in disguise, when a melodious, enchanting voice reached his ears. He inquired after the name of the singer: it was Yossif ben Ali; The sultan took him into his service. A little while later the mu'aḍḍin of the Kutubiya died. The hour of prayer approached, and no one had been found with a voice dignified enough for the sanctity of the task. Fate, which eventually

> befalls all men, befell Yossif ben ʿAli. The sultan, glad for the chance, proposed to him that he serve as mu'aḍḍin. Stupefied, he understood the proposition from this powerful king to be an order. Trapped in a terrible dilemma that tormented him, he hesitated: disobeying the sultan meant certain death; but praying to Muhammad? What a sacrilege! His heart tight, his face glum, he slowly climbed the stairs of the mosque. From the height of the minaret he began calling the believers to prayer. Here different believers give two versions. The Jews pretend that before beginning the prayer he threw himself off the minaret rather than commit this sin. The Arabs believe that just as he finished the prayer, Muhammad took his soul while throwing him off the minaret for fear that he would revert to being Jewish.[33]

Despite the anachronistic invocation of Mawlay Hassan (who may function in this story as a sort of "generic" sultan) and reference to the *mellah* at a time when none yet existed, there is good reason to believe that Sidi Yusuf and Yusuf b. ʿAli (Yossif ben Ali) are in fact the same saint. Consider the following incidents: A Jewish father who killed his son for having stolen some papers is said to have escaped "to the shrine of Mawlay ʿAli Sharif" when his crime was discovered by the authorities.[34] The Jews caught robbing the houses on the *mellah*'s periphery, mentioned earlier, "fled from the walls of the *mellah* and took refuge in the mausoleum."[35] Lastly, a Jew leaving Marrakesh carrying false papers with which to sell the property of a Jewish widow whose husband had died while still in debt to the Makhzan took refuge in a saint's tomb when his plans were discovered.[36] Though the person buried in the place of refuge is named in the first case only, one can nonetheless assume that in all three incidents the place of refuge is the tomb of Yusuf b. ʿAli. Not only is his tomb the most accessible to the *mellah,* located just outside Bab Aghmat to the east of the Jewish and Muslim cemeteries, but in all three cases, the *ḥurm* (sanctuary) was conspicuously respected by the Muslim authorities, who surrounded—but did not enter—it. (In the second case, the thieves' parents were put in jail in order to help lure their sons out). The Jews' presence as spectators in the medina during the annual celebration of Yusuf b. ʿAli's death, involving a bloody bull-run through the city, self-flagellation, and drumming, is further evidence that this is likely the same saint.[37]

While Yusuf b. ʿAli's tomb is located outside the *mellah,* saints whose Jewish identity is more easily verified are buried in the *mellah*'s cemetery. An area near the wall separating the Jewish from the Muslim cemetery is reserved for rabbis and holy men. The most important tomb in this area is that of Hananiya Ha-Cohen, known as "the lion of Marrakesh." Like Murdukhai b. ʿAttar (whose tomb is reputed to be the oldest in the cemetery), Cohen derived his saintliness from having thwarted a tribal attack. But in the place of a flaming barrier, he summoned canon-shooting phantoms and a swarm of wasps to ward off a group of tribal invaders.[38] His tomb is believed to date from the mid-seventeenth century, and is embellished by a tree and a small building (a small mausoleum has recently been added to the site), and it is

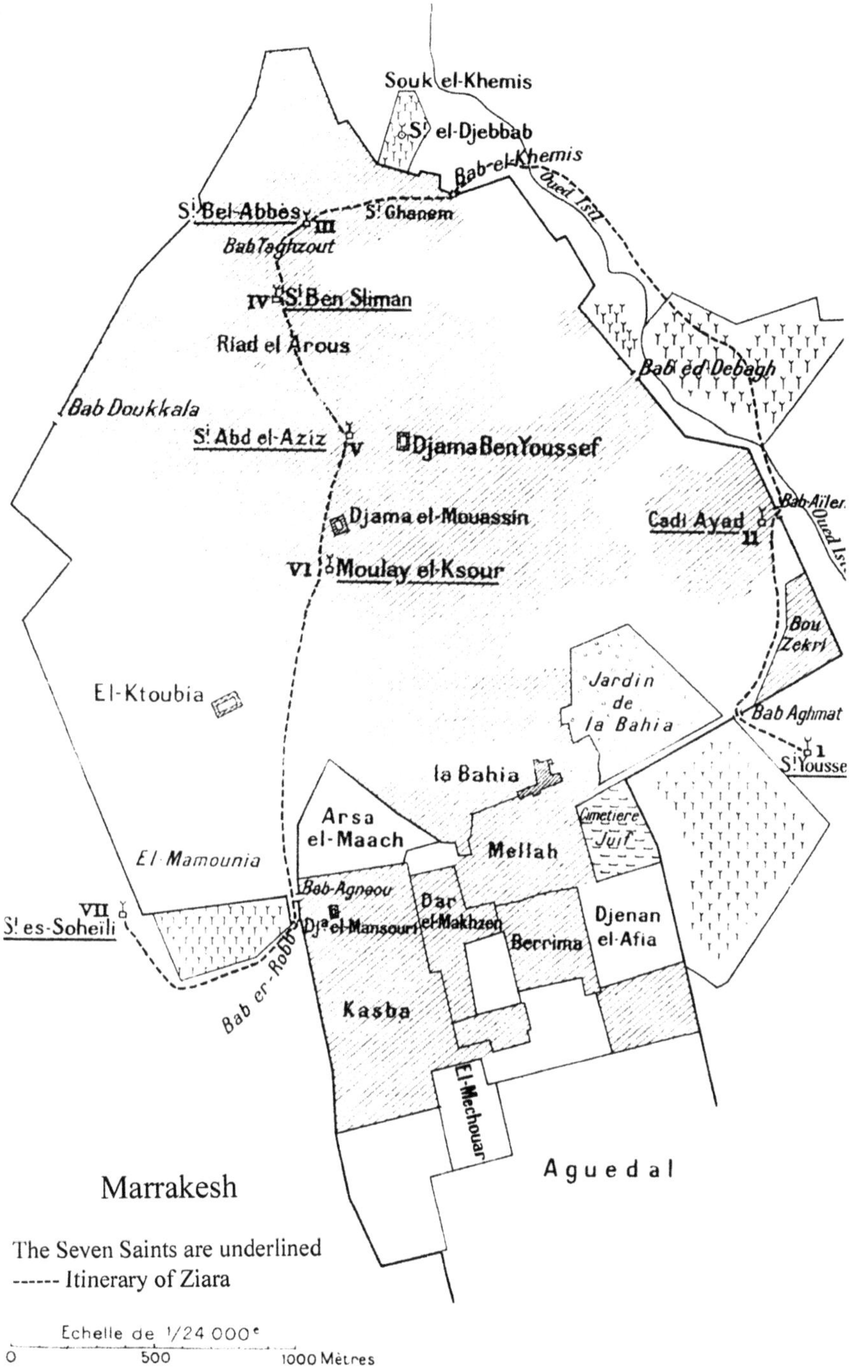

Figure 5.3. The "Seven Saints" of Marrakesh. From Charles Allain and Gaston Deverdun, "Les portes anciennes de Marrakech," *Hespéris* 44 (1957): 85–126.

visited by Muslims as well as Jews. Another pilgrimage site popular among Jews of the region (and even beyond) is the tomb of David b. Tsfat, also known as Sidi Mul Sur ("master of the wall") in recognition of his burial place outside the city's perimeter.[39] (Another saint located just beyond the walls is Masʿud Nahmias, a Marrakesh rabbi who died in Intifa at the beginning of the twentieth century and was brought home for burial.[40]) Other important pilgrimage sites in the Jewish cemetery are the tombs of Shlomo b. Tameshut, dating from 1832,[41] and Pinhas Cohen, the *shaykh al-yahūd* of Taroudant, dating from 1952.[42] An ancient female saint by the name of Lalla Rivqa is also associated with Marrakesh.[43]

As discussed previously, the influx of pilgrims to Marrakesh had significant demographic consequences for the *mellah* and for the city as a whole. But the impact of outbound pilgrimage was perhaps even stronger. Jews from Marrakesh were avid pilgrims,[44] and the surrounding countryside had plenty of sites for them to visit, as Alfred Goldenberg, director of the A.I.U. in Marrakesh in the 1930s, remarked: "No other part of Morocco has in its environs as many saints as the Marrakesh region. Safi has its famous seven rabbis, Ouezzan has its busy pilgrimage, but no city has as many pilgrimages to make as Marrakesh."[45]

The most popular saint in the Marrakesh region (also venerated by Muslims) was David Halevy al-Draʿ,[46] believed to have been a *shaliakh* who came to Morocco following a dispute with the chief rabbi of Palestine. He is buried near an olive grove fifteen kilometers west of Demnat. The anniversary of his death, like that of many Jewish saints, was marked by pilgrimage to his tomb and a festival (*ḥillūla*).[47] In 1933 a spectator described the event:

> A number of Jews are kneeling and praying with fervor, a huge quantity of candles slowly burn . . . An old man lies stretched out on the ground. For eight days he has been in the same place; Upon arrival, [he was] completely paralyzed. Today he can move. He waits and hopes for a full recovery. What can't faith accomplish? A palm tree is near the tomb, to which all the sick pilgrims attach tattered rags. It is the piece of material that carries away the illness. If by some misfortune you detach a knurl from the palm tree, you will contract the disease that has been conjured . . . Afterwards, I made a short prayer and offered a packet of candles, as is customary.[48]

Another saint much venerated by *Marrākshī*s was Solomon (Shlomo) b. al-Hens (al-Ḥanash), whose name refers to the two serpents who once magically appeared to protect his tomb from marauders.[49] His tomb is located about forty kilometers from Marrakesh, at Aït Taghnate in the Ourika valley. Jews from the Marrakesh *mellah* also visited the distant tomb of David Laskar (al-Skar), located in Ighi in the Atlas Mountains, on the Marrakesh-Ouarzazat route. Laskar (also known as Mawlay Ighi for his burial place) was another Palestinian envoy sent to Morocco to collect alms.[50] His adherents included many Jewish women, who passed through a nearby waterfall to enlist the saint's help in becoming pregnant.[51] Other saints in the countryside include Haim b. Diwan (a.k.a. Mul Anzar), the son of a famous rabbi from Wazzan, whose tomb is found in the High Atlas near Zagadir Nbout. According to local sources, Muslims recognized Diwan's saintliness after they threw his tombstone into a river and found it returned to its correct location the following day.[52] The tomb of Musa Tahoné also attracted both Jewish and Muslim pilgrims from Marrakesh.

Saint veneration was a major factor in bringing together urban and rural Jewish (and, for that matter, non-Jewish) populations in the Marrakesh region. Nonetheless, sainthood in Morocco had a distinctly urban orientation that should not be lost sight of. According to Vincent Cornell, the urban saint had a special role to play as an "anchor of the earth" who tied his community to its locality by protecting them and maintaining religious law.[53] Although Cornell is explicitly referring to Muslim saints, his observation also holds true for many of the Jewish saints of Marrakesh, including Ha-Cohen and Ben ʿAttar, both of whom were learned rabbis who had protected the *mellah* from harm. Saint veneration anchored Jews to the city not only religiously but also through its economic impact on the *mellah*. Rural Jews who began their pilgrimages with the customary visit to the Jewish cemetery in Marrakesh contributed to the *mellah*'s economy both directly, by buying candles or glasses of *maḥīya* at the saint's tombs (at prices elevated to include a charitable donation[54]), and indirectly, through the renewal of business contacts in the southern capital. Jews living in Marrakesh itself visited the saints' tombs more regularly, often on Saturday nights after the close of Shabbat. (One former denizen of the *mellah* boasts of having visited the tomb of Hananiya Ha-Cohen three hundred times.[55]) We can assume that Marrakesh's Jewish merchants, like their counterparts of Essaouira, increased the overall commercial flow into the city when they returned home to celebrate major festivals.[56]

The commercial aspect of saint veneration is just one dimension of a larger economic continuum between the *mellah* and its hinterland, which at several points in the late nineteenth and early twentieth centuries formed one of the few links between the southern capital and the intermittently dissident tribal areas of the larger region.[57]

The Mellah and the Rural Economy

As the "*capitale juive*" of southern Morocco and the gateway to the lucrative trade of the Sus, the Sahara, and Timbuktu, Marrakesh was the logical home base for a vast network of Jewish merchants and itinerant traders. Such individuals traveled throughout the south selling the handicrafts and other products of the cities to the rural populations, and at the same time buying local goods like goatskins, wax, cereals, and almonds to resell in Marrakesh. They included members of the *tujjār al-sulṭān*, the sultan's official corps of merchants, who were granted monopolies over certain commodities (recall for example the concessions made to Corcos in the wax trade), exempted from duties, and extended credit from the royal treasury with which to trade. As European commerce continued to penetrate the south, however, more Jews found themselves working in a similar capacity for European firms as *nā'ib*s (agents). Requests for the *simsār*'s (broker's) certificates that accorded this status were made with ever more frequency by French,[58] German,[59] and English[60] firms on behalf of Jewish merchants from Marrakesh. Accordingly, these merchants were increasingly responsible for introducing goods of foreign origin, such as tea, sugar, and textiles, into the countryside.[61]

But economic ties to Europe did not necessarily supplant local ones. Instead, it became common for several functions to overlap in a single person.[62] This web grew increasingly complicated as the sultan lost control not only of Morocco's trade, but also of the very territories into which Jewish merchants ventured to conduct their business. The trade routes around Marrakesh were notoriously unstable, and more than one itinerant merchant was robbed or murdered en route to the capital.[63] Jewish merchants were particularly vulnerable at the eleven or so *nazāla*s (toll stations) that dotted the route between Marrakesh and Essaouira. Only nominally regulated by the Makhzan, these stations probably did more to discourage commerce along this route altogether than to increase the Makhzan's share of profits.[64] Even the most legitimate ones levied special taxes on "beasts, loads of merchandise, and Jews,"[65] but all-out exploitation was more often the rule. Halévy recounts his experience at a *nazāla:*

> It usually takes three days to travel between Mogador [Essaouira] and Maroc [Marrakesh]; it took us three and a half, partly because . . . we made a very short stop due to a disagreement with an Arab who was supposedly authorized to extort money from the Jewish assistant I had with me. The man was a retired officer who had exploited, for a long time and quite fruitfully, the job of customs agent at the expense of our coreligionists. He pretended to turn over half of what he earned to government coffers, thus when I asked to see the Sultan's written confirmation of this, he grew agitated and said he had deposited it in the city archives. The truth is that the upper-level administrators have a share in the booty and close their eyes to acts of brigandage carried out at the very gates of the ancient capital to the detriment of one particular class of citizens and without the knowledge of the sultan. The Jews who try to evade this extortion or simply ask for a small reduction in the sum imposed upon them are severely beaten and have part of their merchandise seized. I formally opposed the extortion of my Jewish servant, and, with the help of the soldier accompanying me, we were able to frustrate the greed of the apocryphal customs agent.[66]

That the *nazāla*s also posed a physical danger to the Jews can be seen in the following incident, which took place in 1874: Masʿud b. Taffa, his two children, and another young man were on their way to Marrakesh from the coast when they were detained at a *nazāla* over a dispute about the toll they were told to pay. When the caravan they were traveling with left them behind, they were forced to find lodging in the area.[67] That night they were robbed and murdered. Two weeks later, a similar event took place in the Haha region, in which three Jews on their way to Marrakesh carrying several thousand dollars worth of merchandise were robbed and murdered.[68]

Marrakesh's Jewish merchants found ways to make the insecurity of the south work to their advantage, however. Claims of robbery were a particularly successful tactic, since compensation was paid by the Makhzan even when the claims were obviously spurious, which was often the case.[69] After a particularly egregious spate of these false claims in the late 1870s and early 1880s, however, the Makhzan began to take the matter more seriously. First, greater care was taken in investigating the details of the Jews' claims. In one case, a young man from the Marrakesh branch of the Corcos family returning home from Oran said he was robbed while spending the night in the home of a Muslim en route. After a detailed inquiry, the Makhzan responded that if a robbery had in fact taken place, "shouting and crying in excess of an hour" would have been heard upon discovery of the crime, when in fact the neighbors heard not a peep. Furthermore, it was argued, the man would not have waited until he arrived in Marrakesh to make his complaint known. On these grounds the claim was rejected.[70] The Makhzan also began to monitor the activities of Marrakesh's Jewish merchants in the countryside more closely. Thus in 1885 the sultan ordered Umalik to require all such individuals to register with an *ʿadl* (juridical official; pl. *ʿadūls*) prior to setting out from the city, "[s]o that the Makhzan is aware of the true amount of the losses if they claim they were robbed, and the people living in the area where the robbery takes place [are made responsible] if it is shown to have occurred within their territory."[71] The *qādī*s of Marrakesh were then instructed to appoint eight trustworthy *ʿadūl*s, "distinguished in their correctness and their piety," to supervise these registrations. The claims of merchants who refused to cooperate would no longer be acknowledged by the authorities.

In addition to protecting the royal treasury from further diminution, the sultan's order had a second, less obvious purpose that can best be understood within the context of growing rural unrest in the south during this period, and the possibility of the Jews' involvement in it. The new rule required the Jews not only to disclose the monetary value of their goods, but also to inform the Makhzan of the precise nature of their merchandise and where they planned to take it. One of the sultan's soldiers (*mukhzanī*) would then be assigned to accompany the merchants throughout their travels. Given these stipulations, it seems likely that the intention was not merely to discourage false claims, but also to monitor the Jews' forays into the countryside, and especially their dealings with potential rebels. The comments of the *wazīr al-kabīr* are quite clear on this matter:

> Previously, when the Jews wished to travel to the interior of the country, they were careful to warn the governors of the localities in which they lived. The latter then provided them with soldiers to escort them. Furthermore, they first registered the nature of their goods, titles, money or merchandise that they carried with them with the authorities, who in turn took care to furnish them with a letter of credit payable at their destination for the value of goods they wished to bring. But today, even in regions where the population has barely been subdued or remains in open revolt, they have the hubris to circulate without even informing the authorities of their departure. As a result, someone who has had 1000 francs stolen from him submits a claim for 10,000. Hence our desire to have the former laws reapplied absolutely.[72]

As the Makhzan's decision to monitor the activities of Marrakesh's Jewish merchants in the countryside demonstrates, the *mellah* was no more removed from the political machinations taking place beyond the city's walls than it was from events within Marrakesh itself. European encroachment in southern Morocco introduced new elements into an already complicated (and not always friendly) set of circumstances governing Marrakesh Jews' interactions with the region's tribes, the ramifications of which would have serious consequences for the whole country.

Jewish-Tribal Relations

The relationship between the Jews and the tribes was in reality many different relationships. On the one hand, Moroccan tribes, as is well known, were not monolithic. In the tumultuous pre-Protectorate period, they were divided into Arab and Berber groups, which in turn were each divided into those that recognized the sultan's authority, either through the payment of taxes or through military service, and those who did not.[73] Divisions also existed within individual tribes, and especially between the tribes and their *qāʾid*s. At this juncture, one might also formally acknowledge divisions that have been mostly implicit thus far, namely those within the *mellah* itself. The *mellah* was divided along the lines of gender, class, age, occupation, education, degree of Westernization, and so on. Because of these divisions, Jews did not have a uniform experience of the tribes. For instance, the vast majority of Jews who had direct contact with the tribes were men. As discussed above, the two main reasons that Marrakesh's Jews went out into the countryside, where the tribes lived, were commerce and pilgrimage. In the case of the former, there is little doubt that all *tujjār* and *nāʾib*s were male. Pilgrimage theoretically encompassed the whole Jewish community, but in practice it too was restricted by gender, with men being much more likely than women to visit saints' tombs located far from their homes.[74] Men also dominated in another important realm in which Jews and tribes came together, namely politics, where, as we'll soon see, the forging of important allegiances was the exclusive prerogative of *qā'ids* and the *shaykh al-yahūd*.

Foundations of the Jewish-Tribal Relationship

Lacking direct ties to the countryside, the majority of the *mellah*'s Jews experienced the tribes as a source of terror above all else. This is reflected in much of the folklore and hagiography treated in the course of this study as well as in the written historical record, in which the Ahmar kidnapping incident constitutes just one of many acts of tribal aggression against urban Jews. Indeed the Ahmar can be considered among the *mellah*'s lesser foes, despite the fact that prior to their kidnapping attempt they had previously caused offense by illegally seizing property in the countryside belonging to Jews from Marrakesh.[75] The *mellah* had much more to fear from the tribes who actually laid siege to Marrakesh, as Jews throughout Morocco tended to bear the brunt of such raids.[76] This was the case in Demnat in 1894,[77] Tetuan in 1903–1904,[78] and Fez in 1907.[79] While El-Hiba and his so-called blue men, Tuaregs from the Sahara whose brief occupation of Marrakesh in 1912 was referred to as a "pogrom" by one eyewitness, must be included in the list of the *mellah*'s tribal enemies,[80] it was from the Rehamna that the *mellah* had the most to fear. The Rehamna were Arabic-speaking Muslim nomads, originally from just north of the Senegal River, who had established themselves in the plains around Marrakesh in the sixteenth century as recruits in the jihad against the Portuguese and Spanish Christians.[81] To the Makhzan's great regret, the Rehamna opted to retain their pastoralist lifestyle rather than become sedentary or provide further military service to the sultan after the jihad was won. Lacking any permanent allegiance to the government, they were free to attack the southern capital repeatedly during the nineteenth century, usually in reaction to European advances. In 1894 they led a joint Misfiwa attack on Marrakesh, which not only terrified the city's inhabitants but also seriously disrupted the flow of trade, injuring local Jewish merchants in particular.[82] The Rehamna again targeted the *mellah* in 1907 by calling for the enforcement of *dhimma* sumptuary regulations as a condition for lifting another planned siege.[83]

Terrifying as these sieges were for the Jews, they nonetheless represent only one aspect of the *mellah*'s interactions with the tribes. Economic concerns, including but not limited to the activities of the itinerant merchants described above, were also significant. In many ways exchanges with the tribes paralleled the inter-communal economic exchanges within Marrakesh itself: Jews of the *mellah* supplied the tribes with *maḥīya*[84] and bail money[85] just as they did their Muslim neighbors in the medina. Quite a few members of the region's tribal population also owned houses in Marrakesh. The chief of the Mtougga was a permanent resident of the capital, leaving his son to see to the tribe's affairs in the countryside,[86] and Lambert's 1867 map of Marrakesh indicates that two adjacent houses in the western part of the city were owned by the *qā'id* of Haha and the *qā'id* of Shiadhma respectively (see figure 3.1). Numerically speaking, however, the city's best-represented tribe was the Rehamna, whose members constituted a full third of the total population of Marrakesh.[87] Some of the tribe's wealthiest individuals had primary residences in Rehamna territory but also maintained homes in Marrakesh from which to see to their affairs. In addition, many of the poorest Rehamna, those who had lost their rights to flocks or pasturelands, likewise settled in the city.[88] The Rehamna population of Marrakesh was concentrated in the northeastern edge of the city near the *zawīya* of Sidi Bel Abbes, a logical location since the tribe's home territory lay northeast of the city. Some tribespeople (though not necessarily Rehamna) may also have owned houses in the *mellah*. This is suggested by the census, which lists the names of two *qā'ids*, al-Shawi ("from the Shawiya") and al-Sahrawi ("from the Sahara"), as property owners. The latter, with five houses, is indeed the *mellah*'s second largest Muslim landlord. At the same time, we also know that at least one of the *mellah*'s Jewish landlords, Rosillio (alt. Rosio), owned land in the countryside (in Misfiwa territory, specifically),[89] and it is likely that other Jews held rural property in anonymous partnerships with Muslims.[90] Finally, other economic arrangements grew more directly out of the rural setting. They included contracts between the *mellah*'s merchants and the tribes guaranteeing the former safe passage from Marrakesh to the coast or elsewhere,[91] as well as loans granted by Jewish financiers to prospective *qā'ids* to purchase taxation and administrative rights over rural territories.[92]

The *mellah* was deeply affected by the troubles, both natural and man-made, that struck the rural south in the decades leading up to the establishment of the French Protectorate. From 1870 onward, an unending cycle of drought and locusts, poor harvests and epidemics devastated Morocco as a whole, and especially this area. The south's impoverishment was literally capitalized upon by the imperial powers, who used credit as a means of entering the once impenetrable markets of the interior. Thus began the painful process whereby the rural economy was transformed from subsistence into production for the larger market in order to pay Morocco's growing foreign debt. The adverse impact of this upon the Jews resulted largely from the fact that rural exchanges were disrupted. Many of the markets that they frequented in the Hawz were abandoned during this period, some for over a decade.[93] Long-distance trade was also interrupted by the unrest, as reported by a local newspaper in 1894:

> The attitude of the Rehamna continues to be a cause for serious concern among the population of Marrakesh, where all commercial movement has been suspended as a result of the inhabitants' sense of panic and the insecurity of the routes.[94]

Early the next year, the same newspaper reported that no caravans had been able to enter Marrakesh for over a month.[95] Moneylending practices had even more direct repercussions on the Jewish-tribal relationship. During times of crisis, the tribes borrowed from the Jews at extremely high interest, and had difficulty making good on their debts. As Ennaji explains, "the lender becomes an integral part of the . . . natural disasters which he accompanies."[96] The economic crisis in the south was destined to exact a political toll as well, which Jews would pay along with everyone else. But in some ways the *mellah* was also in a unique position to influence the outcome.

The Roots of Rural Rebellion in the South

The south has a long history of helping determine Morocco's political destiny. Though the southern roots and orientation of the Saʿdis were used against them in their rivalry with Fez, discussed previously, they were far from unique. Well before the sharifs took power, Ibn Tashfin burst forth from the Sahara to found the city of Marrakesh for the Almoravids. Their successors, the Almohads, had slightly more local roots in the Anti-Atlas. The south also produced more than its fair share of rebels and rogues, as Laroui commented: "It is also a fact that since the Saʿdis, and probably well before, the successful pretenders [to the throne] have always come from the south."[97] Given this history, the established ʿAlawi government, rooted most deeply in Fez, took the prospect of dissidence in the Marrakesh region quite seriously during the pre-Protectorate period. Yet in most cases little could be done to control its underlying causes. The Makhzan was powerless against the drought, famine, and crop failures that ravaged the south in 1877–1883, and not much more effective at stemming the tide of foreign involvement in the region, particularly after the Act of Algeciras granted Europeans increased property ownership rights in the Hawz and elsewhere.[98] When it came to confronting rebellious tribes, however, the Makhzan had both greater experience and a wider variety of methods at its disposal. Potential dissidents could be dissuaded through the use of military devices like the *maḥalla* or the brutal humiliation of captured rebels. The treatment of Tahir b. Sulayman, the Rehamna chief who was paraded around Marrakesh in a cage atop a camel until he nearly died of exposure, was surely meant to serve as an example to potential insurgents.[99] Considerably greater finesse was required in playing the "*grands caïds*" of the Atlas off one another. Gift giving—the granting of Makhzan lands or the donation of a Krupps cannon[100]—was one tactic used. The religious arm of the state could also be extended in the struggle. During one of the Rehamna uprisings, the jurists of Marrakesh ruled that it was more meritorious to engage in jihad against these "perennial pillagers and professional bandits" than against infidels.[101] The tribes' interactions with the urban population could also be controlled in order to thwart potential political alliances. Particularly during periods of strife, the number of tribesmen allowed to enter Marrakesh was limited by the authorities.[102] At times tribes were altogether barred from entering the city, as in the interregnum period following the death of Mawlay Hassan,[103] or chaperones were used to keep an eye on suspicious visitors, as was done for one al-Susi, who, along with ten of his cohorts, planned to come to Marrakesh to spend an evening among the amusements of the Jmaʿ al-Fna.[104] Though more complicated, attempts were also made to monitor the tribes' interactions with *Marrākshīs* in the countryside itself, such as the 1885 order concerning the activities of the *mellah*'s itinerant merchants. How justified were the Makhzan's concerns, and the resulting order? How successful? Insight into this matter can be gained through an examination of the *mellah*'s role in the most serious insurrection of the pre-Protectorate period, Mawlay Hafidh's coup d'état of 1907, known as the *ḥāfiẓīya.*[105]

The Mellah and the Ḥāfiẓīya

The way to revolt was paved by yet another drought and famine that hit the Marrakesh region with great severity in 1905–1906. It was followed by the passage of the Algeciras Act (mentioned above) and French reprisals for the murder of Dr. Mauchamp soon thereafter. As one crisis flowed into the next, Marrakesh and the rest of the south grew increasingly weary of the inept rule of ʿAbd al-ʿAziz. His youth, his fascination with European "toys,"[106] and above all his inability to stop colonial encroachment had given rise to powerful enemies. Foremost among the young sultan's critics was his older brother Hafidh, the serious and scholarly *khalīfa* of Marrakesh. Backed by a tribal coalition of Glaoua, Mtougga, and Rehamna chiefs, Hafidh made his bid for power in the summer of 1907. On August 16 he was proclaimed sultan in Marrakesh, and the cities of the north acquiesced early the next year, after a protracted struggle.[107]

Few were in a better position to contribute to the rise of Mawlay Hafidh than Yeshouʿa Corcos, himself a major participant in the "complicated series of intrigues, treason, and murder that formed the ordinary narrative of Moroccan history," which he recounted to visitors "with ironic detachment."[108] He alone could provide the glue for the crucial alliances of 1907, as affirmed by Mme. Camhy of the A.I.U.: "Always tireless, and thanks to the consideration he is paid by the sultan and the caïds (who called on him to arbitrate their disputes), he tried and succeeded in righting any wrong."[109] Not only was Corcos extremely wealthy (often a prerequisite to influence in Morocco), but he had long-standing ties to all the principal actors of 1907, not least Mawlay Hafidh himself. Walter Harris, the correspondent for the London *Times* during this period, remarked that Hafidh was "on terms of considerable intimacy" with the Jews of Marrakesh.[110] Elsewhere, Corcos is referred to as Hafidh's "Jewish vizier."[111] In particular, Corcos may have had a hand in bringing Hafidh together with another of his patrons, Madani al-

Figure 5.4. Mawlay Hafidh. Postcard, Union Postal Universal Marruecos. Private collection of the author.

Glaoui, a union which provided the initial spark for the revolt.[112] Corcos had long been advising Glaoui on matters pertaining to Moroccan Jewry,[113] and had personally introduced him to the A.I.U. representatives in Marrakesh.[114] In return, Glaoui entrusted Corcos with important missions, such as delivering messages to his main rival, the *qā'id* Goundafa.[115] Nor was Glaoui the only "lord of the Atlas" whose attention Corcos commanded, a crucial fact given that an Atlas alliance was the key to Hafidh's success: "An accord had to be made among all the *caïds*. Only one man, by virtue of his influence, could make the peace: Yeshouʿa Corcos, president of the community."[116] Corcos was also close to Hafidhist sympathizers among local Makhzan officials, including Ibn Dawud, the pasha of the medina in the decade preceding the *ḥāfiẓīya*. Though divested of his power by the time of the revolt, Ibn Dawud was said to have abetted the Rehamna in their 1894 siege of Marrakesh, setting the stage for their involvement in the events of 1907.[117]

Not long after the initial alliance between Glaoui and ʿAbd al-Hafidh had been forged, the *khalīfa* began distributing arms to the Rehamna, possibly from the royal stores in Marrakesh.[118] Was the *mellah* involved in these goings-on? Jews in the Marrakesh region had a long and variegated involvement in the production and trade of arms in Morocco, and from the 1880s onward there was a great expansion in the sale of arms (not to mention an improvement in their quality) in the Moroccan interior.[119] Jews were the fabricators of firearms and other weapons, as well as their carriers, at least in the countryside.[120] Jewish merchants were active participants in the arms trade between Morocco and Europe. From at least the seventeenth century, Moroccan Jews were sent guns by their coreligionists in Europe,[121] and also traveled abroad themselves to make such purchases for the Makhzan.[122] Arms of all sorts were also acquired locally by Jews as collateral on defaulted loans.[123] Given the relatively easy access to arms, the *mellah* became a natural locus for contraband guns and ammunition in World War I, much to the dismay of French authorities.[124]

Finally, who paid for the *ḥāfiẓīya*? Funds were in chronically short supply on both sides of the conflict. At one point in his campaign, ʿAbd al-Hafidh was forced to abrogate the conditional *bayʿa* (oath of allegiance) he had received in Fez by reinstating unpopular taxes and seizing property in order to pay his troops.[125] For his part, ʿAbd al-ʿAziz hocked some of the royal jewels.[126] While the rival sultans leaned hard on Makhzan resources, the *qāʾid*s leaned equally hard on their tribes:

> Large sums of money are being collected from all the tribes, ostensibly for Mulai Hafid, and the report is current that these three great Kaïds are to collect a strong mahalla and march to Rabat and Fez with the men and money they have collected; but whether this move is intended as a support of the Hafidist throne or as a counter-stroke to the growing power of the new Viziers whom Mulai Hafid is summoning to his councils is a matter for conjecture.[127]

Was the *mellah* also exploited as a fiscal resource on this occasion, as it had been so many times in the past? More to the point, did Yeshouʿa Corcos himself underwrite Hafidh's victory by funneling money to the tribes?[128] There are certainly historical precedents that suggest so. For instance, when fighting broke out between the tribes of al-Jalmima and al-Asrir in 1850, the Makhzan was advised to bring an end to the *fitna* (strife) by using money from the local Jews to manipulate allegiances: "Write to the al-Jalmima and tell them to get the Jews from both areas, who are all very rich on account of usury, to pay 1000 *mithqāls* and the other tribe, al-Asrir, to pay 400, to make a tribal coalition."[129]

Moreover, the Rehamna were well known among the moneylenders of the *mellah*. The danger of such alliances had been clearly understood by Mawlay Hassan in his day. He ordered Umalik to make a list of the names of the Rehamna and Jews involved and the sums that had changed hands. Each tribesman was then contacted directly and told to cease this "irresponsible behavior" (which was of course fervently denied).[130] There were also precedents for dissenting tribes' buying arms with money borrowed from Jewish lenders.[131] Finally, the Jews' financial involvement in the *ḥāfiẓīya* may be alluded to in the Ahmar kidnapping incident. Many of the tribes around Marrakesh, including the Ahmar, associated Jews with blood and buried treasure. We have already dealt with the blood aspect of the story, but what about the treasure? Its association with Jews, recorded by Thomson in another form,[132] becomes significant in the present discussion when we learn of how ʿAbd al-Hafidh's financial problems were finally solved:

> The usual reports of Mulai Hafid's departure from Marakesh are current. His horses are said to have been sent into camp outside the town, a sign of an impending move . . . There is a report that his financial difficulties have been relieved by a find of treasure in Marakesh to the amount of 20,000 Spanish doubloons (about £75,000). This rumour is supported by the assertion of couriers from Marakesh that Mulai Hafid's men are being paid in gold.[133]

The rock under which the treasure was said to have been found was identified by Françoise Legey as one of Marrakesh's most important relics. It stands not far from the *mellah* at Bab al-Rubb on the western side of the Kasbah.[134] Could the buried treasure be an allusion to Corcos's deep pockets? The answer may be beyond our grasp, as Bénech acknowledges:

> Given his very close relations with Madani El Glaoui, he [Corcos] certainly was aware of the conspiracy by which the latter pushed Mawlay Hafidh to the Moroccan throne. In what measure did he finance the operation? This we will never know.[135]

The circumstances outlined above that suggest that the Jews of Marrakesh were in a unique position to contribute to the *ḥāfiẓīya* revolt. What has yet to be addressed is the question of why they would choose to do so. On the positive side of the equation, Mawlay Hafidh's attractions for the Jews can best be understood in the context of the larger north-south rivalry in Morocco. A sultan with deep roots in Marrakesh was always preferable to the city's Jews, who benefited from the local experience and especially the likely physical presence of their main protector. Paybacks to those directly involved in the coup were probably also a consideration (as was the potential for punishment, had it not succeeded). The prospect of a new Makhzan in which the clerical class of *Fāsī* Arab notables would be replaced by southern chieftains with strong patronage ties to Jews was also something to be welcomed.[136] The prominence of the Glaoui brothers in the new government, with Madani as *wazīr al-kabīr* and Thami as pasha of Marrakesh, did indeed prove an immediate boon for the *mellah.* According to the local A.I.U. representative, Glaoui's rule marked a major turning point in its history:

> There is little use in recalling the painful trials and tribulations experienced by the Jews during the period between August 1900 and the coming [to power] of Al-Glawi. With Si Madani, everything changed as if by magic. [Endowed with a] vivacious and hardy spirit, immediately understanding the sympathy that would accrue to the new regime as a result of tolerant and firm policies, he called all the authorities of the city and the environs to his side and urged them to protect the Jews. Moreover, he outlawed the bastinado and fines, and only with the authorization of M. J. [Yeshouʿa] Corcos, whose power in the mellah is equivalent to that of a pasha, does he allow for the imprisonment of Jews.[137]

But the *ḥāfiẓīya* also held clear disadvantages for the Jews. Condoning the Rehamna's actions was undoubtedly a bitter pill for the *mellah* to swallow. The tribe's 1894 attack was still fresh in Jewish memory when Hafidh agreed to strengthen *dhimma* restrictions, just months before he became sultan. Somewhat less clear, however, is how Jews may have received the anti-European stance of the *ḥāfiẓīya,* at least prior to the concessions the new sultan was forced to make. We know that the Muslim population of Marrakesh was in complete sympathy with Hafidh's call for the evacuation of all Europeans from the city.[138] Were the Jews? Judging from the conviction with which Corcos urged Nessim Falcon, the A.I.U. director, to leave Marrakesh and close the school for the good of the local community, the *mellah*'s ambivalence about the European presence in Marrakesh, which has been documented throughout the preceding chapters, remained strong in 1907:

> The president of the community himself came to beg me to leave Marrakesh. As I sought to make him understand that there was no way I could compromise the entire program of the Alliance by closing the schools and seeking safety for myself, M. Corcos demonstrated to me that our presence in the mellah did more harm to our coreligionists than good, given that the [ḥāfiẓīya] movement is exclusively anti-European and that the humiliations the Jews have suffered are the solely the consequence of their sympathy for foreigners.[139]

Nor was Corcos the only influential Jew in Marrakesh to have pro-Hafidhist tendencies, or at least to cultivate the appearance of such. The German Jewish doctor Judah Holzmann was a vocal proponent of Hafidh's bid for power, and traveled to the countryside on his behalf to meet with tribal leaders. His activities earned him the wrath of both Nessim Falcon and Emile Mauchamp.[140]

Though lacking a shared *Marrākshī* identity to mitigate the tensions inherent in rural-urban relations, Marrakesh Jewry's ties to the hinterland were nonetheless sufficiently strong to fix the *mellah* firmly within a wide network of regional interests, a position that could in turn be used to effect specific outcomes. While the exchanges that helped build this network were largely economic in nature, it did not follow that Jews "could achieve nothing more than wealth by means of it," as Geertz has argued in trying to explain the political neutrality of Jewish merchants in the Middle Atlas region.[141] Rather, whatever influence could be mustered among Jews' contacts in both city and countryside was successfully brought to bear on the events of 1907.

Epilogue

Ḥāy al-Salām

The area of Marrakesh once known as the *mellah* is today called Ḥāy al-Salām, its name a nostalgic (or perhaps even ironic) nod to the more positive aspects of the complex sets of interactions once carried out within its walls. Jews have all but disappeared from the *mellah,* and indeed from the city as a whole. At the time of this writing, approximately two hundred Jews remain in Marrakesh, most of them old, with only one or two families still residing in the *mellah* itself. (The rest live in the newer quarters of the city.) Four Jewish businesses continue to operate in the *mellah* or on its periphery: a spice shop, two textile merchants (the owner of one also serves as a rabbi), and a stationer. On *Derb al-Tijara,* the Corcos home reveals the demise of this community with particular poignancy. The former residence of one of the most powerful men in the city's history, described by the Tharaud brothers in 1920 as being "full of children,"[1] now sits empty. The lively sounds of piano-playing, humming sewing machines, and chickens being slaughtered for Shabbat have long since been silenced. When I first visited the *mellah* in the mid-1990s, the Corcos home functioned as a home for the aged, and the only sounds to be heard came from two severely senile Jews, but now they too have died. A portrait of Yeshouʿa Corcos hangs in a corner room on the second floor, but the house itself is uninhabited.

The Jews of Marrakesh slowly began leaving the *mellah* in the decades fol-

Figure e.1. Yeshouʿa Corcos. Photograph by the author.

lowing the establishment of the French Protectorate in 1912, first for the new European parts of the city, known as Gueliz, then for Morocco's coastal cities, particularly Casablanca, and eventually for foreign lands. The reasons that they left are many and overlapping. The few Zionist officials who came to Marrakesh in the 1920s and 1930s did their best to entice the local Jews to go to Palestine,[2] but Zionist feeling was weak in Morocco during the Protectorate period, at least partly due to the countervailing influence of the A.I.U., whose assimilationist doctrine was antithetical to Jewish nationalism.

Figure e.2. Jewish spice merchant in the *mellah,* 2004. Photograph by the author.

(French governmental policy in Morocco was likewise opposed to Zionism.) Thus Jews who could afford to do so often emigrated to France or elsewhere in Europe, and eventually to distant cities like Montreal, Buenos Aires, Los Angeles, and New York. For many decades an almost constant flow of Jewish immigrants to Marrakesh from the countryside compensated for this exodus, with the *mellah* registering its first decrease in population only in the 1940s.[3] But the trend became irreversible with the general instability and political unrest surrounding the independence movement, and by 1960 only ten thousand Jews remained in Marrakesh.[4] Jews had been made equal citizens of the Moroccan state in 1956, but the Middle Eastern wars of 1967 and 1973 convinced the majority of Moroccan Jews that life in their native land had become untenable, resulting in mass emigration—at this point mostly to Israel—and the closing of most of the country's Jewish institutions for good. A 1980 census determined that just 1,820 Jews lived in Marrakesh.[5] A decade later, the only Jews left were "a handful of the old and sick, waiting for their end."[6]

Although Muslims have all but replaced Jews in the *mellah,* if one looks closely enough, a multitude of signs recalling the ebb and flow of the latter's four-hundred-year habitation of this space are still visible. Multistory houses attest to a difficult history of overcrowding; because of the perimeter walls, the only direction to expand was upward, despite Islamic religious

Figure e.3. Jewish cloth merchant in the *mellah,* 2004. Photograph by the author.

Figure e.4. Jewish resident of the *mellah,* 2004. Photograph by the author.

Figure e.5. Jewish resident of the *mellah,* 2004. Photograph by the author.

injunctions to the contrary.[7] The faded image of a *khamsa,* scorpion, or serpent on the door of a home recalls the tenacity of traditional religious expression in defiance of the numerous attempts by the A.I.U. and other Western organizations to "modernize" and "civilize" this and other Jewish communities in Morocco. On another house, a Spanish-style wrought iron balcony bears witness to the social, economic, and demographic impact of the expulsion from *Sefarad* (Heb., Spain). It also reminds us of Judaism's weaker constraints on female visibility and the impact of this discrepancy on Muslim perceptions of Jewish space. Finally, the candle stubs and small stones placed on top of the tombs in the adjacent cemetery evoke the saints who anchored the Jews' most intense religious aspirations (and those of many Muslims as well) to the very earth of Marrakesh and the surrounding countryside. All are evidence of the vibrant, engaged, and resolutely *Marrākshī* community that once inhabited the *mellah.*

In this traversing of the "*grandes lignes*" of the history of the *mellah* of Marrakesh, the disposition of space has been treated as a manifestation of the underlying social order; as Norbert-Schulz has remarked, "Life interprets itself as space, in taking possession of the environment."[8] The idea that spatial arrangements not only allowed for but actually helped shape inter- and intra-communal relations has been examined at several crucial junctures in the history of the *mellah.* These include how the creation of the *mellah* formed a key ideological component of the Saʿdi quest for legitimacy, how crowding in the *mellah* was subsumed into the Makhzan's pre-Protectorate reform program, how the growing influence of Europe affected traditional spatial and social arrangements in Marrakesh, and how the *mellah* fit into wider regional networks, including both Jewish and tribal populations of the countryside. At the core of this study lies a firm belief in the permeability of the *mellah,* which allowed for the development of extensive and highly nuanced relations between Jews and Muslims that had a lasting impact on the identities of both populations, mutually reinforcing their sense of what Mohammed Naciri has termed "*mudaniyya,*"[9] being both in and of a place, particularly a city, in this case Marrakesh.

While asserting the integral role of the *mellah* in the larger life of the city, this study has at the same time recognized the durability of the dominant Moroccan point of view on the disposition of space in Marrakesh and its effect on inter-communal relations. With this idea in mind, I hope to have avoided the shortcoming—or at least what would be a shortcoming in the case of Marrakesh—of seeing European agency, i.e., foreign involvement in Moroccan affairs and its byproducts (migration to the coasts, the protégé system, Westernization, etc.), as the defining factor in the history of the *mellah.* By guiding the discussion back to the evolution of the cityscape itself, we can see that Jews in Marrakesh were in fact subject to many of the same influences and shared many of the same reactions as their Muslim neighbors, and that these elements, rather than a unilateral, accelerated entry into a world-system, were primarily responsible for shaping their daily lives and destinies.

NOTES

INTRODUCTION

1. For a detailed description of this incident, see Susan Miller, "Saints et laïcs dans le Tanger juif du XIXe siècle," in *Mémoires juives d'Espagne et du Portugal,* ed. Aron Rodrigue and Esther Benbassa (Paris: Publisud, 1996), 171–173.

2. Although the edict was promulgated in early 1864, it was subsequently nullified on the grounds of redundancy by a decree issued soon after Montefiore's departure. For a debate as to the meaning of the so-called Montefiore *dahir* and its retraction, see Norman Stillman, *The Jews of Arab Lands in Modern Times* (Philadelphia: The Jewish Publication Society of America, 2003), 14–15; and, from a Moroccan perspective, Mohammed Kenbib, *Juifs et musulmans au Maroc, 1859–1948* (Rabat, Morocco: Faculté des Lettres et des Sciences Humaines, 1994), 153–173.

3. Jean-Louis Miège, *Le Maroc et l'Europe: 1830–1894* (Rabat, Morocco: Editions la Porte, 1989), 2:563 n.7.

4. Joseph Hooker and John Ball, *Journal of a Tour in Morocco and the Great Atlas* (London: Macmillan, 1878), 137. The wall blocking the entrance was knocked down so that Hooker and Ball could be lodged in the house in question.

5. A very large body of scholarship exists on the topic of the "Islamic city." See in particular the work of William Marçais, in which its prototypical elements are defined: "L'islamisime et la vie urbaine," *L'académie des inscriptions et belles-lettres, comptes rendus* (1928): 86–100. The concept is further developed in the work of his brother Georges Marçais, who is the first to suggest a specific morphology: "La conception des villes dans l'islam," *Revue d'Alger* 2 (1945): 517–533. The topic is again taken up throughout the remainder of the century, most notably in Ira Lapidus, *Muslim Cities in the Later Middle Ages* (Cambridge: Cambridge University Press, 1984); and André Raymond, *The Great Arab Cities in the Sixteenth–Eighteenth Centuries: An Introduction* (New York: New York University Press, 1984). For an overview of the various academic debates surrounding the topic, see Albert Hourani and S. M. Stern, eds., *The Islamic City* (Philadelphia: University of Pennsylvania Press, 1970), which was based on a conference held at Oxford University in 1965; Janet Abu-Lughod, "The Islamic City: Historical Myth, Islamic Essence, and Contemporary Relevance," *International Journal of Middle Eastern Studies* 19 (1987): 155–176; and Masashi Hanedi and Toru Miura, eds., *Islamic Urban Studies* (London: Kegan Paul International, 1994). More recently, Paul Wheatley has rendered the "Islamic city" debates irrelevant and perhaps even exhausted with his alternative, altogether more flexible understanding of Islamic urban forms as part of a dynamic system, one that not only has no difficulty accommodating the concept of Jewish space but also facilitates a better understanding of

its actual function within cities like Marrakesh: "A city comprises a set of functionally interrelated social, political, administrative, economic, cultural, religious, and other institutions located in close proximity in order to exploit scale economies. A group of such institutional sets, together with their attributes and mutual relationships, constitutes an urban system, an arrangement in which the concurrent operation of agglomerative tendencies and accessibility factors tends to induce a hierarchical arrangement of the constituent parts." Paul Wheatley, *The Places Where Men Pray Together* (Chicago: University of Chicago Press, 2001), 59.

6. The more familiar European spelling will be used here. For a discussion of the etymology of the term "*mellah,*" see the seminal work by Simon Levy, "Ḥāra et mellāḥ: Les mots, l'histoire et l'institution," in *Histoire et linguistique*, ed. Abdelahad Sebti (Rabat, Morocco: Université Mohammed V, Publications de la Faculté des Lettres et des Sciences Humaines, 1992), 41–50.

7. Susan Miller, "Un *mellaḥ* désenclavé: L'espace juif dans une ville marocaine; Tanger, 1860–1912," in *Perception et réalités au Maroc: Relations judéo-musulmanes,* ed. Robert Assaraf and Michel Abitbol (Casablanca: Najah El Jadida, 1998), 325.

8. Antoine Fattal, *Le statut légal des non-musulmans en pays d'Islam* (Beirut: Imprimerie Catholique, 1958), 93.

9. All the city's quarters were locked at night, a detail that is often overlooked in discussions emphasizing the isolation of the *mellah,* as is the fact that the *mellah* was locked from the inside, by the Jews themselves, and not from the outside. The *mellah* remained closed on Jewish holidays in addition to during Shabbat.

10. Daniel Schroeter, "The Jewish Quarter and the Moroccan City," in *New Horizons in Sephardic Studies,* ed. Yedida Stillman and George Tucker (Albany: State University of New York Press, 1993), 67.

11. The early Orientalists' search for a suitable methodology by which to compare European cities to Middle Eastern ones, conducted under the influence of the sociologist Max Weber, was a significant factor in the development of the "Islamic city" model. Although the conclusions reached using comparative methodologies (including the idea that Islamic society was stagnant while European society was dynamic) have rightly been criticized by later scholars, the potential benefits of such an approach on the microcosmic level of Jewish urban history, comparing, for example, the European ghetto, the *mellah,* and the North American Jewish neighborhood (e.g., New York's Lower East Side), are, in my view, still worth scholarly consideration.

12. This term was coined by Norman Stillman to replace Goitein's biological metaphor of symbiosis. Given the cultural context of southern Morocco, where the Sephardic influence was much weaker than in the north of the country, "commensality" is preferable to the alternative Spanish term, "*convivencia.*" See Norman Stillman, "The Commensality of Islamic and Jewish Civilizations," *Middle Eastern Lectures* 2 (1997): 81–94.

13. Daniel Noin, *La population rurale du Maroc* (Paris: Presses universitaires de France, 1970), 1:42.

14. The ʿAynayniya, a lodge associated with the Saharan rebel and religious figure Ma al-ʿAynayn, operated in Marrakesh during the first decade of the twentieth century.

15. Miège is referring to Thami al-Glaoui, who served as pasha of Marrakesh from 1908 to 1956. See chapter 5 for more on al-Glaoui.

16. Jean-Louis Miège, *Morocco,* trans. O. C. Warden (Paris: Arthaud, 1952), 191–193.

17. Marrakesh is somewhat unique in its municipal administration, in that it had not one but two pashas. The first was the pasha or *qāʾid* of the medina (sometimes referred to as the "governor" in European sources). The second, known simply as the pasha, was responsible for the Kasbah and the *mellah,* and by extension the Jewish communities of the countryside around Marrakesh. His jurisdiction is confirmed in the following: "Thus the Jews living in the countryside are under our authority as Jews of the Kasbah, and they will be ruled by the same law that rules over the Jews of Marrakesh." Direction des archives royales, Rabat (hereafter D.A.R.), Marrakesh 7, 18 Ṣafar 1303/26 November 1885, Umālik. The pasha also named the *shaykh al-yahūd* for the region: Archives de l'Alliance Israélite Universelle, Paris (hereafter A.I.U.), Maroc VII.B.1852/2, 1914, Danon. The Jewish communities the pasha of Marrakesh supervised included those of the Atlas Mountains and pre-Saharan oasis towns, but not those of Tafilalt, which were officially linked to Meknes. See Harvey Goldberg, "The Mellahs of Southern Morocco: Report of a Survey," *Maghreb Review* 8 (1983), 61–69.

18. Gaston Deverdun, *Marrakech des origines à 1912* (Rabat, Morocco: Editions Techniques Nord-Africaines, 1959), 1:117.

19. There is some disagreement about whether Marrakesh was founded in 1062 or 1070, with most scholars now favoring the later date. See Vincent Lagardère, *Les Almoravides jusqu'au règne de Yûsuf b. Tâsfîn (1039–1106)* (Paris: L'Harmattan, 1989); and Ronald Messier, "Rereading Medieval Sources through Multidisciplinary Glasses," in *The Maghrib in Question: Essays in History and Historiography,* ed. Michel Le Gall and Kenneth Perkins (Austin: University of Texas Press, 1997), 176–178.

20. Joseph Thomson, *Travels in the Atlas and Southern Morocco* (London: George Philip and Son, 1889), 350. Casablanca surpassed Marrakesh as home to the largest Jewish community in the 1930s.

21. Fully 90 percent of the Jews of Marrakesh were bilingual Berber and Arabic speakers. See José Bénech, *Essai d'explication d'un mellah (ghetto marocain): Un des aspects du judaïsme* (Paris: Larose, 1940), xvii.

22. Pierre Flamand, inspector of primary education for the Department of Education of French Morocco and part-time ethnographer, was responsible for much of this work. In addition to his study of Demnat, *Un mellah en pays berbère: Demnate* (Paris: Librairie Generale de Droit & de Jurisprudence, 1952), see also his *Diaspora en terre d'Islam,* vol. 1, *Les communautés israélites du Sud-Marocain* (Casablanca: Imprimerie Réunies, 1959–1960). More recent examples can be found in Michel Abitbol, ed., *Communautés juives des marges sahariennes du Maghreb* (Jerusalem: Imprimerie Daf-Chen, 1982). See also Andre Levy and Yoram Bilu, "Nostalgia and Ambivalence: The Reconstruction of Jewish-Muslim Relations in Oulad Mansour," in *Sephardi and Middle Eastern Jewries: History and Culture in the Modern Era,* ed. Harvey Goldberg (Bloomington: Indiana University Press, 1996), 288–311.

23. The colonial ethnography by Bénech, *Essai d'explication d'un mellah,* based exclusively on European secondary sources, has descriptive value for the contemporary historian. Jane Gerber's *Jewish Society in Fez, 1450–1700* (Leiden, Netherlands: E. J. Brill, 1980) deals with some of these issues in passing but its main focus remains internal Jewish communal life and not Jewish-Muslim relations *per se.* To the extent that Essaouira can be considered on a similar urban scale as Marrakesh or Fez, see

also Daniel Schroeter, *Merchants of Essaouira: Urban Society and Imperialism in Southwestern Morocco, 1844–1886* (Cambridge: Cambridge University Press, 1988).

24. Bernard Lewis, *Jews of Islam* (Princeton, N.J.: Princeton University Press, 1987), 149. The historians Norman Stillman and Michael Laskier, though clearly cognizant of the differences separating the two entities, nonetheless use the two terms interchangeably, as does Albert Memmi in describing the Tunisian *ḥāra* where he grew up in his semi-autobiographical *Pillar of Salt* (the subject of which, not surprisingly, is the author's struggle to come to terms with his Franco-Maghrebi identity). See Albert Memmi, *The Pillar of Salt* (Boston: Beacon Press, 1992), 94; Stillman, *The Jews of Arab Lands in Modern Times,* 80; and Michael Laskier, *The Alliance Israélite Universelle and the Jewish Communities of Morocco: 1862–1962* (Albany: State University of New York Press, 1983), 13. Janet Abu-Lughod rejects the term *mellah* entirely, referring only to Morocco's "Jewish ghettos," the origins of which she inexplicably dates to the nineteenth century. See Abu-Lughod, "The Islamic City." A compromise is struck by the French-Moroccan historian Germaine Ayache, who prefers a hyphenated amalgamation of the two terms, "*mellah*-ghetto." See his "La minorité juive dans le Maroc précolonial," *Hespéris-Tamuda* 25 (1987): 150.

25. Muhammad al-Nasiri, as quoted in Mohammed Kenbib, "Changing Aspects of State and Society in Nineteenth-Century Morocco," in *The Moroccan State in Historical Perspective, 1850–1985,* ed. Abdelali Doumou, trans. Ayi Kwei Armah (Dakar, Senegal: Codesria, 1990), 11.

26. Through most of history, Jews in the Islamic world generally enjoyed greater political autonomy and religious freedom than did Jews in Christian Europe. By the pre-colonial period, however, the prospect of full equality for Jews, as promised by the French Revolution and the various Enlightenment legislation that was promulgated in Europe, was seen as vastly preferable to Jews' second-class status in the Middle East and North Africa. With the establishment of the French Protectorate over Morocco in 1912, the Alliance Israélite Universelle argued forcefully for the granting of French nationality to Moroccan Jews, as had been done for Algerian Jews with the Crémieux decree of 1870, but this request was rejected by the French authorities. See Laskier, *The Alliance Israélite Universelle and the Jewish Communities of Morocco,* 163–171.

27. Leland Bowie, "An Aspect of Muslim-Jewish Relations in Late Nineteenth-Century Morocco: A European Diplomatic View," *International Journal of Middle Eastern Studies* 7 (1976), 4.

28. Schools for the children of Muslim notables were opened in Marrakesh during the first decades of the Protectorate.

29. A similar dynamic is discussed in the context of Zionism, whereby the Ashkenazi-dominated Zionist authorities of the Yishuv (and later the Israeli government) attempted to de-Orientalize the so-called Mizrahim in order for Israel to gain acceptance as a European-style nation-state, in Amnon Raz-Krakotzkin, "The Zionist Return to the West and the Mizrahi Jewish Perspective," in *Orientalism and the Jews,* ed. Derek Penslar and Ivan Kalmar (Waltham, Mass.: Brandeis University Press, 2005), 162–181.

30. Laskier, *The Alliance Israélite Universelle and the Jewish Communities of Morocco,* 353.

31. Eugene Aubin, *Morocco of Today* (London: E. B. Dutton, 1906), 290.

32. Oren Kosansky, "All Dear unto God: Saints, Pilgrimage, and Textual Practice in Jewish Morocco" (Ph.D. dissertation, University of Michigan, 2003), 73.

33. The phrase is borrowed from Shlomo Deshen, *The Mellah Society: Jewish Communal Life in Sherifian Morocco* (Chicago: University of Chicago Press, 1989).

34. A.I.U., Maroc XXVII.E.417–442, 30 December 1901, Moïse Levy. See chapter 3.

1. MELLAHIZATION

An earlier version of the first part of this chapter previously appeared in the *International Journal of Middle Eastern Studies.*

1. The Pact of ʿUmar is thought to have been modeled on a capitulation treaty between the caliph ʿUmar b. al-Khattab (r. 634–644) and the patriarch of Jerusalem. Its terms were eventually extended to other conquered non-Muslim minorities (including Jews), so long as the belief systems to which they subscribed were monotheistic and scripturally based, and pre-dated Islam. The *ahl al-dhimma* (those granted the status of *dhimmī*) were accorded the state's protection, which guaranteed them the right to life, property, and the practice of their religion. In exchange, they were required to pay a special poll tax (*jizya*) and in some cases, particularly in the early Islamic period, a land tax (*kharāj*). *Dhimmīs* were also subject to a series of disabilities intended to underline their humility (and thus perhaps induce them to choose Islam), including sumptuary laws, building codes, and bans on public displays of religion. The application of these regulations varied considerably in practice, as did the fulfillment of the guarantee of protection. For a more complete treatment of *dhimma* status and a translation of the Pact of ʿUmar, see Norman Stillman, *The Jews of Arab Lands in Modern Times* (Philadelphia: The Jewish Publication Society of America, 2003), 25–28, 157–158, passim. For its application in Marrakesh, see chapters 2 and 4 of this book, which deal with *jizya* and sumptuary laws respectively.

2. According to the twelfth-century geographer al-Idrisi, the Almoravid sultan ʿAli b. Yusuf (r. 1106–1142) forbade Jews to spend the night in Marrakesh, though they were permitted (perhaps even encouraged) to enter the city during the day to pursue "the business and services that are their particular specialty." Reinhart Dozy and Michael De Goeje, eds. and trans., *Description de l'Afrique et de l'Espagne, par Edrisi* (Leiden, Netherlands: E. J. Brill, 1866), 1:80.

3. Leo Africanus, *Description de l'Afrique,* ed. and trans. Alexis Epaulard, 2 vols. (Paris: Librairie d'Amerique et d'Orient, 1956). Technically, Leo was not a foreigner in the Islamic world, since he was born in Granada. He spent time in Fez as a teenager before being captured by Christian corsairs and subsequently liberated, and baptized, by the pope.

4. Leo Africanus, *Description de l'Afrique,* 1:101–102.

5. Leo Africanus, *Description de l'Afrique,* 1:102.

6. See Weston Cook, *The Hundred Years War for Morocco* (Boulder, Colo.: Westview Press, 1994), 175; and Pierre de Cenival, "Les emirs des hintata, 'rois' de Marrakech," *Hespéris* 24 (1937): 245–261.

7. Leo Africanus, *Description de l'Afrique,* 1:85–86.

8. Mercedes García-Arenal, "Spanish Literature on North Africa in the XVI Century: Diego de Torres," *Maghreb Review* 8, nos. 1–2 (1983): 53–59.

9. Ellen Friedman, *Spanish Captives in North Africa in the Early Modern Age* (Madison: University of Wisconsin Press, 1983), 56.

10. Luis del Marmol Carvajal, *Descripción general de Africa,* 2 vols. (Granada: Rene Rabut, 1573).

11. Torres was in fact one of the first European travelers to have had the idea to disguise himself as a Jew in order to move around the country more easily.

12. Diego de Torres, *Relación del origen y suceso de los Xarifes y del estado de los reinos de Marruecos, Fez, y Tarudante que tienen usurpados* (Seville: Casa Francisco Perez, 1586). A French translation of Torres's work appears as "Histoire des cherifs, et de royaumes de Maroc, de Fez, de Tarudant, et autres provinces" in Luis del Marmol Carvajal, *L'Afrique de Marmol,* trans. Nicolas Perrot (Paris: L. Billaine, 1667), vol. 3; and a modern reprint has been edited by Mercedes García-Arenal: *Relación del origen y suceso de los Xarifes y de los reinos de Marruecos, Fez, y Tarudante* (Madrid: Siglo Veintiuno, 1980). All subsequent references are to the latter edition unless indicated otherwise.

13. Luis del Marmol Carvajal, *L'Afrique de Marmol,* 3 vols., trans. Nicolas Perrot (Paris: L. Billaine, 1667). All subsequent references are to this edition.

14. Marmol Carvajal, *L'Afrique de Marmol,* 59.

15. The existence of two distinct neighborhoods may be an indication that the newly arrived Jewish exiles from Spain lived separately from the established Jewish community during this period. Gaston Deverdun, *Marrakech des origines à 1912* (Rabat, Morocco: Editions Techniques Nord-Africaines, 1959), 1:338.

16. Whether Torres meant a thousand inhabitants in each quarter or combined is unclear from the text, though judging from Marmol's estimate of three thousand households, the former seems more plausible. See Torres, *Relación del origen,* 93.

17. Torres, *Relación del origen,* 295.

18. Marmol Carvajal, *L'Afrique de Marmol,* 59.

19. Lucette Valensi points out that it is through the giving of a date in the Hebrew calendar that events are introduced into "sacred time" and thus become part of Jewish collective memory. "From Sacred History to Historical Memory and Back: The Jewish Past," *History and Anthropology* 2 (1986): 289. Valensi discusses the significance of similar mnemonic devices in relation to Moroccan historical memory in *Fables de la mémoire: La glorieuse bataille des trois rois* (Paris: Seuil, 1992).

20. Dov Noy, *Moroccan Jewish Folktales* (New York: Herzl Press, 1966), 80–81.

21. See David Corcos, *Studies in the History of the Jews of Morocco* (Jerusalem: Rubin Mass, 1976), 81; and Maurice de Périgny, *Au Maroc: Marrakech et les ports du sud* (Paris: P. S. Roger, 1917), 138.

22. Noy, *Moroccan Jewish Folktales,* 76–78.

23. See Vincent Cornell, *Realm of the Saint: Power and Authority in Moroccan Sufism* (Austin: University of Texas Press, 1998), 259.

24. Mercedes García-Arenal, "Sainteté et pouvoir dynastique au Maroc: La résistance de Fès aux Sa'diens," *Annales E.S.C.* 4 (1990): 1026–1027.

25. Pierre de Cenival, "Le palais d'El Bedi et l'œuvre de Matham: Introduction critique," in *Les sources inédites de l'histoire du Maroc,* première série, *Archives et bibliothèques des Pays-Bas,* ed. Henry de Castries (Paris: E. Leroux, 1906–1923), 4:573.

26. The architectural program of Henri IV is treated extensively in Hillary Ballon, *The Paris of Henri IV: Architecture and Urbanism* (Cambridge, Mass.: M.I.T. Press, 1991).

27. Deverdun, *Marrakech,* 1:359. Al-Ifrani goes to great lengths to refute allegations that al-Ghalib used alchemy. See Muḥammad al-Ifrānī, *Nuzhat al-ḥādī bi-akhbār mulūk al-qarn al-ḥādī,* ed. Octave Houdas (Paris: E. Leroux, 1889), 51–53, translated into French by Houdas as *Histoire de la dynastie saâdienne au Maroc, 1511–1670* in the same volume. All subsequent references are to the Arabic text unless indicated other-

wise. Saʿdi enterprises in Marrakesh were more likely financed by a combination of extraordinary taxation and economic revitalization as a result of peace with the Portuguese.

28. This paternalistic relationship between the Jews and the sultan also reinforces Jews' ties to their Muslim neighbors, insofar as all are the sultan's subjects. As Kosansky has shown, this political ideology continues to serve a similar purpose in the contemporary period by tying Muslims and Jews, including those that no longer live in Morocco, to the Moroccan nation. Kosansky, "All Dear unto God," 210–211.

29. Georges Vajda, *Un recueil de textes historiques judéo-marocains* (Paris: Larose, 1951).

30. Vajda, *Un recueil de textes historiques judéo-marocains,* 13. For a discussion of this epidemic using Vajda and other sources, see Hamid Triki and Bernard Rosenberger, "Famines et epidémies au Maroc aux XVIe et XVIIe siècles," *Hespéris-Tamuda* 14 (1973): 109–175; 15 (1974): 5–103.

31. Vajda, *Un recueil de textes historiques judéo-marocains,* 11.

32. Vajda, *Un recueil de textes historiques judéo-marocains,* 14.

33. Although such an argument is admittedly far from conclusive, it is worth noting that the same logic is employed in debates concerning the date of the founding of Marrakesh itself: the complete omission of the place name by al-Bakri, who wrote in 1067–1068, is cited as proof that the southern capital was founded not in 1062 but in 1070. See Ronald Messier, "Rereading Medieval Sources through Multidisciplinary Glasses," in *The Maghreb in Question: Essays in History and Historiography,* ed. Michel Le Gall and Kenneth Perkins (Austin: University of Texas Press, 1997), 177.

34. José Bénech, *Essai d'explication d'un mellah (ghetto marocain): Un des aspects du judaïsme* (Paris: Larose, 1940), 15.

35. *Encyclopaedia Judaica,* 1st ed. (Jerusalem: Encyclopaedia Judaica, 1971), s.v. "Marrakesh."

36. Deverdun, *Marrakech,* 1:368.

37. Al-Ifrānī, *Nuzhat al-ḥādī,* 51. Note that Houdas's Arabic transcription gives the date incorrectly as 1070; it is correctly given as 970 in the French translation (page 93). For a discussion of al-Ifrani as a source for Saʿdi history, see Mercedes García-Arenal, "Mahdi, Murabit, Sharif: L'avènement de la dynastie Sa'dienne," *Studia Islamica* 71 (1990): 80–81. The Muwwasin complex expanded to include a monumental fountain and a student hostel (*madrasa*), which in recent times functioned as an orphanage for girls of sharifian descent. Dale Eickelman, *Knowledge and Power in Morocco* (Princeton, N.J.: Princeton University Press, 1985), 76–77.

38. Such transfers are not without historical precedent. In Fez, for instance, a Jewish neighborhood that pre-dated the construction of the *mellah* had been displaced by the building of the Qarawiyyin. See Deverdun, *Marrakech,* 1:367; Jane Gerber, *Jewish Society in Fez, 1450–1700* (Leiden, Netherlands: E. J. Brill, 1980), 123; Ibn Abī Zarʿ al-Fāsī, *Rawḍ al-Qirṭās,* translated into French by Auguste Beaumier as *Histoire des Souverains du Maghreb* (Paris: Imprimerie imperiale, 1860), 75.

39. Al-Ifrani does not, however, go on to suggest that 1562 is the definitive date of the *mellah*'s creation, which Deverdun clearly implies it is. Only al-Khamlishi recognizes Deverdun's error. See ʿAbd al-ʿAzīz al-Khamlīshī, "Ḥawal musa'ala binā' al-millāḥāt bi-l-mudun al-maghribīya," *Dar al-Nīyāba* 19–20 (1988): 37 n.17.

40. Al-Ifrānī, *Nuzhat al-ḥādī,* 53. The interdiction against trespassing on the graves of non-believers is shared by both Jews and Muslims in Morocco. See Edward West-

ermarck, *Ritual and Belief in Morocco* (New York: University Books, 1968), 2:539. Westermarck adds that many Muslims believe that the reason that walking on Jewish graves is forbidden is because it gives relief to the dead "infidel" within, who is understood to be writhing in torture.

41. Bénech, *Essai d'explication d'un mellah,* 15.

42. Janet Abu-Lughod, "The Islamic City: Historical Myth, Islamic Essence, and Contemporary Relevance," *International Journal of Middle Eastern Studies* 19 (1987): 172.

43. Michael Meyer, "Where Does the Modern Period of Jewish History Begin?" *Judaism* 24, no. 3 (1975): 329–338.

44. Jacques Meunié and Henri Terasse, *Nouvelles recherches archéologiques à Marrakech* (Paris: Arts et métiers graphiques, 1957), 47–48.

45. Reprinted and discussed in Henri Koehler, "La kasba saadienne de Marrakech, d'après un plan manuscrit de 1585," *Hespéris* 27 (1940): 1–19.

46. These include Henry Roberts in 1585–1589 (see Thomas Willan, *Studies in Elizabethan Foreign Trade* [Manchester, England: Manchester University Press, 1959], 225); John Smith (better known for his travels to the New World and relationship with Pocahontas) in 1604 (see *Les sources inédites de l'histoire du Maroc,* première série, *Archives et bibliothèques d'Angleterre,* 3 vols., ed. Henry de Castries, Pierre de Cenival, and Philippe de Cossé Brissac [Paris: E. Leroux, 1918–1935]); and Jean Mocquet in 1601–1607 (see Jean Mocquet, "Voyage de Jean Mocquet au Maroc," in *Les sources inédites de l'histoire du Maroc,* première série, *Archives et bibliothèques de France,* ed. Henry de Castries [Paris: E. Leroux, 1905–1926], 2:404).

47. Vajda, *Un recueil de textes historiques judéo-marocains,* 44.

48. Georges Colin, ed., *Chronique anonyme de la dynastie saadienne* (Rabat, Morocco: F. Moncho, 1934), 56.

49. Georg Höst, *Nachrichten von Marokos und Fès* (Copenhagen: Verlegts, 1781), 77. Höst served as Danish consul in Marrakesh during the period 1760–1768.

50. For an explanation of the events leading up to the massacre of Jews in Fez, see Gerber, *Jewish Society in Fez,* 19.

51. Susan Gilson Miller, Attilio Petruccioli, and Mauro Bertagnin, "Inscribing Minority Space in the Islamic City: The Jewish Quarter of Fez (1438–1912)," *Journal of the Society of Architectural Historians* 60, no. 3 (2001): 313. I often heard similar explanations for the origins of various *mellahs* from Moroccan Jews during the course of my own research.

52. See Corcos, *Studies in the History of the Jews of Morocco,* 82; and also Périgny, *Au Maroc,* 138. Among Moroccan Jews and other Sephardic groups, these prayers are recited nightly throughout the Hebrew month of Elul preceding the High Holidays.

53. Gerber, *Jewish Society in Fez,* 19–20.

54. Mocquet, "Voyage de Jean Mocquet au Maroc," 400.

55. Fernand Braudel, *The Mediterranean and the Mediterranean World in the Age of Philip II,* trans. Siân Reynolds (New York: Harper and Row, 1972), 1:326.

56. Marmol Carvajal, *L'Afrique de Marmol,* 62.

57. Deverdun, *Marrakech,* 1:359.

58. They included many rural Jews who came to Marrakesh in search of more secure lives and livelihoods, initiating strong links between the *mellah* and the surrounding countryside which would become increasingly important to the city as a whole in the coming centuries. (See chapter 5.)

59. Al-Ifrānī, *Nuzhat al-ḥādī,* 103.

60. Willan, *Studies in Elizabethan Foreign Trade,* 94–95.

61. On the subject of Dutch trade with Morocco during the Saʿdi period, see *Les sources inédites de l'histoire du Maroc: Pays-Bas,* especially vols. 5 and 6.

62. The earlier figure is given by Leon Godard, *Description et histoire du Maroc* (Paris: C. Tanera, 1860), 426; the later by Pierre Dan, *Histoire de Barbarie et de ses corsaires, des royaumes et des villes d'Alger, de Tunis, de Salé, et de Tripoly* (Paris: P. Rocole, 1637), 231, 251.

63. See the discussion in Friedman, *Spanish Captives in North Africa,* 88–90.

64. Friedman, *Spanish Captives in North Africa,* 88–90.

65. For Lion's operations in Marrakesh, see Willan, *Studies in Elizabethan Foreign Trade,* 246–248.

66. Willan, *Studies in Elizabethan Foreign Trade,* 205. What kind of living a fishmonger could make in Marrakesh, the gateway to the Sahara, is open to debate.

67. Deverdun, *Marrakech,* 1:452.

68. Willan, *Studies in Elizabethan Foreign Trade,* 136.

69. For the history of the Franciscan church in Morocco, see Pierre de Cenival, "L'église chrétienne de Marrakech au XIIIe siècle," *Hespéris* 7 (1927), 69–83.

70. Francisco Jesus Maria de San Juan del Puerto, *Mission historial de Marruecos* (Seville: Francisco Garay, 1708), 421.

71. Al-Ifrānī, *Nuzhat al-ḥādī,* 51.

72. Fernand Braudel, "Espagnols et mauresques," *Annales E.S.C.* 4 (1947): 403, cited in Deverdun, *Marrakech,* 1:442.

73. Haim Ben-Sasson, ed., *History of the Jewish People* (Cambridge, Mass.: Harvard University Press), 631.

74. Bénech, *Essai d'explication d'un mellah,* 16.

75. Both Torres and Del Puerto, a Spanish Franciscan, remarked on the overwhelming use of the Spanish language by Jewish merchants in Marrakesh. See Torres, *Relación del origen,* 93; and Francisco del Puerto, *Mission historial de Marruecos,* 245.

76. Deverdun, *Marrakech,* 1:462. This leaves open the question of Deverdun's opinion of the Kutubiya, one of the most outstanding examples of Almohad architecture.

77. For a discussion of Saʿdi attitudes toward Iberian exiles, see Muhammad Hajji, *L'activité intellectuelle au Maroc a l'epoque Sa'dide* (Rabat, Morocco: Dar El-Maghrib, 1976), 1:77–80, 318–335.

78. John Hunwick, "Al-Mahili and the Jews of Tuwat: The Demise of a Community," *Studia Islamica* 61 (1985): 155–183.

79. Roger le Tourneau, "Notes sur les lettres latines de Nicolas Clénard relatant son séjour dans le royaume de Fés," *Hespéris* 19 (1934): 52–53. Also in Mohammed Kenbib, "Les relations entre musulmans et juifs au Maroc, 1859–1945: Essai bibliographique," *Hespéris-Tamuda* 23 (1985): 32 n.53.

80. Henry Koehler, *L'église chrétienne du Maroc et la mission franciscaine* (Paris: Société d'éditions franciscaines, 1934), 105–107.

81. For a full description of the affair, see Bénech, *Essai d'explication d'un mellah,* 21–22; Koehler, *L'église chrétienne,* 111–112; and Francisco del Puerto, *Mission historia del Marruecos,* 757–762, who tells of the request for "imprisonment of all missionaries by petition of the mayor of the Jews."

82. *Encyclopaedia Judaica,* s.v. "Marrakesh."

83. Torres, "Histoire des cherifs," 174 (*Relación del origen,* 238).

84. Albert Savine, *Dans les fers du Moghreb: Récits de chrétiens esclaves au Maroc, XVIIe et XVIIIe siècles* (Paris: Société des éditions, 1912), 20.

85. *Les sources inédites de l'histoire du Maroc: France,* 3:729.

86. Torres, "Histoire des cherifs," 109; also cited in Deverdun, *Marrakech,* 1:421.

87. Mocquet, "Voyage de Jean Mocquet au Maroc," 400.

88. Willan, *Studies in Elizabethan Foreign Trade,* 224.

89. Mocquet, "Voyage de Jean Mocquet au Maroc," 400.

90. Savine, *Fers du Moghreb,* 12.

91. Koehler, *L'église chrétienne,* 85. Francisco del Puerto reports being received by the *muqaddam* (guardian) of the captives at his residence in the *mellah* (*Mission historial de Marruecos,* 240–243). Captives were also held in the Fez *mellah.* Mercedes Garcia-Arenal and Gerard Wieggers, *A Man of Three Worlds: Samuel Pallache, a Moroccan Jew in Catholic and Protestant Europe* (Baltimore: Johns Hopkins University Press, 2003), 25.

92. Savine, *Fers du Moghreb,* 13.

93. For a detailed discussion of the siege and its consequences, see al-Ifrānī, *Nuzhat al-ḥādī,* 27–29; and García-Arenal, "Sainteté et pouvoir dynastique," 1022–1026. The first entry in the Ibn Danan chronicle also describes these events.

94. Colin, *Chronique anonyme de la dynastie saadienne,* cited in García-Arenal, "Sainteté et pouvoir dynastique," 1024.

95. Al-Ifrānī, *Nuzhat al-ḥādī,* 30.

96. Vajda, *Un recueil de textes historiques judéo-marocains,* 12.

97. See García-Arenal, "Sainteté et pouvoir dynastique," 1026.

98. Deverdun, *Marrakech,* 1:355.

99. Aḥmad b. Khālid al-Nāṣirī, *Kitāb al-Istiqṣāʾ li-Akhbār Duwal al-Maghrib al-Aqṣā* (Casablanca: Dar al-Kitab, 1949), 5:29.

100. Although these were more appendages than monuments in their own right, the siting is not without symbolic value. By adding their mark to the Qarawiyyin, the Saʿdis were able to establish high Islamic culture credentials where, despite all their efforts in Marrakesh, they still counted most. The development of Marrakesh came to full fruition during the rule of Mawlay Ahmad al-Mansur (r. 1578–1603), whose ambitious building projects rivaled those of any European capital at the time. See Garcia-Arenal and Wieggers, *A Man of Three Worlds,* 27–28.

101. Al-Ifrānī, *Nuzhat al-ḥādī,* 29.

102. Al-Ifrānī, *Nuzhat al-ḥādī,* 83.

103. Al-Ifrānī, *Nuzhat al-ḥādī,* 51; Deverdun, *Marrakech,* 1:368.

104. Pascalle Saisset, *Heures juives au Maroc* (Paris: Rieder, 1930), 145–146.

105. Quoted in Willan, *Studies in Elizabethan Foreign Trade,* 225.

106. Mohammed Kenbib, *Juifs et musulmans au Maroc, 1859–1948* (Rabat, Morocco: Faculté des Lettres et des Sciences Humaines, 1994), 33.

107. Mocquet, "Voyage de Jean Mocquet au Maroc," 400.

108. Pierre Champion, *Rabat et Marrakech* (Paris: H. Laurens, 1926), 112.

109. Mocquet, "Voyage de Jean Mocquet au Maroc," 408. While daily life may have been relatively peaceful in Saʿdi Marrakesh, it should not be forgotten that cataclysmic events nonetheless did occur during this period, including the violent sacking of the *mellah* by al-Mutawakkil with the participation of the townspeople: "*wa dakhala ʿalā-l-millāḥ wa akhathahu wa salabahu wa ẓafara bi-māl kathīr wa naẓarahu ahl Marrākush.*" Colin, *Chronique anonyme,* 56.

110. Matham accompanied the Dutch ambassador, Antoine de Liedekerke, to Morocco, arriving on 1 September 1640 and remaining until 12 November 1641. For extracts from his journal and reproductions of his paintings as well as a critical introduction by Pierre de Cenival, see *Les sources inédites de l'histoire du Maroc: Pays-Bas,* 4:570–647.

111. Berrima again reverted to the Jews' control when the A.I.U. acquired permission to expand into the area in the early 1930s.

112. Deverdun, *Marrakech,* 1:366.

113. For a treatment of the grid in urban history, see Spiro Kostof, *The City Shaped: Urban Patterns and Meanings through History* (Boston: Little, Brown, 1991), 95–157.

114. For some preliminary remarks on the subject, see David Elalouf, "Une architecture juive?" in *Les juifs du Maroc,* ed. André Goldenberg (Paris: Editions du Scribe, 1992), 303–307.

115. Marrakesh is known for the correspondence between the names of its gates and their neighborhoods: "For the most part, the names of gates refer to the people and activities which surround them, and through their lists . . . the tribal and economic organization of the city can be reconstructed." Oleg Grabar, "Cities and Citizens: The Growth and Culture of Urban Islam," in *The World of Islam,* ed. Bernard Lewis (London: Thames and Hudson, 1976), 97. See also Charles Allain and Gaston Deverdun, "Les portes anciennes de Marrakech," *Hespéris* 44 (1957): 85–126, especially 88–92 for Bab Aghmat.

116. Vajda, *Un recueil de textes historiques judéo-marocains,* 44.

117. Deverdun, *Marrakech,* 1:492.

118. See Gerber, *Jewish Society in Fez,* 19 n.85.

119. Henry de Castries, ed. and tr., *Une description du Maroc sous le règne de Moulay Ahmed El-Mansour, 1596* (Paris: E. Leroux, 1909), 119.

120. For the Jews of Fez, confinement in the *mellah* was seen as "a sudden and a bitter exile." Stillman, *The Jews of Arab Lands in Modern Times,* 80. A Jewish text of the period, *Ne'r Hama'arav,* offers the following account: "In the year 5198 [1438], Jews who had been living in the Fez medina since the foundation of the city were expelled from it with a fierce brutality. Some Jews were killed, while others embraced Islam. A few families left the medina and built the *mellah.*" Quoted in Miller, Petruccioli, and Bertagnin, "Inscribing Minority Space in the Islamic City," 313. For a discussion of the similar phenomenon of *sürgün* in the Ottoman context, see Benjamin Braude and Bernard Lewis, *Christians and Jews in the Ottoman Empire* (New York: Holmes and Meier, 1982), 1:11.

121. A.I.U., Maroc II.B.9–13, 10 March 1929, Goldenberg.

122. A.I.U., Maroc II.B.9–13, 10 March 1929, Goldenberg. Also recounted by Jacky Kadoch, president of the Jewish community of Marrakesh-Essaouira, in my interview of him in June 2004.

123. See Issachar Ben-Ami, *Saint Veneration among the Jews in Morocco* (Detroit, Mich.: Wayne State University Press, 1998), 252.

124. Deverdun, *Marrakech,* 1:366. An inundation described by Deverdun killed 480 Muslims but not one Jew. Nor was a single synagogue destroyed, though many houses and possessions were swept away. The Jews of Fez attached similar sentiments to their *mellah.* When an earthquake killed 2500 Muslims in their well-built houses but spared the flimsier homes of the *mellah,* it was understood as an act of God. See Vajda, *Un recueil de textes historiques judéo-marocains,* 42–43.

125. Germain Mouette, "Histoire des conquestes de Mouley Archy," in *Les sources inédites de l'histoire du Maroc,* deuxième série, *Archives et bibliothèques de France,* ed. Henry de Castries, Pierre de Cenival, and Philippe de Cossé Brissac (Paris: E. Leroux, 1922–1960), 2:176.

126. Marmol Carvajal, *L'Afrique de Marmol,* 59.

127. Mocquet, "Voyage de Jean Mocquet au Maroc," 402.

128. Marmol Carvajal, *L'Afrique de Marmol,* 59.

129. Francisco del Puerto, *Mission historial de Marruecos,* 79.

130. *Les sources inédites de l'histoire du Maroc: France,* 3:729.

131. An eighteenth-century observer summarized the situation thus: "The custom of the *megorashim* is accepted in Fez and all the cities of the Maghreb except for Tafilalt and its surroundings, while in Marrakesh some do this and some do that." Quoted in Shlomo Deshen, *The Mellah Society: Jewish Community Life in Sherifian Morocco* (Chicago: University of Chicago Press, 1989), 125 n.7. Tafilalt is also known as the area of Morocco where Jews absorbed the fewest Sephardic influences.

132. Vajda, *Un recueil de textes historiques judéo-marocains,* 14. The author of the entry goes on to say that the number of Jewish dead in Marrakesh reached a total of 7500.

133. Deverdun, *Marrakech,* 1:439.

134. Moses Pallache's activities are described in the following anonymous description from 1638: "I may add to this Mousa Peliachi, a Jew, Sheck of all the rest that live in the Judaria; . . . He is a good linguist and excellent speaker, used by the King as a necessary minister at audience of Embassadours and in other foraigne negotiations. He hath had the happiness, notwithstanding theis late changes, to be retained by all the fower Kings successively, now being very gratious with Mahamet Sheck." See "Relation sur le Maroc: 1638," in *Les sources inédites de l'histoire du Maroc: Angleterre,* 3:483. Moses put his skills to use by making tours of the Mediterranean region to preach to victims of the Spanish expulsion. Ironically, his most famous speech, concerning the ethics of Judaism, was given at the behest of the Spanish ambassador in Marrakesh. He later published two important works, *Va-Yakhel Moshe* (1597) and *Ho'il Moshe* (1597), comprising homilies, eulogies, sermons, and an autobiography. See *Encyclopaedia Judaica,* s.v. "Pallache." For a detailed biography of Samuel Pallache, see García-Arenal and Wiegers, *A Man of Three Worlds.*

135. Vincent Cornell, "Socioeconomic Dimensions of Reconquista and Jihad in Morocco: Portuguese Dukkala and the Saʿdid Sus, 1450–1557," *International Journal of Middle Eastern Studies* 22 (1990): 396.

136. Braudel, *The Mediterranean and the Mediterranean World in the Age of Philip II,* 1:182.

137. John Pory, "A Summarie Discourse of the Manifold Religions Professed in Africa: And First of the Gentiles," in Leo Africanus, *The History and Description of Africa* (London: Haklyut Society, 1896), 3:1005.

138. Jews were also involved in sugar processing. See Jean Célérier, "Le Maroc: Pays du sucre et d'or," *France-Maroc* 79 (1923): 114; also Deverdun, *Marrakech,* 1:437.

139. "Requête de marchands trafiquant au Maroc au conseil privé: 25 April 1567," in *Les sources inédites de l'histoire du Maroc: Angleterre,* 1:93.

140. Gerber, *Jewish Society in Fez,* 173.

141. Al-Ifrānī, *Nuzhat al-ḥādī,* 103.

142. As cited in Deverdun, *Marrakech,* 1:400.

143. The captives held in Marrakesh were both male and female. Mocquet, "Voyage de Jean Mocquet au Maroc," 2:404.

144. Friedman, *Spanish Captives in North Africa,* 59.

145. "Mémoire des trafiquants d'Amsterdam: 3 October 1651," *Les sources inédites de l'histoire du Maroc: Pays-Bas,* 5:290.

146. "Lettre de Henrique de Noronha à Jean III: 4 June 1541," in *Les sources inédites de l'histoire du Maroc,* première série, *Archives et bibliothèques de Portugal,* ed. Pierre de Cenival, David Lopes, Robert Ricard, and Chantal de La Véronne (Paris: Paul Geuthner, 1934–1953), 3:417, 421.

147. Marmol Carvajal, *L'Afrique de Marmol,* 59–60.

148. Mocquet, "Voyage de Jean Mocquet au Maroc," 402.

149. Roger le Tourneau, as quoted in Deverdun, *Marrakech,* 1:352.

2. COUNTING JEWS IN MARRAKESH

1. Daniel Nordman, "Les expéditions de Moulay Hassan: Essai statistique," *Hespéris-Tamuda* 19 (1980–1981): 123–152.

2. It is noteworthy, for example, that the *mellah* observed the traditional Jewish period of mourning for Mawlay Hassan upon his death. See Gaston Deverdun, *Marrakech des origines à 1912* (Rabat, Morocco: Editions Techniques Nord-Africaines, 1959), 1:521.

3. Public Record Office, London (hereafter P.R.O.), FO 174: 291, 13 May 1874, Bargash.

4. *Times of Morocco,* 8 October 1892.

5. Such gifts typically included a silk scarf and three to five dollars: *Times of Morocco,* 30 June 1887.

6. *Le réveil du Maroc,* 20 December 1886.

7. The sultan supplied the following provisions for the feast: "8 bullocks, 36 sheep, 10 cwts. flour, 4 karrobas peas, 100 lbs. oil, 5 lbs. saffron, 50 lbs pepper, 10 cwts. coal, 4 cwts. potatoes, 18 cwts. sugar, 4 chests tea, 1700 eggs, 350 fowls, 1 cwt. almonds, 150 lbs. honey, and $400 for buying brandy, wine, and other necessities." *Times of Morocco,* 21 January 1891.

8. Paul Pascon, *Le Haouz de Marrakesh* (Rabat, Morocco: Editions marocaines et internationals, 1977), 2:415; partially published in English as *Capitalism and Agriculture in the Haouz of Marrakesh* (London: Kegan Paul International, 1986).

9. D.A.R., Al-tartīb al-ʿāmm, 6 Rabīʿ II 1308/19 November 1890. This invaluable source was brought to my attention by Khalid Ben Srhir (Khālid b. Ṣaghīr), who has published an Arabic transliteration of it in "Wathīqa ghayr munshūra ʿan millāḥ Marrākush fī-l-qarn al-tāsiʿ ʿashar," *Hespéris-Tamuda* 35, no. 2 (1997): 25–71.

10. *Times of Morocco,* 27 October 1892.

11. Archives du ministère des affaires etrangères, Paris (hereafter A.A.E./P.), Nouvelle série (hereafter N.S.) Maroc 405, 6 January 1903, French legation at Tangier.

12. See Hyman Alterman, *Counting People: The Census in History* (New York: Harcourt, Brace, and World, 1969), 17–35, 37.

13. For more on the *defter* and its use as a source for Ottoman history, see Omer Barkan, "Essai sur les données statistiques des registres de recensement dans l'empire ottoman au XVe et XVIe siècles," *Journal of Economic and Social History of the Orient* 1, no. 1 (1957): 9–21; and by the same author, "Research on the Ottoman Fiscal

Surveys," in *Studies in the Economic History of the Middle East,* ed. Michael Cook (London: Oxford University Press, 1970), 163–171.

14. David Herlihy, *Medieval Households* (Cambridge, Mass.: Harvard University Press, 1985).

15. D.A.R., Al-tartīb al-ʿāmm, 6 Rabīʿ II 1308/19 November 1890. It should be noted that two pages of the text, covering houses 55–60 in the *mellah*'s fourth quarter, are missing from the original document, though the total numbers of houses, rooms, and individuals are provided on the top of page 41. All conclusions based on other types of information in the census were arrived at without reference to these two pages.

16. For more on the figure of Meir Maqnin (also known as "Macnin"), see Daniel Schroeter, *The Sultan's Jew: Morocco and the Sephardi World* (Stanford, Calif.: Stanford University Press, 2002).

17. Polygamy was not uncommon in the nineteenth-century *mellah.* The census records fourteen men with two wives each, and one man with three.

18. See Hans Wehr, *Dictionary of Modern Written Arabic,* ed. J. Milton Cowan, 4th ed. (Ithaca, N.Y.: Spoken Language Services, 1994); Elias Antoon Elias, *Elias' Modern Dictionary, Arabic-English,* 31st ed. (Cairo: Elias' Modern Pub. House, 1990); and J. G. Hava, *Al-Faraid Arabic-English Dictionary* (Beirut: Catholic Press, 1964), s.v. "*ayyim.*"

19. See Edward William Lane, *Arabic and English Lexicon* (Lahore, Pakistan: Islamic Book Center, 1978); and Muḥammad b. Manẓūr, *Lisān li-lisān* (Beirut: Dar al-Kutub al-ʿIlmiyah, 1993), s.v. "*ayyim.*"

20. Payton, the English consul in Essaouira, observed in his "Report on Slave Trade in Mogador and District": "Although the holding of slaves is supposed to be a privilege of the 'true believers' only, and denied to Christians or Jews, yet I am informed that the Moors are no great sticklers now-a-days for their exclusive right to the 'institution,' for slaves are often *virtually* held by Christians and Jews, who, though they cannot purchase them in their own names, get possession of them through some friendly Mohammedan, who figures in the notarial deed of purchase as the owner, but hands over the 'chattel' to the Jew or Christian." P.R.O., FO 174: 292, 30 May 1883. The English author James Richardson likewise noted that "all the merchants of Mogador, Christians and Jews, more or less aid and abet the slave-trade, all having connections with slave-dealers." James Richardson, *Travels in Morocco* (London: Charles J. Skeet, 1860), 2:27–28. That slaves were not only bought and sold by Essaouira's Jews but also kept as domestic help is related by Aubin: "I have even seen, in a Jewish house in Mogador, a little negress from the South who was growing up to perform the same servile offices as the slaves bought by Mohammedan families." Eugene Aubin, *Morocco of Today* (London: E. B. Dutton, 1906), 291. For a study of the slave trade in Morocco, see Daniel Schroeter, "Slave Markets and Slavery in Moroccan Urban Society," in *The Human Commodity: Perspectives on the Trans-Saharan Slave Trade,* ed. Elizabeth Savage (London: Frank Cass, 1992), 185–213.

21. Slaves were so integrated into some families that when they died confusion often ensued as to whether they should be buried in the Jewish cemetery, especially since many had converted to Judaism. See Haim Zafrani, *Mille ans de vie juive au Maroc: Histoire et culture, religion et magie* (Paris: Maisonneuve et Larose, 1983), 124.

22. The number of males counted by the census is 2030. Added together, this gives us a total of 4887 individuals, as opposed to the 5032 of the census's *talkhīṣ* (summary) on its last page. I believe that the former number, based on my recount

of named individuals, is closer to the correct figure, particularly in light of the frequency of computing errors in the census.

23. D.A.R., Al-tartīb al-ʿāmm, 6 Rabīʿ II 1308/19 November 1890.

24. For a discussion of legibility as a hallmark of *niẓām*, see Timothy Mitchell, *Colonising Egypt* (Cambridge: Cambridge University Press, 1988), 45–46.

25. Bardukh's house had twice as many rooms as the typical *mellah* home (which had 6.05, according to the census), and hence double the average total number of inhabitants. Its per-room density exceeded the average in the *mellah* by .88 people (4.83 as compared to 3.95). According to a report in the *Times of Morocco,* the dimensions of a room in a typical courtyard house in the Marrakesh *mellah* were the same as in the Essaouira *mellah,* i.e., 8 feet × 6 feet (*Times of Morocco,* 25 October 1890). According to a Jewish chronicle from 1879, the situation in Fez was comparable, with an average house in its *mellah* said to have 25 occupants (compared to 23.96 in Marrakesh, according to the census's findings) and 4 inhabitants per room. See Y. D. Sémach, "Une chronique juive de Fès: Le 'Yahas Fès' de Ribbi Abner Hassarfaty," *Hespéris* 19 (1934): 79–94.

26. Montefiore's travel companion in 1863–1864, Thomas Hodgkin, reported that the Marrakesh *mellah* was "densely inhabited" and that the narrowness of the streets made it "extremely difficult to move through the crowd," even when blows were used to clear the way. Thomas Hodgkin, *Narrative of a Journey to Morocco in 1863 and 1864* (London: T. C. Newby, 1866), 85.

27. The French officer Jules Erckmann, who came to Marrakesh in 1877 as part of a military mission, commented that the *mellah* was remarkable for two things: "the dirtiness of its streets and the density of its population." Jules Erckmann, *Le Maroc moderne* (Paris: Challamel Ainé, 1885), 190.

28. Since the nineteenth-century *mellah* covered 17.5 hectares, its population density, according to calculations based on the census, was 287 inhabitants per hectare. By the twentieth century, the population of the *mellah* exceeded 1000 inhabitants per hectare. Deverdun, *Marrakech,* 1:563.

29. José Bénech, *Essai d'explication d'un mellah (ghetto marocain): Un des aspects du judaïsme* (Paris: Larose, 1940), 2.

30. A.I.U., Maroc XXV E 394–397, 5 October 1917, Eskanazi.

31. Ali Bey al-Abassi, *Travels of Ali Bey in Africa and Asia: 1803–1807* (Philadelphia: M. Carey, 1816), 1:173. "Ali Bey" was the pseudonym for the Spanish traveler General Domingo Badia y Leblich.

32. D.A.R., Marrakesh 6, 7 Dhū al-Qaʿda 1301/29 August 1884, Makhzan.

33. *Times of Morocco,* 9 June 1888.

34. See *Times of Morocco,* 1 March 1890 and 24 May 1890.

35. *Times of Morocco,* 1 March 1890.

36. See Aubin, *Morocco of Today,* 291. The census also describes several multistory houses.

37. D.A.R., Marrakesh 4, 11 Muḥarram 1297/25 December 1879, Umanāʾ al-Amrās.

38. Bibliothèque générale, Rabat (hereafter B.G./R.) D3410, Risāʾil muḥtasib Marrākush Mawlāy ʿAbdallāh al-Būkīlī: 6, 13 Muḥarram 1309/19 August 1891.

39. P.R.O., FO 413: 21 and 25 April 1894, Satow.

40. Class stratification among Moroccan Jews is discussed in Louis Massignon, "Enquête sur les corporations d'artisans et des commerçants au Maroc," *Revue du monde musulman* 58 (1924): 151.

41. D.A.R., Marrakesh 8, 22 Shawwāl 1307/11 June 1890, Umālik.

42. P.R.O., FO 413: 48, n/d, Nairn. Another such report is found in A.A.E./P., Correspondence politique des consuls (hereafter C.P.C.), Maroc 2, 10 August 1888, French consul at Mogador [Essaouira].

43. For a summary of gender issues and the A.I.U., see Aron Rodrigue, "The Emancipation and Reformation of Women," in his *Jews and Muslims: Images of Sephardi and Eastern Jewries in Modern Times* (Seattle: University of Washington Press, 2003), 80–93. For discussion of this same topic in the context of Tangier, see Susan Miller, "Gender and the Poetics of Emancipation: The Alliance Israélite Universelle in Northern Morocco, 1890–1912," in *Franco-Arab Encounters,* ed. Leon Carl Brown and Mathew Gordon (Beirut: The American University of Beirut Press, 1996), 229–252.

44. A.I.U., Maroc VII.B, Dossiers déclassés et manquant à l'intérieur des comités et communautés, 24 January 1913, Danon.

45. A.I.U., Maroc XXV.E.394–397, 8 June 1915, Danon.

46. A.I.U., Maroc XXVI.E.398–416, 18 June 1924, Falcon.

47. A.I.U., Maroc XXVII.E.417–442, 16 September 1901, Coriat.

48. *Times of Morocco,* 15 December 1888.

49. *Times of Morocco,* 30 November 1889.

50. Daniel Schroeter, *Merchants of Essaouira: Urban Society and Imperialism in Southwestern Morocco, 1844–1886* (Cambridge: Cambridge University Press, 1988), 65–66, 200–202. See also P.R.O., FO 174: 85, 4 May 1875, Hay; and *Times of Morocco,* 30 November 1889.

51. *Times of Morocco,* 26 December 1891.

52. *Times of Morocco,* 7 December 1889.

53. *Times of Morocco,* 8 November 1890.

54. *Times of Morocco,* 25 April 1891.

55. *Times of Morocco,* 20 June 1891.

56. Jean-Louis Miège, *Une mission française à Marrakech en 1882* (Aix-en-Provence: La pensée universitaire, 1968), 344–345 n.237.

57. *Times of Morocco,* 9 July 1892. The sultan sent the delegates back to Marrakesh with an order to the pasha to allow each man to build a new house for himself, and also with a *taẓhīr* (certificate of endorsement) attesting to the holder's good reputation.

58. *Jewish Missionary Intelligence,* September 1894.

59. See the schedule of the sultan's movements in Nordman, "Les expéditions de Moulay Hassan," 123–152; and also the calculations of Mohamed Aafif, "Les harkas hassaniennes d'après l'œuvre d'A. Ibn Zidane," *Hespéris* 19 (1980–1981): 159, both of which are based on Arabic primary source materials.

60. Al-ʿAbbās b. Ibrāhīm al-Marrākushī, *Al-Iʿlām bi-man ḥalla Marrākush wa Aghmāt min al-aʿlām* (Rabat, Morocco: Al-Maṭbaʿa al-Malakīya, 1974–1983), 3:179–180.

61. Aḥmad b. Khālid al-Nāṣirī, *Kitāb al-Istiqṣāʾ li-Akhbār duwal al-Maghrib al-Aqṣā* (Casablanca: Dar al-Kitab, 1949), 4:253.

62. Nordman, "Les expéditions de Moulay Hassan," 133. The physical presence of the sultan or another high-ranking official was often a prerequisite for breaking ground on new urban projects, as indicated by al-Marrākushī above.

63. B.G./R. D3410, Risāʾil muḥtasib Marrākush Mawlāy ʿAbdallāh al-Būkīlī: 173, 23 Rabīʿ I 1309/27 October 1891.

64. Bibliothèque royale, Rabat, kunāsh 425, "Mā ṣīrahu al-amīn al-ḥājj ʿAbd al-

Raḥmān b. ʿAbd al-Kabīr al-Marrākushī ʿalā sūr al-millāḥ," Rabīʿ I 1314/August–September 1896. Reference is also made to this report in D.A.R., Marrakesh 11, 6 Ṣafar 1314/17 July 1896, Muḥammad Muṣṭafā.

65. *Times of Morocco,* 14 March 1891.

66. See, for example, the "Congratulatory address to the Emperor," from the Anglo-Jewish Association, asking Mawlay Hassan to continue his good treatment of the Jews: P.R.O., FO 174: 291, 9 January 1874.

67. Among the *mellah*'s *ḥubus* properties, ironically, was a building endowed in the name of Qādī ʿAyad, one of Marrakesh's "Seven Saints," who, according to some sources, was murdered by a Jew in one of the city's bath houses in the twelfth century. Henry de Castries, "Les sept patrons de Merrakech," *Hespéris* 4 (1924): 266.

68. With only their names to go by, it is impossible to confirm the religion of property owners with complete accuracy. The criteria I have used here include onomastic clues, such as whether the name carries a Jewish title such as *ḥazān* (rabbi); whether the person lives in the house being counted or can be located as a resident in another *mellah* home; and whether the person's religion is known from other sources. For a guide to Moroccan Jewish names, see Abraham Laredo, *Les noms des juifs du Maroc* (Madrid: Consejo Superior de Investigaciones Científicas, Instituto "B. Arias Montano," 1978). Also useful is Paul Pascon and Daniel Schroeter's study of Jewish names on tombs in Iligh: "Le cimetière juif d'Iligh, 1751–1955: Etude des épitaphes comme documents d'histoire démographique," in *La maison d'Iligh et l'histoire sociale du Tazerwalt,* ed. Paul Pascon (Rabat, Morocco: SMER, 1984), esp. 123–134.

69. Eleven, if we are to count that of his presumed relative Saʿdan Corcos. Their exact relation is unknown, as Saʿdan Corcos is not included in the extensive Corcos family tree reconstructed by Michel Abitbol. See his *Temoins et acteurs: Les Corcos et l'historie du Maroc contemporain* (Jerusalem: Institut Ben-Zvi, 1977).

70. It was transgressed elsewhere in Morocco, however. For example, Gerber has found evidence that at least one house in the medina of Fez was still owned by Jews several centuries after the community's transfer to the *mellah.* Jane Gerber, *Jewish Society in Fez, 1450–1700* (Leiden, Netherlands: E. J. Brill, 1980), 128.

71. According to a letter from the French consul, "it is precisely in the medina that the trading posts and commercial establishments of the principal Jewish merchants are located." A.A.E./P., C.P.C., Maroc 2, 10 December 1885.

72. It is nonetheless worth mentioning that two individuals with the surname of ʿAbd al-Haq, a name virtually unknown among Jews, are listed among the *mellah*'s inhabitants by the census. For more on Jews and Muslim names, see Pascon and Schroeter, "Le cimetière juif d'Iligh," 126.

73. It is possible that in periods when the *mellah* was less crowded individual houses were inhabited by a single family, or members of an extended family. By the time of the census, however, most houses contained people not obviously related to each other. According to Erckmann, even the wealthiest families had access to at most two rooms. Erckmann, *Maroc moderne,* 191.

74. A.I.U., Maroc XXVII.E.417–442, 16 September 1901, Levy.

75. A.I.U., Maroc XXV.E.394–397, 25 March 1913, Danon.

76. A.I.U., Maroc XXV.E.394–397, 25 March 1913, Danon.

77. Richardson, *Travels in Morocco,* 1:145: "Morocco has its fashions and manias as well as Europe. House building is now the rage. They say it is not so easy for the Sultan to fleece the people of their property when it consists of houses. Almost

every distinguished Moor in the interior has built, or is building himself a spacious house."

78. Around this time the shops of Jewish metalworkers were moved to an area outside the walls just west of the new *mellah* area. Individuals whose property in the *mellah* was appropriated by Ba Ahmad, the grand vizier of Mawlay Hassan, to build his Bahia Palace were also relocated at this time. (Ba Ahmad seized part of the Jewish cemetery as well. Mawlay ʿAbd al-ʿAziz [r. 1894–1908] also seized Jewish property in order to expand his palace and gardens.) See Deverdun, *Marrakech,* 1:538; and Bénech, *Essai d'explication d'un mellah,* 27. For Ba Ahmad's appropriations specifically, see *Le réveil du Maroc,* 27 October 1893 and 9 March 1899; *Al-Moghreb al-Aksa,* 29 October 1898; and Maurice de Perigny, *Au Maroc: Marrakech et les ports du sud* (Paris: P. S. Roger, 1917), 148–149.

79. B.G./R. D3410, Risāʾil muḥtasib Marrākush Mawlāy ʿAbdallāh al-Būkīlī: 129, 3 Ramaḍān 1310/21 March 1893.

80. B.G./R. D3410, Risāʾil muḥtasib Marrākush Mawlāy ʿAbdallāh al-Būkīlī: 150, 17 Shawwāl 1309/15 May 1892.

81. A.I.U. teachers in the 1920s and 1930s complained bitterly about the proximity of the Behira quarter to their school, claiming it threatened the "dignity" and "prestige" of their "*beautiful schools.*" A.I.U., Maroc XXIII.E.359–384, 4 September 1931, Bibasse. Not surprisingly, Behira was often the site of epidemics. A.I.U., Maroc XXIII.E.359–384, 28 February 1927, Bibasse. It was also where potential benefactors were first taken during their visits to Marrakesh to ensure their sympathies. A.I.U., Maroc XXIV.E.384–393, 19 April 1935, Bibasse.

82. Aubin, *Morocco of Today,* 285.

83. D.A.R., Al-tartīb al-ʿāmm, 21 Ṣafar 1309/26 September 1891, Ibn Sussan and Corcos.

84. Mohammed Kenbib, "Les relations entre musulmans et juifs au Maroc, 1859–1945: Essai bibliographique," *Hespéris-Tamuda* 23 (1985): 85.

85. For a detailed explanation of the tax responsibilities of *dhimmīs* see the *Encyclopedia of Islam,* 2nd ed. (Leiden, Netherlands: Brill, 1960), s.v. "Djizya"; and also Antoine Fattal, *Le statut légal des non-musulmans en pays d'Islam* (Beirut: Imprimerie Catholique, 1958), 286–287.

86. *Jewish Missionary Intelligence* 8 (1894): 120.

87. Susan Gilson Miller, "Dhimma Reconsidered: Jews, Taxes, and Royal Authority in Nineteenth-Century Tangier," in *In the Shadow of the Sultan: Culture, Power, and Politics in Morocco,* ed. Rahma Bourqia and Susan Gilson Miller (Cambridge, Mass.: Harvard University Press, 1999), 103–128. Miller's point is complemented by Deshen's argument that wealthy Jews, particularly the *shaykh al-yahūd,* may nonetheless have had the coercive power to collect from their poorer counterparts in the form of goods and services, if not money: Shlomo Deshen, *The Mellah Society: Jewish Community Life in Sherifian Morocco* (Chicago: University of Chicago Press, 1989), 60–61.

88. Aubin, *Morocco of Today,* 296.

89. Germain Mouette, "The Travels of the Sieur Mouette in the Kingdoms of Fez and Morocco," in *A New Collection of Voyages and Travels,* ed. John Stevens (London, 1711), 102.

90. William Lemprière, *A Tour through the Dominions of the Emperor of Morocco* (Newport: Tayler, 1813), 180. (Marrakesh, from which the country as a whole derives its name, was sometimes referred to as Morocco City or versions thereof.)

91. D.A.R., Marrakesh 2, 13 Jumādā II 1283/23 October 1866, Ibn Danī.
92. *Times of Morocco,* 26 May 1887 and 30 June 1887.
93. D.A.R., Marrakesh 6, 20 Rajab 1301/16 May 1884, Umālik.
94. *Times of Morocco,* 10 October 1891.
95. D.A.R., Marrakesh 9, 12 Rabīʿ II 1310/3 November 1892. For the acknowledgment of reception of the *jizya* for these years by the local *umanāʾ*, see D.A.R., Marrakesh 9, 7 Jumādā I 1310 /27 November 1892, al-Ridānī, al-Ṣubān, and Ibn Shaqrūn.
96. See reports in *Jewish Missionary Intelligence,* August 1894; and in *Jewish Chronicle,* 14 March 1894.
97. Efforts to standardize space in the "model villages" in Egypt and in French Algeria are discussed in Mitchell, *Colonising Egypt,* 44–48.
98. For discussion of the trade between Marrakesh and the coast, see Jean-Louis Miège, *Le Maroc et l'Europe: 1830–1894* (Rabat, Morocco: Editions la Porte, 1989), vol. 2.
99. *Times of Morocco,* 22 May 1885.
100. *Times of Morocco,* 14 July 1887.
101. Miège, *Le Maroc et l'Europe,* 3:16.
102. Miège, *Le Maroc et l'Europe,* 3:13.
103. Miège, *Le Maroc et l'Europe,* 3:13.
104. Miège, *Le Maroc et l'Europe,* 3:22.
105. Miège, *Le Maroc et l'Europe,* 3:367.
106. Miège, *Le Maroc et l'Europe,* 3:28.
107. See the chart in Friedrich Schwerdtfeger, *Traditional Housing in African Cities* (New York: J. Wiley, 1982), 421. Daniel Schroeter also makes the point that Morocco's inland cities were neither in demographic nor in economic decline in the nineteenth century. Schroeter, *Merchants of Essaouira,* 3.
108. It is evident from the context that Miège's use of the term "Berber" is meant to indicate Berber Muslims and not Berber Jews. In a footnote elsewhere, Miège acknowledges Jewish migration to Marrakesh from the Atlas and further south, but insists on its redirection to the coast after 1875. Miège, *Le Maroc et l'Europe,* 3:28 n.3.
109. Lt. Washington, as cited in Richardson, *Travels in Morocco,* 2:150.
110. John Davidson, *Notes Taken during Travels in Africa* (London: J. L. Cox and Sons, 1839), 39; Richardson, *Travels in Morocco,* 2:150; and Paul Lambert, "Notice sur la ville de Maroc," *Bulletin de la Société de géographie de Paris* (November–December 1868): 440–441.
111. Miège, *Le Maroc et l'Europe,* 3:367.
112. A.I.U., France IX.A.67–73, 8 August 1876, Halévy.
113. *Bulletin de l'Alliance Israélite Universelle,* 2nd series, 25 (1900): 95.
114. Aubin, *Morocco of Today,* 295.
115. The phenomenon of child marriage among Jews is commented upon frequently (and disapprovingly) in the colonial ethnographic and travel literature on Morocco, though typically without the further explanation that such marriages were usually not consummated for several years. See Aubin, *Morocco of Today,* 292; and a detailed report on "*le marriage précoce*" by an A.I.U. teacher in Marrakesh: A.I.U., Maroc XXVI.E.398–416, 11 May 1930, Graziani. For a detailed account of the various local traditions surrounding marriage rituals among Moroccan Jews, see Zafrani, *Mille ans de vie juive au Maroc,* 78–91.

116. *Times of Morocco*, 29 September 1888.

117. Aubin, *Morocco of Today*, 292. A 1902 smallpox epidemic also hit the *mellah* quite hard, claiming the lives of three hundred Jewish children. Elias Harrus, *L'Alliance en action: Les écoles de l'Alliance Israelite Universelle dans l'Empire du Maroc (1862–1912)* (Paris: Nadir, 2001), 81. Aubin may have had his dates wrong and been actually referring to one of these epidemics.

118. Françoise Legey was a French doctor who set up a clinic catering especially to Jewish women in Marrakesh under the auspices of the Protectorate. While in Morocco she compiled an extensive collection of local folklore, which she published under the title of *Essai de folklore marocain* (Paris: Paul Geuthner, 1926), later published in English as *The Folklore of Morocco* (London: G. Allen and Unwin, 1935).

119. For more on Mauchamp and the events surrounding his murder in 1907, see Pascon, *Capitalism and Agriculture in the Haouz of Marrakesh*, 75; and Jonathan Katz, "The 1907 Mauchamp Affair and the French Civilising Mission in Morocco," in *North Africa, Islam, and the Mediterranean World: From the Almoravids to the Algerian War*, ed. Julia Clancy-Smith (London: Frank Cass, 2001), 143–166.

120. For correspondence dealing with this enigmatic figure, see A.I.U., Maroc XXVII.E.417–442, 10 February 1902, Levy; A.I.U., XXVI.E.398–416, 13 August 1905, n/a; and A.I.U., Maroc VII.B, *déclassé*, 10 October 1907, Falcon.

121. See chapter 3 for more on this organization.

122. A.I.U., France IX.A.67–73, 8 August 1876, Halévy.

123. Two important caveats must immediately be added to this figure. The first is that the census does not include small children. While I assume that the same is true of the European sources, it should be recognized that, even if we were to add an average number of young children to each married couple in the census (older offspring were already included) in order to arrive at a typical family size, the resulting increase would still not fill the gap between the two types of population estimates. (In any event, it is the gap itself that is of greater interest to the current discussion than the precise population of the *mellah*.) The second caveat is that we do not know definitively how much of the *mellah* is included in the census. The introduction (translated into English above) is somewhat unclear as to whether all the houses in the *mellah* or just the "full" ones were to be counted. The Arabic reads, "*lammā ishtakā ʿalā-l-aʿtāb al-sharīfa . . . ahl dhimma . . . Marrākush. . . . anna al-suknā ḍāqat ʿalayhim bi-l-millāḥ wa aṣdara amra mawlānā dāma ʿalāhu bi-taqyīd al-dūr allatī bihi muḍayaqa al-suknā.*" For the following reasons, I have decided to treat the 210 houses counted by the census as the total number of residential homes in the *mellah*. First, as I argue above, the Makhzan's reason for conducting the census was derived in large part from the wish to increase the Jews' *jizya* payments, which would have required a new head count of the total male population. Second, the introduction to the census states that the units to be counted are the crowded houses. Given the overwhelming emphasis in European sources on overcrowding in the *mellah*, it is difficult to imagine that any home would have been excluded by this criterion. At the same time, the census is fairly liberal in its definition of "crowded." Many of the houses it counts contain fewer than ten residents (for example, house 24 in the first quarter, house 21 in the second quarter, house 53 in the third quarter, and houses 52 and 731 in the fourth quarter), and one house has only five occupants (house 4 in the first quarter). Moreover, despite the connection between poverty and crowding, the residences of the wealthiest members of the Jewish community

are counted in the census, including that of Haim Corcos, the father of Yeshouʿa (house 17 in the second quarter). Lastly, insofar as one can determine the original boundaries of the *mellah* from aerial photographs, its division into four quarters corresponds closely with the census, as does the number of houses, particularly when we exclude a certain number as non-residential (synagogues, stores, markets, *funduq*s, etc.). See Deverdun, *Marrakech*, 2, plate 72; and ʿAbd al-Hādī al-Tāzī, *Qaṣr al-badīʿ bi-Marrākush* (Rabat, Morocco: Wizārat al-Dawlat al-Mukallafat bi-l-Shuʾūn al-Thaqāfīya, 1977), 28.

124. *Bulletin de l'Alliance Israélite Universelle,* 2nd series, 25 (1900), 95. Ribbi's report of six hundred houses is possibly an exaggeration to justify the opening of an A.I.U. school in Marrakesh.

125. On the subject of Jewish emigration to Palestine, Halévy writes, "In contrast to other pilgrims, the immigrants from Morocco almost all exercise useful trades and as such can earn their livelihoods honorably in Palestine. It seems to me that emigration from Morocco merits encouragement." A.I.U., France IX.A.67–73, 8 August 1876, Halévy.

126. Although Jews may have been tempted to exaggerate their numerical importance to European visitors (or conversely claim diminished numbers to the Moroccan authorities in an effort to decrease their tax burden), the estimates of the rabbinical authorities were probably fairly accurate, insofar as the rituals associated with birth and death required that careful track be kept of the population at all times. While it has not been possible to locate the full records of the Marrakesh *bayt din* for this period, it is safe to assume that Europeans had access to at least some of those who held this information during their visits to Marrakesh.

127. Paul Odinot, as quoted in Jean Gaignebet, "Marrakesh: Grand carrefour des routes marocaines," *Revue de géographie marocaine* 7 (1928): 273–274.

128. The permanent population was 149,263: *Encyclopedia of Islam,* 2nd ed., s.v. "Marrākush." In 1913, the floating population was estimated at 30,000. See Louis Botte, "Marrakech une année après la conquête," *L'Afrique française* 12 (1913): 431.

129. The ever-gloomy Ali Bey al-Abassi described Marrakesh around 1803 thus: "This unfortunate town, partly destroyed by wars and partly by the plague, is without any trade. Arts and sciences are entirely out of the question, as there is hardly a school of any note. It would be impossible to believe such an astonishing and rapid decline, if it were not proved by its large walls, its immense masses of ruins, the great number of conduits become useless, and its vast church-yards." *Travels of Ali Bey,* 176.

130. D.A.R., Marrakesh 2, 26 Jumādā II 1282/16 November 1865, al-Mashāwarī.

131. Jews' involvement in the trade in Ketama tobacco in Marrakesh is frequently discussed in the royal correspondence of the late 1880s and early 1890s. See, for example, D.A.R., Marrakesh 7, 2 Rabīʿ II 1305/18 December 1887, Umālik; D.A.R., Marrakesh 8, 22 Shawwāl 1307/11 June 1890, Umālik; and B.G./R. D3410, Risāʾil muḥtasib Marrākush Mawlāy ʿAbdallāh al-Būkīlī: 41, Ramaḍān 1310/19 March–17 April 1893.

132. *Times of Morocco,* 15 December 1888.

133. The term "*ḥaraka,*" also associated with this institution, refers to the sultan and his entourage in movement, i.e., on expedition, whereas "*maḥalla*" refers to the settled camp. For additional comments on the subject, see Jocelyne Dakhlia, "Dans la mouvance du prince: Symbolique du pouvoire itinérant au Maghreb," *Annales E.S.C.* 43, no. 3 (1988): 735–760; and also Abderrahmane El Moudden, "Etat et société

rurale à travers la *harka* au Maroc du XIXème siècle," *Maghreb Review* 8, nos. 5–6 (1983): 141–145.

134. The story of the sultan's death and the concealment of his badly decaying corpse as the campaign continued to Rabat is recounted in detail in Walter Harris, *Morocco That Was* (London: Eland, 1983), 10–14.

135. Joseph Thomson, *Travels in the Atlas and Southern Morocco* (London: George Philip and Son, 1889), 350. Under Mawlay ʿAbd al-ʿAziz (and this was typical of his excesses), even the royal pet elephant was brought along to pass the winter in the warmer climes of the south. See *Le réveil du Maroc,* 29 November 1896.

136. Pierre Flamand, *Diaspora en terre d'Islam,* vol. 1, *Les communautés israélites du Sud-Marocain* (Casablanca: Imprimerie Réunies, 1959), 121–122.

137. *Le réveil du Maroc,* 9 March 1899.

138. *Le réveil du Maroc,* 28 October 1897.

139. A.I.U., Maroc XXVII.E.417–442, 10 February 1902, Levy.

140. *Le réveil du Maroc,* 9 March 1899.

141. Bénech, *Essai d'explication d'un mellah,* 50.

142. A.I.U., France IX.A.67–73, 8 August 1876, Halévy. The line of Jewish seamstresses seems to have been a regular fixture in the medina even when the *maḥalla* was not in town (see chapter 4).

143. D.A.R., Marrakesh 6, 22 Rajab 1301/18 May 1884, *Umanāʾ* of Marrakesh.

144. Thomson, *Travels in the Atlas and Southern Morocco,* 290.

145. Works dealing extensively with the *tujjār al-sulṭān* include Schroeter, *Merchants of Essaouira;* Abitbol, *Temoins et acteurs;* and Abitbol, *Tujjâr al-sultân: Une élite économique judeo-marocaine au XIXème siècle* (Jerusalem: Institut Ben-Zvi, 1994) (Hebrew).

146. Richardson, *Travels in Morocco,* 1:147.

147. See the report concerning the summons of Demnat's Jewish leaders to Marrakesh in the *Times of Morocco,* 25 September 1896. For further discussion of the meaning of the *hadīya* in nineteenth-century Morocco, see Rahma Bourqia, "Don et théâtralité: Réflexion sur le rituel du don (hadiya) offert au sultan au XIXe siècle," *Hespéris-Tamuda* 31 (1993): 61–75.

148. Issachar Ben-Ami, *Culte des saints et pèlerinages judéo-musulmans au Maroc* (Paris: Editions Maisonneuve & Larose, 1990), 179.

149. Ben-Ami, *Culte des saints et pèlerinages judéo-musulmans au Maroc,* 179.

150. In a parallel pattern, the most promising Muslim students from the countryside also came to Marrakesh to continue their religious educations at the Yusufiya or Muwwasin *madrasas*. Dale Eickelman has written a biography of one such student, who went on to become an important rural *qāḍī*. Dale Eickelman, *Knowledge and Power in Morocco* (Princeton: Princeton University Press, 1985).

151. Nahum Slouschz, *Travels in North Africa* (Philadelphia: Jewish Publication Society of America, 1927), 443.

152. The story of Abisrour is told in Sanford Bederman, *God's Will: The Travels of Rabbi Mordochai Abi Serour* (Atlanta: Georgia State University, Department of Geography, 1980); and also in Y. D. Sémach, "Un rabbin voyageur marocain: Mordochée Aby Serour," *Hespéris* 8 (1928): 385–399. Abisrour is buried in the Jewish cemetery of Marrakesh.

153. The composition of the student body in a course in Talmud taught at the A.I.U. school in 1935 may be representative. Most students were from the immediate environs of Marrakesh; one was from the Ourika region in the High Atlas; and

two others came from pre-Saharan villages beyond the Atlas, a twenty-four-hour drive from Marrakesh. A.I.U., Maroc XXVI.E.398–416, 10 December 1935, Goldenberg.

154. A.I.U., Maroc XXVI.E.398–416, 10 December 1935, Goldenberg.

155. For Demnat, see *Times of Morocco,* 5 September 1884. For Tamarzit, see *Le réveil du Maroc,* 7 December 1899.

156. P.R.O., FO 413: 42, 21 March 1906, Ghanjaoui.

157. A.I.U., Maroc XXVI.E.398–416, 22 June 1905, Falcon.

158. For a copy of a 1903 letter sent to the Marrakesh *mellah* asking for alms for the poor of Safed during the holiday of Shavuot, see Central Archives for the History of the Jewish People, Jerusalem, MA/MR.2111, Jewish Community of Safed to Rabbi Shlomo b. Haim. For a more thorough discussion of the role of the *shaliakh* in Moroccan Jewish communal life, see Zafrani, *Mille ans de vie juive au Maroc,* 31–34.

159. See H. Z. Hirschberg, *A History of the Jews in North Africa* (Leiden, Netherlands: Brill, 1974–1981), 2:247.

160. Aubin, *Morocco of Today,* 290–291.

161. For example, see the request made by Dawid b. Murdukh of Jerusalem to travel from Essaouira to Demnat: D.A.R., Marrakesh 2, 12 Ṣafar 1283/26 June 1866, al-Swiri to al-Simlali.

162. Aubin, *Morocco of Today,* 290.

163. Paul Valence, "La yeshiba," *Bulletin de l'énseignment publique au Maroc* 26, 1–2 (1939): 3–12.

164. A.I.U., France IX.A.67–73, 8 August 1876, Halévy.

165. P.R.O., FO 413: 42, 26 May 1906, Lowther.

166. A.I.U., Maroc VII.B 7368/8, 15 February 1904, Danon.

167. A.I.U., Maroc XXV.E.394–397, 1 May 1911, Danon.

168. Périgny, *Au Maroc,* 141.

169. Mention is made of homeless Jews occupying the cemetery in A.I.U., Maroc XXV.E.394–397, 25 March 1913, Danon; in A.I.U., Maroc XXIV.E.384–393, 9 December 1934, Bibasse; and in Pascalle Saisset, *Heures juives au Maroc* (Paris: Rieder, 1930), 146. Reference to the "mad Muslim" living in the Jewish cemetery can be found in *Jewish Missionary Intelligence* 11 (1892): 180.

170. This phenomenon occurs in other Middle Eastern cities as well, Cairo's "City of the Dead" being the most famous example.

171. P.R.O., FO 174: 85, 4 May 1875, Hay.

172. A.A.E./P., Mémoires et documents (hereafter M.D.) Maroc 10, March 1867, Beaumier.

173. A.A.E./P., Maroc, 1917–1940 (MA17–40), c. 1917, n/a.

174. A.A.E./P., Affaires diverses politiques (hereafter A.D.P.) Maroc 5, 15 January 1880, Asseraf.

175. For the arrival in Oran of Jewish refugees, see A.A.E./P., A.D.P. Maroc 3, 22 May 1857, Ministre secretaire d'état de la guerre.

176. *Jewish Missionary Intelligence* 10 (1892): 163.

177. The same phenomenon among Jews from Tangier is discussed at length by Susan Gilson Miller in "Kippur on the Amazon: Jewish Emigration from Northern Morocco in the Late Nineteenth Century," in *Sephardi and Middle Eastern Jewries: History and Culture in the Modern Era,* ed. Harvey Goldberg (Bloomington: Indiana University Press, 1996), 190–209.

178. A.A.E./P., A.D.P. Maroc 2, 8 October 1851, Le garde des sceaux. For more

on the situation of families left behind in such instances, see A.I.U., Maroc II.B.9–13, 27 March 1911, Danon; and A.I.U., Maroc VII.B, Dossiers déclassés et manquant à l'intérieur des comités et communautés, 24 January 1913, Danon.

179. D.A.R., Al-tartīb al-ʿāmm, 6 Rabīʿ II 1308/19 November 1890.

180. Daniel Noin, *La population rurale du Maroc* (Paris: Presses universitaires de France, 1970), 1:21.

3. MUSLIMS AND JEWISH SPACE

An earlier version of this chapter previously appeared in *Jewish Social Studies.*

1. Ronald Messier, "Rethinking the Almoravids, Rethinking Ibn Khaldun," in *North Africa, Islam, and the Mediterranean World: From the Almoravids to the Algerian War,* ed. Julia Clancy-Smith (London: Frank Cass, 2001), 70.

2. Eugene Aubin, *Morocco of Today* (London: E. B. Dutton, 1906), 292; Paul Lambert, "Notice sur la ville de Maroc," *Bulletin de la Société de géographie de Paris* (November–December 1868): 435.

3. Although Thomson says that the Jews' cells were superior to those of the Muslims, a more reliable report from the British consul suggests otherwise: "The rooms on the right of the doorway are used for Jewish prisoners, while the five rooms opening from the passage on the left are reserved for prisoners of the better class who can afford to pay for the better accommodation and other privileges." See Joseph Thomson, *Travels in the Atlas and Southern Morocco* (London: George Philip and Son, 1889), 416; and P.R.O., FO 174: 281, 23 November 1911, Lennox.

4. P.R.O., FO 413: 18, 24 October 1892, Payton to Eliot. The inmates of the *māristān* should be kept in mind during the discussion of prostitution in the *mellah,* below, particularly as we are told by the French explorer Paul Lambert that "In general, only women of bad lives or reputed to be such who are encountered in the streets at night are held in the Morstan." Lambert, "Notice sur la ville de Maroc," 437. A fourth prison, located in the Kasbah, was used for prisoners of state. I have found no evidence that Jews were incarcerated there.

5. Ali Bey al-Abassi, *Travels of Ali Bey in Africa and Asia: 1803–1807* (Philadelphia: M. Carey, 1816), 1:175.

6. Lambert, "Notice sur la ville de Maroc," 445.

7. Jules Erckmann, *Le Maroc moderne* (Paris: Challamel Ainé, 1885), 37. According to Erckmann, the *ḥāra*'s inhabitants suffered from syphilis rather than leprosy. This is consistent with a European newspaper report from the period claiming that syphilis was the "national disease" of Marrakesh: *Times of Morocco,* 24 November 1888.

8. Self-segregation reflects the need for close proximity to the institutions (synagogue, *mikvah,* kosher butcher, etc.) that allow Jews to fulfill their religious obligations, particularly on Shabbat when travel is limited. See Jacob Katz, *Tradition and Crisis* (New York: Schocken, 1971), 13. As explained by Hirschberg, "[Territorial concentration] was caused by the need to enable every Jew to live in accordance with religious law. The particular conditions for Jewish residence that a city or quarter had to meet are stated in a second-century *Baraita,* which says, *inter alia:* 'A Torah student must not live in a city which does not have a court empowered to implement its decisions; a charity chest administered in accordance with the Law; a synagogue; a bath; a scribe and a teacher for children (Sanhedrin 17b).'" Haim Z. Hirschberg,

"The Jewish Quarter in Muslim Cities and Berber Areas," *Judaism* 17 (1968): 406. As seen earlier, Jews in Marrakesh were concentrated in two distinct neighborhoods well before their segregation became institutionalized with the creation of the *mellah* in the sixteenth century.

9. Budgett Meakin, *The Land of the Moors: A Comprehensive Description* (London: Darf, 1986), 302.

10. D.A.R., Marrakech 4, 17 Muḥarram 1297/31 December 1879, ʿAbdallāh b. Ibrāhīm. This defense was rejected by the sultan, however, who reminded the *muḥtasib* with some severity that Umalik, as pasha of the Kasbah, retained full authority in the *mellah,* markets included: D.A.R., Marrakech 3, 14 Dhū al-Ḥijja 1296/29 November 1879. The pasha of the Kasbah thus appropriated the authority of the *muḥtasib* over the behavior of *dhimmīs*, his usual prerogative in addition to markets and morals. The particularity of Marrakesh with regard to the limited role of the *muḥtasib* is attributed by Massignon to the fierce competition among the region's *qāʾids*: "The power of the great indigenous chiefs in the city of Marrakesh effectively created, insofar as the corporations are concerned, a very particular situation very different from what one observes in other towns of the Empire . . . The pasha, wishing to affirm his authority, took over certain of the *muḥtasib*'s allotments related to the supervision of the corporations, especially the designation of the *amīns*, who are named by the pasha, on the basis not of their professional competence but of their loyalty to him; the *muḥtasib* is quite limited in the normal exercise of his functions by this situation, which rather explains the conflict between the Glaoua and Mtougga clans." Louis Massignon, "Enquête sur les corporations d'artisans et des commerçants au Maroc," *Revue du monde musulman* 58 (1924): 118.

11. D.A.R., Marrakesh 4, 17 Muḥarram 1297/31 December 1879, ʿAbdallāh b. Ibrāhīm.

12. D.A.R., Al-tartīb al-ʿāmm, 6 Rabīʿ II 1308/19 November 1890. With the exception of six *ḥabūs* properties, the remaining houses were all owned by Jews.

13. See A.A.E./P., N.S. Maroc 405: B.6.1, 6 January 1903, French legation at Tangier, in which it is noted that some Christian students also attended the school.

14. A.I.U., Maroc XXVI.E.398–416, 3 April 1910, Falcon.

15. See Issachar Ben-Ami, *Saint Veneration among the Jews in Morocco* (Detroit: Wayne State University Press, 1998), 240–242.

16. Françoise Legey, *The Folklore of Morocco* (London: G. Allen and Unwin, 1935), 189.

17. Legey, *The Folklore of Morocco,* 186.

18. Legey, *The Folklore of Morocco,* 187. The ashes were added to other ingredients to make an amulet that was placed under the bed of an adulterous husband, causing him to be struck with a severe toothache each time he tried to lie down with a woman other than his wife.

19. According to the recipe, the couscous must be stirred using the hands of a newly buried corpse, dug up for this purpose. Legey, *Essai de folklore marocain,* 180–181. Westermarck also observed several rituals involving the urine of a Jew, though not in Marrakesh: Edward Westermarck, *Ritual and Belief in Morocco* (New York: University Books, 1968), 2:301, 555.

20. Erckmann, *Maroc moderne,* 191.

21. Gaston Deverdun, *Marrakech des origines à 1912* (Rabat, Morocco: Editions Techniques Nord-Africaines, 1959), 1:608.

22. Turner himself borrowed the term from Arnold van Gennep's formulation of "*rites de passage*": see Victor Turner, *Drama, Fields, and Metaphors: Symbolic Action in Human Society* (Ithaca, N.Y.: Cornell University Press, 1974), 231. For a discussion of liminality in the context of Moroccan history, see Amira Bennison, "Liminal States: Morocco and the Iberian Frontier between the Twelfth and Nineteenth Centuries," in Clancy-Smith, *North Africa, Islam, and the Mediterranean World,* 11–28, in which the author employs the concept "to denote . . . a permeable barrier across which peoples and ideas passed to and fro, creating a rich zone of transition" (27 n.5).

23. Quoted in Thomas Willan, *Studies in Elizabethan Foreign Trade* (Manchester, England: Manchester University Press, 1959), 225.

24. Erckmann, *Maroc moderne,* 190–191.

25. A.I.U., Maroc XXVII.E.417–442, 16 September 1901, Levy.

26. Henriette Celarié, *Un mois au Maroc* (Paris: Hachette, 1923), 71.

27. See the 1899 map of Marrakesh by N. Larras in Deverdun, *Marrakech,* vol. 2, plate 103.

28. P.R.O., FO 174: 292, 26 November 1886, Payton.

29. A.A.E./P., C.P.C. Maroc 2, 10 August 1888, French consul at Mogador [Essaouira].

30. I am grateful to Sarah Levin for bringing this saying to my attention.

31. *Bulletin de l'Alliance Israélite Universelle,* 2nd series, 26 (1901): 77. While heavy consumption of alcohol in the *mellah* may have been damaging to the social fabric, its economic benefits were unquestionable. As many as 227 Jews were involved in the production and sale of alcohol in Marrakesh: A.I.U., Maroc XXVII.E.417–442, 10 February 1902, Levy. In addition to the local product, imported alcohol was also widely available in the *mellah* through the intermediary efforts of Jewish merchants. Akkan Corcos, a native of Marrakesh, was one well-known trafficker: P.R.O., FO 174: 85, 1 March 1874, Beaumier. Consumption of foreign alcohol even supplanted that of local *maḥīya* in years when crop failures in the Marrakesh region made its ingredients prohibitively expensive: P.R.O., FO 413: 34, 11 June 1902, Pearson; and in the same folder, 12 May 1902, MacLeod. In 1902, for example, three-quarters of all alcohol imported from Germany to Morocco went directly to the southern capital: Deverdun, *Marrakech,* 1:561.

32. *Bulletin de l'Alliance Israélite Universelle,* 2nd series, 26 (1901): 77. See also A.I.U., Maroc XXVII.E.417–442, 16 September 1901, Levy.

33. A.I.U., Maroc XXIV.E.384–393, 22 January 1934, Bibasse.

34. See for example, A.I.U., Maroc III.C.10, 12 November 1911, Danon.

35. A.I.U., Maroc III.C.10, 19 August 1925, Falcon.

36. P.R.O., FO 909: 1219, 5 February 1929, n/a.

37. A.I.U., Maroc XXVII.E.417–442, 30 December 1901, Levy.

38. Erckmann, *Maroc moderne,* 191.

39. Jews selling cigarettes in the medina risked incurring the wrath of the *muḥtasib:* D.A.R., Marrakesh 9, 28 Rajab 1310/15 February 1893, ʿAbdallāh.

40. D.A.R., Marrakesh 3, 29 Jumādā I 1284/28 September 1867, Makhzan.

41. A.I.U., Maroc XXVI.E.398–416, 1 March 1928, Goldenberg. In Tunis as well, prostitution, alcohol, and gambling were concentrated in particular areas, including the Jewish quarter. See Mohamed Kerrou and Moncef M'halla, "La prostitution dans la médina de Tunis au XIXe et XXe siècles," in Fanny Colonna and Zakya Daoud, eds., *Etre marginal au Maghreb* (Paris: CNRS Editions, 1993), 201–221.

42. Masashi Haneda and Toru Miura, eds., *Islamic Urban Studies: Historical Review and Perspectives* (London: Kegan Paul International, 1994), esp. pp. 4–5.

43. Janet Abu-Lughod, "The Islamic City: Historical Myth, Islamic Essence, and Contemporary Relevance," *International Journal of Middle Eastern Studies* 19 (1987): 163.

44. A.I.U., Maroc XXVII.E.417–442, 10 February 1902, Levy.

45. Al-Abassi, *Travels of Ali Bey,* 174.

46. Thomas Hodgkin, *Narrative of a Journey to Morocco in 1863 and 1864* (London: T. C. Newby, 1866), 86–87.

47. Walter Harris, *The Land of an African Sultan: Travels in Morocco, 1887, 1888, and 1889* (London: Sampson Low, Marston, Searle, & Rivington, 1889), 219.

48. The French ethnographer Pierre Flamand represents a prime example of this tendency. See, for example, his discussion of "*droit de cuissage*" in the hiring of Jewish seamstresses: Pierre Flamand, *Un mellah en pays berbère: Demnate* (Paris: Librairie générale de droit & de jurisprudence, 1952), 131.

49. In one instance, a Jew thought to have been murdered was eventually found in the cupboard of his lover's house, where he had hidden when the woman's husband arrived home unexpectedly. See P.R.O., FO 413: 21, 25 April 1894; and also *Le réveil du Maroc,* 2 May 1894.

50. *Times of Morocco,* 24 November 1888.

51. A.I.U., Maroc VII.B, Dossiers déclassés et manquant à l'intérieur des comités et communautés, 24 January 1913, Danon. In another report, it was noted that one aspect of "*l'esprit Marrakshi*" was that Jews made poor spouses: A.I.U., Maroc XXIV.E. 384–393, 9 April 1937, Cohen.

52. In the contemporary Israeli context, this takes the form of anti-Mizrahi bias.

53. For several examples of this phenomenon, see Vivian Mann, ed., *Morocco: Jews and Art in a Muslim Land* (London: Merell in association with the Jewish Museum, 2000).

54. William Lemprière, *A Tour through the Dominions of the Emperor of Morocco* (Newport, England: Tayler, 1813), 15.

55. Flamand, *Un mellah en pays berbère,* 131.

56. Gavin Maxwell, *Lords of the Atlas: The Rise and Fall of the House of Glaoua, 1893–1956* (London: Arrow, 1991), 167. See also James Gray Jackson, *An Account of the Empire of Marocco* (Philadelphia: 1810), 362–363.

57. Deverdun, *Marrakech,* 1:609. A more direct, if no doubt exaggerated, appraisal is offered by Arthur Koestler in the American popular press: "Marrakesh, the trading center and playground of the Sahara, had one of the most picturesque red-light districts in the world; it was one of its principal industries. Its Pashas used to pay their armies with their revenues from prostitution, which was taxed like any other trade. The French troops stationed in Marrakesh added to the boom; when the brothels were finally abolished in 1955 by the present Sultan, there were 27,000 officially registered prostitutes in the town, which had a total population of 240,000. A little arithmetic yields the astonishing result that over 10 percent of the total population; that is, 20 percent of the female population; that is, 40 percent of all females of childbearing age, exercised that profession." Arthur Koestler, "Reports and Comment: Marrakech," *Atlantic Monthly* (December 1971): 26.

58. Hamid Triki and Bernard Rosenberger, "Famines et épidémies au Maroc aux XVIe et XVIIe siècles," *Hespéris-Tamuda* 15 (1974): 9–10.

59. A.I.U., Maroc XXVI.E.398–416, 30 August 1905, Falcon.

60. A.I.U., Maroc XXVI.E.398–416, 30 November 1905, Falcon. The collusion of municipal officials in prostitution was in fact quite common in Marrakesh. See Thomson, *Travels in the Atlas and Southern Morocco,* 362, in which a local *qā'id,* along with many of the city's prominent sharifs, are thus accused. As for the *shaykh al-yahūd,* it should be kept in mind that this position was typically bestowed upon the wealthiest and most powerful member of the Jewish community and did not necessarily connote moral or religious authority.

61. Several documents deal with the abandonment of Jewish women in the *mellah* by their spouses. See, for example, A.A.E./P., A.D.P. Maroc 2, 8 October 1851, Le garde des sceaux; A.I.U., Maroc VII.B, Dossiers déclassés et manquant à l'intérieur des comités et communautés, 24 January 1913, Danon; and A.I.U., Maroc II.B.9–13, 27 March 1911, Danon.

62. A.I.U., Maroc VII.B, Dossiers déclassés et manquant à l'intérieur des comités et communautés, 24 January 1913, Danon.

63. This figure is based on the A.I.U.'s estimate of a Jewish population of twelve thousand for Marrakesh at the time of the establishment of the French Protectorate in 1912. A.I.U., Maroc XXVI.E.398–416, 15 March 1936, Goldenberg.

64. A.I.U., Maroc XXVI.E.398–416, 30 August 1905, Falcon.

65. For a fuller treatment of this flamboyant figure, see Khalid Ben Srhir, *Britain and Morocco during the Embassy of John Drummond Hay, 1845–1886,* tr. Malcolm Williams and Gavin Waterson (London: Routledge/Curzon, 2005).

66. Aubin, *Morocco of Today,* 36.

67. D.A.R., Marrakesh 8, beginning of Muḥarram 1307/end of August 1889, Torres.

68. See also D.A.R., Marrakesh 7, 2 Rabīʿ II 1305/18 December 1887, Umālik, in which a Jew is arrested for bringing contraband tobacco into the *mellah* that he claims to be selling on the behalf of Ghanjaoui.

69. Though this may simply be a scribal error, it is worth noting that while miscalculations are fairly common in the census, mistakes in pronoun and suffix use and in grammar are rare. 6 Rabīʿ II 1308/19 November 1890, 5.

70. D.A.R., Marrakesh 9, 27 Shawwāl 1310/14 May 1893, ʿAbbas b. Dawud. The text of the letter reads as follows: "The *ʿamil* [prefect] of the residential quarters [was commissioned] to prevent the women of the medina from entering the *mellah* in order to protect them from the degradation of frequenting the shops of the *dhimmīs* and to cause any doubt about them to be cast aside." Mohammed Ennaji interprets this letter somewhat differently. He suggests that the purpose of restricting Muslim women's access to the *mellah* was to prevent them from pawning their belongings in times of scarcity. Mohammed Ennaji, *Expansion européenne et changement social au Maroc* (Casablanca: Editions Eddif, 1996), 64.

71. A.I.U., Maroc XXVI.E.398–416, 3 April 1910, Falcon.

72. Jean Baudry, "Une ambassade au Maroc en 1767," *Revue des questions historiques* 36 (1906): 193.

73. The empty building was still visible to the English merchant and consul James Jackson in the early nineteenth century: "In this quarter stands the Spanish convent, which, till lately, was inhabited by two or three friars; but it is now deserted." Jackson, *An Account of the Empire of Marocco,* 115.

74. Deverdun, *Marrakech,* 1:551.

75. A.I.U., France IX.A.67–73, 8 August 1876, Halévy.

76. See Jonathan Katz, "The 1907 Mauchamp Affair and the French Civilising Mission in Morocco," in Clancy-Smith, *North Africa, Islam, and the Mediterranean World,* 154.

77. Jean-Louis Miège, *Le Maroc* (Paris: Presses universitaires de France, 1950), 2:474. Halévy, however, indicates that there were no Christians in Marrakesh when he visited in 1876. A.I.U., France IX.A.67–73, 8 August 1876.

78. The attitude of the French doctor Mauchamp was representative of this new breed of Europeans, who, said one commentator, "parad[ed] their feelings of superiority as ostentatiously as their European dress." The same author suggests that Mauchamp, who was murdered by a mob in Marrakesh on 19 March 1907, was ultimately the "victim of his own arrogance." Helen Titus, "Among Competing Worlds: The Rehamna of Morocco on the Eve of French Conquest" (Ph.D. dissertation, Yale University, 1978), 234–237. Burke takes a slightly broader view of the causes of the Mauchamp murder: "The volatile atmosphere at Marrakech made such an event likely; the insensitivity of Mauchamps [*sic*] made it inevitable." Edmund Burke III, *Prelude to Protectorate in Morocco: Precolonial Protest and Resistance, 1860–1912* (Chicago: University of Chicago Press, 1976), 92.

79. Leland Bowie tells of a Moroccan Jewish merchant by the name of David Darmon, who had been naturalized in Algeria, and who was trafficking in contraband arms along the Moroccan-Algerian border when his shipment of rifles was stolen. Though his merchandise was hardly legitimate, he nonetheless submitted a claim to the Makhzan for reimbursement of losses. This outraged the sultan, who was at the time busy trying to suppress tribal dissidence in the frontier area. See Leland Bowie, "An Aspect of Muslim-Jewish Relations in Late Nineteenth-Century Morocco: A European Diplomatic View," *International Journal of Middle Eastern Studies* 7 (1976): 9.

80. James Richardson, *Travels in Morocco* (London: Charles J. Skeet, 1860), 1:144.

81. *Times of Morocco,* 15 December 1888.

82. *Le réveil du Maroc,* 21 October 1891.

83. See D.A.R., Marrakesh 12: 7 Dhū al-Qaʿda 1321/25 January 1904, Muḥammad Znībar.

84. A.I.U., Maroc III.C.10, 22 November 1912, Danon.

85. See A.I.U., Maroc XXVI.E.398–416, 20 March 1907, Falcon. There are several different explanations of what Mauchamp actually put on his roof and why. See Katz, "The 1907 Mauchamp Affair," 155.

86. Thomson, *Travels in the Atlas and Southern Morocco,* 364, 416–418.

87. A.I.U., Maroc III.C.10, 13 September 1915, Azoulai.

88. A.I.U., Maroc VII.B.188/2, 2 September 1907, Falcon.

89. P.R.O., FO 174: 105, 27 March 1881, Payton.

90. The incident is reported in the *Times of Morocco* on the following dates in 1890: 31 May; 7, 12, 14, and 28 June; 23 August.

91. ʿAbd al-Raḥmān b. Zaydān, *Itḥāf aʿlām al-nās bi-jamāl akhbār ḥāḍirat Miknās* (Casablanca: Idiyāl, 1990), 3:392–394.

92. P.R.O., FO 909: 1214, 19 March 1927, vice consul of Marrakesh.

93. See a letter from a French ship's captain, in which he discusses the plans of an English missionary named Markham to leave Rabat in order to preach in the interior: A.A.E./P., M.D. Maroc 10, 31 July 1853.

94. Missionaries of Russian-Jewish origin who were active in Morocco include Paulus Dressler of the Mildmay Missions, J. B. Crighton Ginsburg and a Mr. Miscovitch of the London Society for the Conversion of the Jews, and the missionary Markham mentioned in the previous note. For more on the work of Protestant missionaries in Morocco, see Jean-Louis Miège, "Les missions protestantes au Maroc, 1875–1905," *Hespéris* 42 (1955): 153–186.

95. A.I.U., France IX.A.67–73, 8 August 1876, Halévy.

96. P.R.O., FO 836: 18, 11 February 1935, Nairn.

97. P.R.O., FO 836: 18, 11 February 1935, Nairn; also P.R.O., FO 836: 18, 31 July 1935, Vaughan-Russel.

98. Aubin, *Morocco of Today*, 37–38.

99. A.A.E./P., C.P.C. Maroc 1, 5 May 1878. Ginsburg did little to endear himself to the Jewish commercial elite of Essaouira, judging from these remarks: "Let England, let Christendom clearly understand this, that persecution was not brought about by the native authority, or by the religious fanaticisms of the Jews or Mahommedans, but by the ill will, jealousy, and malice of a handful of disaffected Jews, enjoying British protection under, and abetted by, English officials." J. B. Ginsburg, *An Account of the Persecution of the Protestant Mission among the Jews, at Mogador, Morocco* (London: Edward G. Allen, 1880), 40.

100. P.R.O., FO 174: 292, 26 November 1886, Payton.

101. P.R.O., FO 174: 95, 31 December 1875, Maclean.

102. See P.R.O., FO 99: 189, 12 March 1877, Hay.

103. In addition to Moses Montefiore, the scholar Nahum Slouschz and the chief rabbi of Metz also published accounts of their visits to Marrakesh, as did Elias Canetti in a later period. Such accounts often paid special attention to the *mellah.*

104. Judah Holzmann was an Ottoman subject who converted to Islam while in Morocco and married a local Muslim woman.

105. Many of these individuals were in fact Ottoman subjects who had attended A.I.U. schools in the Balkans or Anatolia before going to Paris for more advanced pedagogical training.

106. A.I.U., Maroc XXVI.E.398–416, 2 April 1905, Falcon.

107. Michael Laskier, "The Alliance Israelite Universelle and the Struggle for Recognition within Moroccan Jewish Society, 1862–1912," in *The Sepharadi and Oriental Jewish Heritage: Studies,* ed. Issachar Ben-Ami (Jerusalem: Magnes Press, Hebrew University, 1982), 191–207.

108. See the list of donors in A.I.U., Maroc XXVI.E.398–416, 13 August 1905, n/a.

109. A.I.U., Maroc III.C.10, 20 December 1900, Levy.

110. A.I.U., Maroc XXVI.E.398–416, 12 April 1907, Falcon.

111. A.I.U., Maroc XXVI.E.398–416, 5 May 1905, Falcon.

112. A.I.U., Maroc II.B.9–13, 27 March 1911, Danon, in which the author, then the director of the boys' school, gives the following three reasons for the Jews' failure to entrust their children to the A.I.U.: 1) "fanaticism and ignorance"; 2) competition by the rabbis' schools; 3) the fact that tuition is required of those deemed able to pay it.

113. P.R.O., FO 174: 292, 11 December 1885, Johnston.

114. The school's director relates, "We have lost all influence with the authori-

ties; we are considered suspect, and even our coreligionists ardently wish that we would leave Marrakesh as quickly as possible." A.I.U., Maroc XXVI.E.398–416, 1 April 1907, Falcon.

4. JEWS AND MUSLIM SPACE

1. Haim Z. Hirschberg, "The Jewish Quarter in Muslim Cities and Berber Areas," *Judaism* 17 (1968): 406.

2. Most official Moroccan documents dealing with Jews during this period place the term *al-dhimmī* or *min ahl al-dhimma* ("from among the *dhimmī* people" of a specific town) after a Jewish person's name.

3. Norman Stillman, *The Jews of Arab Lands in Modern Times* (Philadelphia: The Jewish Publication Society of America, 2003), 158–159.

4. *Encyclopedia of Islam*, 2nd ed. (Leiden, Netherlands: Brill, 1960), s.v. "Dhimma."

5. Mohamed El Mansour, *Morocco in the Reign of Mawley Sulayman* (Wisbech, England: Middle East & North African Studies Press, 1988), 15.

6. William Lemprière, *A Tour through the Dominions of the Emperor of Morocco* (Newport, England: Tayler, 1813), 185.

7. Budgett Meakin, *The Land of the Moors: A Comprehensive Description* (London: Darf, 1986), 301.

8. For a full description of Jewish men's attire in Marrakesh, see Walter Harris, *The Land of an African Sultan: Travels in Morocco, 1887, 1888, and 1889* (London: Sampson Low, Marston, Searle, & Rivington, 1889), 218; and also A.I.U., France IX.A.67–73, 8 August 1876, Halévy. The blue kerchief with white dots was commonly worn by older Jewish men, often scholars, in Berber regions in the south. Yeshouʿa Corcos wears such a scarf in his portrait (see figure e.1).

9. See Donald Mackenzie, *The Khalifate of the West* (London: Simpkin, Marshall, Hamilton, Kent, 1911), 61; and Records of the Board of Deputies of British Jews, Greater London Record Office (hereafter B.D.J.), Acc3121.B2.9.6, Cohen.

10. A.I.U., France IX.A.67–73, 8 August 1876, Halévy.

11. Lemprière, *A Tour through the Dominions of the Emperor of Morocco*, 180.

12. A similar incident occurred in late 1885, also involving Umalik, in which Jews were again forbidden to wear slippers outside the *mellah*. See P.R.O., FO 174: 292, 11 December 1885, Johnston; and A.A.E./P., C.P.C. Maroc 2, 10 December 1885, French consul at Mogador.

13. A.A.E./P., Correspondance politique (hereafter C.P.) Maroc 38, 10 July 1873, Tissot.

14. A.I.U., Maroc VII.B, *déclassé*, 5 May 1907, Falcon. See also Helen Titus, "Among Competing Worlds: The Rehamna of Morocco on the Eve of French Conquest" (Ph.D. dissertation, Yale University, 1978), 148–149.

15. A.I.U., Maroc III.C.10, 22 November 1912, Danon.

16. A.I.U., Maroc XXVI.E.398–416, 23 July 1907, Falcon.

17. Letter of 26 October 1908, Glaoui, reprinted in "L'Alliance Israélite et le gouvernement marocain," *L'univers israélite* (October 1908): 7–8.

18. A.A.E./P., C.P.C. Maroc 1, 16 Adar 5641/1–2 January 1880, fifteen Jews of Marrakesh.

19. A.I.U., Maroc XXVII.E.417–442, 30 May 1902, Levy.

20. James Richardson, *Travels in Morocco* (London: Charles J. Skeet, 1860), 1:viii.

21. A.A.E./P., C.P.C. Maroc 1, 16 Adar 5641/1–2 January 1880, fifteen Jews of Marrakesh.

22. A.I.U., Maroc III.C.10, 8 October 1907, Bonjo.

23. *Jewish Missionary Intelligence* (October 1892).

24. See, for instance, the story of Yusuf b. ʿAli in the next chapter.

25. Possibly Mawlay Sulayman (r. 1793–1822), who is often referred to as dark-skinned.

26. A.I.U., Maroc II.B.9–13, 6 June 1929, Camhy.

27. A statement prepared by the Board of Jewish Deputies to the secretary of state for foreign affairs seeking the latter's support at the 1888 Madrid Conference lists among the "principal disabilities" of Moroccan Jews the fact that a Jew who renounces his or her religion is required to convert to Islam, and any return to Judaism is punishable by death. B.D.J., Acc3121.B2.9.6, 3 February 1888, Cohen.

28. D.A.R., Marrakesh 9, 11 Ramaḍān 1310/29 March 1893, al-Muṣṭafā.

29. For correspondence regarding this case, see P.R.O., FO 413: 20, 8 October 1893, Board of Jewish Deputies to Montagu; and also the letter from Yashuʿa Pinto, a prominent Marrakesh rabbi, to Isaac Abensur: B.D.J., Acc3121.B2.9.6, 22 January 1894.

30. See relevant correspondence between Eliot and the earl of Rosebury in P.R.O., FO 413: 19.

31. *Le réveil du Maroc,* 6 December 1893.

32. See, for example, the conversion of Yosh b. Hanina of the Marrakesh *mellah:* D.A.R., Marrakesh 11, late Dhū al-Qaʿda 1314/early May 1897, *ʿudūl* of Marrakesh.

33. A.I.U., Maroc III.C.10, 28 October 1904, Souessia.

34. A.I.U., Maroc VII.B, *déclassé,* 10 October 1907, Falcon.

35. D.A.R., Marrakesh 8, 20 Ṣafar 1309/25 September 1891, al-Fāsī.

36. D.A.R., Marrakesh 10, 23 Rabīʿ II 1312/24 October 1894, ʿAbdallāh.

37. Paul Pascon, *Capitalism and Agriculture in the Haouz of Marrakesh,* ed. John R. Hall, trans. C. Edwin Vaughan and Veronique Ingman (London: Kegan Paul International, 1986), 75.

38. P.R.O., FO 413: 36, 7 January 1904, Griffin.

39. See Jean-Louis Miège, *Le Maroc et l'Europe: 1830–1894* (Rabat, Morocco: Editions la Ports, 1989), 3:57, 59–60, 85, 94–95. For the slave trade in particular, see T. Zerbib, "Slave Caravans in Morocco," *Anti-Slavery Reporter* (May–June 1887): 97–99.

40. A.I.U., France IX.A.67–73, 8 August 1876, Halévy.

41. See for example Abdellah Laroui, *Les origines sociales et culturelles du nationalisme marocain, 1830–1912* (Paris: F. Maspero, 1977), 210–211; and Mohammed Kenbib, "Changing Aspects of State and Society in Nineteenth-Century Morocco," in *The Moroccan State in Historical Perspective, 1850–1985,* ed. Abdelali Doumou, trans. Ayi Kwei Armah (Dakar: Codesria, 1990), 11–27, in which the detrimental effects of the protégé system on Moroccan independence are discussed at length. Moroccan Jews are more explicitly linked to the loss of Moroccan independence in Kenbib's longer study, *Juifs et musulmans au Maroc, 1859–1948* (Rabat, Morocco: Faculté des Lettres et des Sciences Humaines, 1994).

42. With regard to the Hawz, Pascon squarely places the responsibility for facilitating European penetration of the region with the local *zawīyas* (Sufi lodges) and *qāʾids*, calling them the "most active partners in the process of foreign colonization."

See Pascon, *Capitalism and Agriculture in the Haouz of Marrakesh*, 59. Ennaji, meanwhile, includes Jews along with these other groups, emphasizing their role in furthering European-style capitalism in the Moroccan countryside. Mohammed Ennaji, *Expansion européenne et changement social au Maroc* (Casablanca: Editions Eddif, 1996), 57–58.

43. A.I.U., Maroc XXVII.E.417–442, 10 February 1902, Levy.

44. José Bénech, *Essai d'explication d'un mellah (ghetto marocain): Un des aspects du judaïsme* (Paris: Larose, 1940), 48.

45. Al-Glaoui was one such "high-profile" customer, though his reputation among jewelers suffered because he did not always pay his debts. In one instance, a jeweler was forced to borrow money from another Jew to cover Glaoui's debt, and was put in jail when he could not repay on time. See A.I.U., Maroc VII.B.1752/2, 2 March 1911, Danon.

46. Gaston Deverdun, *Marrakech des origines à 1912* (Rabat, Morocco: Editions Techniques Nord-Africaines, 1959), 1:563. (See also B.G./R. D3410, Risāʾil muḥtasib Marrākush Mawlāy ʿAbdallāh al-Būkīlī: 150, 17 Shawwāl 1309/15 May 1892, for the Makhzan's collection of taxes from this *sūq*.) Bénech implies that the jewelers actually lived in their ateliers, making them the only Jews to reside outside the *mellah* in this period, though this cannot be corroborated by other sources. Bénech, *Essai d'explication d'un mellah*, 47.

47. According to one report, up to fifty women could be seen squatting in the dirt patching uniforms on a given day: A.I.U., Maroc XXVII.E.417–442, 16 September 1901, Levy. The sewing of soldiers' uniforms was also a Jewish occupation in Fez: P.R.O., FO 174: 95, 4 October 1879, Maclean.

48. Joseph Thomson, *Travels in the Atlas and Southern Morocco* (London: George Philip and Son, 1889), 361. Halévy witnessed the same phenomenon more than a decade earlier (see chapter 2).

49. This Jewish tailor was eventually murdered by his client's companions, which is how he enters into the historical record. See D.A.R., Marrakesh 9, 24 Rajab 1310/11 February 1893, Ibn Dāwūd.

50. A.I.U., Maroc III.C.10, 16 November 1911, Danon.

51. A.I.U., Maroc III.C.10, 12 January 1912, Danon.

52. See A.I.U., Maroc III.C.10, 7 March 1912, Danon; and also A.I.U., Maroc III.C.10, 12 January 1911 [*sic;* actually 1912], Danon.

53. Jules Erckmann, *Le Maroc moderne* (Paris: Challamel Ainé, 1885), 38.

54. Eugene Aubin, *Morocco of Today* (London: E. B. Dutton, 1906), 34.

55. See for example P.R.O., FO 174: 281, 26 Jumādā I 1325/7 July 1907, n/a (Arabic).

56. Jérome Tharaud and Jean Tharaud, *Marrakech, ou les seigneurs de l'Atlas* (Paris: Librairie Plon, 1920), 132.

57. See the 1890 census of the Marrakesh *mellah* for Rosillio's property holdings. The barley contract can be found in D.A.R., Al-Yahūd 2, 15 Dhū al-Qaʿda 1323/11 December 1905, ʿAbd al-Ḥāfiẓ.

58. D.A.R., Marrakesh 6, 18 Shaʿbān 1301/12 June 1884, the two *amīn*s of Marrakesh, Buzid and Bināni. Corcos's right to these markets was revoked in 1893: B.G./R. D3410, Risāʾil muḥtasib Marrākush Mawlāy ʿAbdallāh al-Būkīlī: 119, 23 Dhū al-Ḥijja 1310/8 July 1893.

59. Paul Lambert, "Notice sur la ville de Maroc," *Bulletin de la Société de géographie de Paris* (November–December 1868): 438. Presumably this was the *funduq* that was

restored in 1879. For a report on the hiring of carpenters and other laborers for this project, see D.A.R., Marrakesh 4, 11 Muḥarram 1297/25 December 1879, Umanā' of Marrakesh.

60. Miège, *Le Maroc et l'Europe,* 2:568 n.5. See also D.A.R., Marrakesh 4, 19 Shawwāl 1298/14 September 1881, in which a Muslim guard is hired to watch a Jew's *funduq* overnight, indicating that the storehouse was in the medina, as Muslims were prohibited from spending the night in the *mellah.*

61. A.A.E./P., C.P.C. Maroc 2, 10 December 1885, French consulate in Mogador (Essaouira).

62. P.R.O., FO 174: 292, 11 December 1885, Johnston: "They say that most of the business of their Hebrew agents in Marocco is carried on in the Medeena."

63. P.R.O., FO 174: 95, 19 December 1878, Maclean. Cotton was sold by Jewish merchants from Marrakesh as far away as Tinduf, deep in the Sahara: Y. D. Sémach, "Un rabbin voyageur marocain: Mordochée Aby Serour," *Hespéris* 8 (1928): 389.

64. Daniel Schroeter, "Slave Markets and Slavery in Moroccan Urban Society," in *The Human Commodity: Perspectives on the Trans-Saharan Slave Trade,* ed. Elizabeth Savage (London: Frank Cass, 1992), 192.

65. The English were vigorously opposed to the slave trade, while the French were more apathetic. See various reports in P.R.O., FO 413: 56, including 19 February 1912, Foreign Office to Anti-slavery and Aborigines' Protection Society; and "Report on Slavery in Morocco," 23 January 1912, Mackenzie.

66. Mordukhai Abisrour was the patriarch of this group (see chapter 2).

67. Richardson, *Travels in Morocco,* 1:68.

68. P.R.O., FO 174: 85, 12 April 1876, Hay. Ennaji makes the same estimate for the years 1876–1880. Mohammed Ennaji, *Soldats, domestiques, et concubines: L'esclavage au Maroc au XIXe siècle* (Paris: Balland, 1994), 173. Daniel Schroeter has studied several *kanānīsh* (registers) related to the slave market in Marrakesh during a slightly later period. He estimates that between 7 September 1888 and 4 July 1894, the average number of slaves sold in Marrakesh each year was close to five thousand. See Schroeter, "Slave Markets and Slavery in Moroccan Urban Society," esp. charts on pp. 189, 199.

69. P.R.O., FO 174: 85, 12 April 1876, Hay. Europeans were also forbidden to attend the slave auctions, but many still managed to observe the sales surreptitiously.

70. D.A.R., Marrakesh 8, beginning of Muḥarram 1307/end of August 1889, Torres.

71. D.A.R., Marrakesh 1, 27 JumādāI 1261/3 June 1845, n/a.

72. D.A.R., Marrakesh 2, 28 Jumādā I 1282/19 October 1865, Ibn al-Mushāwrī.

73. D.A.R., Marrakesh 2, 21 Muḥarram 1283/5 June 1866, Ibn Hīma.

74. D.A.R., Marrakesh 2, 23 Ṣafar 1283/7 July 1866, al-Binānī.

75. D.A.R., Marrakesh 8, 9 Shaʿbān 1307/31 March 1890, Umālik.

76. D.A.R., Marrakesh 2, end of Muḥarram 1283/mid-June 1866, Ibn Danī.

77. See for example D.A.R., Marrakesh 2, 24 Jumādā I 1282/15 October 1865, Ibn Ṭāhir.

78. See D.A.R., Marrakesh 6, 4 Shawwāl 1301/27 July 1884, Umālik.

79. D.A.R., Marrakesh 2, 24 Jumādā I 1282/15 October 1865, Ibn Ṭāhir.

80. D.A.R., Marrakesh 2, 24 Jumādā I 1282/15 October 1865, Bargash.

81. D.A.R., Marrakesh 4, 29 Ramaḍān 1297/4 September 1880, Ibn Hīma; and D.A.R., Marrakesh 6, 4 Shawwāl 1301/27 July 1884, Umālik.

82. Lemprière, *A Tour through the Dominions of the Emperor of Morocco,* 180.

83. D.A.R., Marrakesh 6, 15 Shaʿbān 1301/9 June 1884, Umālik. In the same folder, see the letter of 23 Dhū al-Ḥijja 1301/14 October 1884, in which the Makhzan acknowledges receipt of the *amīns*' report.

84. This was equally true of Muslim homes. The subject is treated extensively in Juan Campo, *The Other Sides of Paradise: Explorations into the Religious Meanings of Domestic Space in Islam* (Columbia: University of South Carolina Press, 1991).

85. *Times of Morocco*, 8 December 1887. The newspaper offers the following translation of the imprecation: "O scorpion, daughter of a scorpion, be thou accursed by the strength of every power that exists. From the mouth of the Prophet Joshua, the son of Nun; from the mouth of the High Priest Judah Bar Eli; and also from the mouth of the High Priest Judah Bar Ezekiel; so that you may not pass the threshold of this door, nor hurt any Israelite or son of an Israelite, now and for evermore. This is by command of the High Priest, Simon Bar Yuli [Yochai]. Amen."

86. *Times of Morocco*, 8 December 1887.

87. A.I.U., Maroc II.B.9–13, 11 March 1929, Camhy.

88. A.I.U., Maroc II.B.9–13, 12 March 1929, Goldenberg.

89. Françoise Legey, *The Folklore of Morocco* (London: G. Allen and Unwin, 1935), 28–29.

90. Legey, *The Folklore of Morocco*, 71.

91. A.I.U., Maroc II.B.9–13, 12 March 1929, Goldenberg.

92. Legey, *The Folklore of Morocco*, 35.

93. Legey, *The Folklore of Morocco*, 48.

94. Elie Malka, *Essai d'ethnographie traditionnelle des mellahs* (Rabat, 1946) 29; see also Legey, *Essai de folklore marocain*, 135. Bab al-Khamis was the site of the big Thursday market in Marrakesh, so Jews were quite familiar with this area of the city.

95. Legey, *The Folklore of Morocco*, 217–218.

96. P.R.O., FO 413: 18, 24 October 1892, Payton.

5. HINTERLANDS

1. The first two elements may bring to mind the European blood libel, i.e., the belief that Jews required Christian blood for their rituals and magic, which spread through Europe between the twelfth and sixteenth centuries and reappeared sporadically in later periods. Though any parallels with the Ahmar incident are most likely coincidental, it is still possible that Moroccan tribes had gained familiarity with the basic elements of the blood libel through their contact with European travelers, some of whom, as we have seen earlier, were well versed in anti-Semitic rhetoric. The subject of blood libels is treated generally in R. Po-chia Hsia, *The Myth of Ritual Murder: Jews and Magic in Reformation Germany* (New Haven, Conn.: Yale University Press, 1988). Several useful references can be found on page 2, note 3. For a reading of the blood libel as folklore, see Alan Dundes, ed., *The Blood Libel Legend: A Casebook in Anti-Semitic Folklore* (Madison: University of Wisconsin Press, 1991). A relatively late blood libel occurred in the Arab world, though it was perpetrated by French and local Catholics. See Ronald Florence, *Blood Libel: The Damascus Affair of 1840* (Madison: University of Wisconsin Press, 2004).

2. In Moroccan Arabic, *siḥr* refers to an occult practice utilizing sacred writing to achieve divine or supernatural intercession in the realms of money, health, romance and marriage, etc.

3. D.A.R., Al-tartīb al-ʿāmm, 4 Muḥarram 1309/10 August 1891, Makhzan. Additional details of these events can be found in the *Times of Morocco,* 8 August 1891; and A.A.E./P., C.P.C. Maroc 2, 6 August 1891, Hugonnet.

4. D.A.R., Al-tartīb al-ʿāmm, 4 Muḥarram 1309/10 August 1891, Makhzan.

5. D.A.R., Al-tartīb al-ʿāmm, 4 Muḥarram 1309/10 August 1891, Makhzan. In his response, the *khalīfa,* Mawlay Muhammad, sought to exonerate himself from these accusations by insisting that the Jews were at least partly responsible for the disturbances. See D.A.R., Marrakesh 8, 20 Ṣafar 1309/25 September 1891, Muḥammad al-Fāsī.

6. For an overview of the literature on this topic, see R. Stephens Humphreys, *Islamic History: A Framework for Inquiry* (Minneapolis, Minn.: Bibliotheca Islamica, 1988), 284–308.

7. Daniel Schroeter, *Merchants of Essaouira: Urban Society and Imperialism in Southwestern Morocco, 1844–1886* (Cambridge: Cambridge University Press, 1988).

8. ʿUmar Afā, *Al-Ṣaḥrāʾ wa-Sūs min khilāl al-wathāʾiq wa-al-makhṭuṭat* (Rabat, Morocco: Kullīyat al-Ādāb wa-al-ʿulūm al-Insānīya, 2001).

9. As noted (but not seconded) by Dale Eickelman, *Knowledge and Power in Morocco* (Princeton, N.J.: Princeton University Press, 1985), 76.

10. *Khaṭṭāra*s are man-made springs which tap groundwater and subsurface runoff from irrigation from the Tensift tributary basins.

11. Edmond Doutté, *Missions au Maroc: En tribu* (Paris: Paul Geuthner, 1914), 8. Mention should also be made of the magnificent date palm plantation, comprising several hundreds of thousands of trees, just northwest of the city. According to local traditions, it was inadvertently planted by a date pit spat out of the mouth of the founder of Marrakesh himself, though the careful fertilizing and watering required by a plantation of this size suggests that far greater planning was involved. See Gaston Deverdun, *Marrakech des origines à 1912* (Rabat, Morocco: Editions Techniques Nord-Africaines, 1959), 1:89–90.

12. For correspondence dealing with the ownership of land by Jews in the area of Aït Saʿada, see D.A.R., Marrakesh 4, 28 Rajab 1297/6 July 1880, Makhzan. Fifty families of the Atlas village of Asni were counted among the Moroccan Jews who earned their livelihoods primarily through agriculture: A.I.U., Maroc VII.B.1852/2, 1914, Danon.

13. Pierre Flamand, "Quelques renseignements statistiques sur la population israélite du Sud marocain," *Hespéris* 37 (1950): 363–397; by the same author, *Diaspora en terre d'Islam,* vol. 1, *Les communautés israélites du Sud-Marocain* (Casablanca: Imprimerie Réunies, 1959).

14. Eugene Aubin, *Morocco of Today* (London: E. B. Dutton, 1906), Schroeter has identified some of the mythological underpinnings of scholarly assumptions regarding the so-called Berber Jews, including the nature of the Jews' patronage ties to the tribal *qāʾid*s. See his "La découverte des juifs berbères," in *Relations judéo-musulmanes au Maroc: Perceptions et réalités,* ed. Michel Abitbol (Paris: Stavit, 1997), 169–187.

15. Nahum Slouschz, *Travels in North Africa* (Philadelphia: Jewish Publication Society of America, 1927), 455. Jerba is a small island off the coast of Tunisia which historically had a Jewish majority, though it too looked to its more urbane and sophisticated coreligionists in Tunis to meet many of its needs.

16. Pierre Flamand, *Un mellah en pays berbère: Demnate* (Paris: Librairie Générale de Droit & de Jurisprudence, 1952), 142 n.1.

17. Slouschz, *Travels in North Africa,* 455.

18. P.R.O., FO 174: 196, 17 March 1886, David Amar.

19. Theft within the Marrakesh Jewish community was also fairly common. See A.I.U., Maroc XXIV.E.384–393, 10 May 1910, Bonjo; and A.I.U., Maroc XXVI.E.398–416, October–December 1906, Falcon, in which the author reports, "The hungry crowd sets out to steal and [engage in] debauchery. Bands of thieves have coalesced, and all the houses have been victims of their assaults. They even go so far as to set fire to stores to take advantage of the chaos." The attempt to break into and rob *mellah* homes by boring through the peripheral wall, as discussed in chapter 2, can also be noted in this context.

20. D.A.R., Marrakesh 2, 11 Rabīʿ II 1282/3 September 1865, Muḥammad b. ʿAzūz; and D.A.R., Marrakesh 2, 23 Rabīʿ II 1282/15 September 1865, Muḥammad b. ʿAzūz.

21. A.I.U., Maroc III.C.10, 5 July 1923, Falcon.

22. Hirschberg has introduced the Khaldunian term *ʿaṣabīya* into the discourse on Jewish quarters in Morocco and elsewhere in the Arab-Islamic world, suggesting that the *mellah* should be interpreted as a spatial expression of group feeling rather than a symbol of degradation. Haim Z. Hirschberg, "The Jewish Quarter in Muslim Cities and Berber Areas," *Judaism* 17 (1969): 406–407.

23. P.R.O., FO 413: 22, 4 September 1894, Abensur. Objects of Judaica, some apparently authentic, can be easily found in the *sūq*s of Marrakesh today, though their intended buyers are more likely to be Jewish tourists than locals.

24. A.I.U., Maroc II.B.9–13, 10 March 1930, Goldenberg.

25. *Times of Morocco,* 12 October 1889.

26. A.I.U., Maroc VII.B, 3 January 1909 (date received), Jewish community of Taroudant. Corcos criticized Taroudant's *shaykh al-yahūd,* Pinhas Cohen, for involving the A.I.U. in the matter: A.I.U., Maroc XXVI.E.398–416, 11 January 1909, Falcon. For more on these events, see A.I.U., Maroc XXVI.E.398–416, 22 December 1908, Falcon.

27. A.I.U., Maroc VII.B, 1914, Danon. The Jews of Marrakesh had themselves been the victims of an abusive *shaykh al-yahūd* in 1876–1877. The *shaykh,* by the name of Arrobas, was accused of ordering four of his henchmen to beat a member of the community and throw him in jail. The ramifications of the incident were felt well beyond the boundaries of the local Jewish community, with the French legation at Tangier threatening to demand reparations for those Jews injured by Arrobas who were naturalized French persons or protégés: A.A.E./P., C.P.C. Maroc 1, 14 February 1877, Le Rée. Umalik's involvement in the affair resulted in yet another letter of reprimand from the Makhzan: A.A.E./P., C.P.C. Maroc 1, 3 Dhū al-Ḥijja 1293/20 December 1876, Moussa b. Hamed. The fact that the Moroccan system of justice was involved in this case alongside the foreign powers supports Ahmed Toufiq's argument that it remained relevant to Moroccan Jews in the second half of the nineteenth century: Ahmed Toufiq, "Les juifs de Demnate au 19e siècle," in *Juifs du Maroc: Identité et dialogue* (Grenoble, France: Pensée Sauvage, 1980), 160.

28. A pioneering work in the field is Edward Westermarck, *Ritual and Belief in Morocco,* 2 vols. (New York: University Books, 1968). See also Ernest Gellner, *Saints of the Atlas* (Chicago: University of Chicago Press, 1969); and Vincent Cornell, *Realm of the Saint: Power and Authority in Moroccan Sufism* (Austin: University of Texas Press, 1998). Saint veneration among Moroccan Jews is treated in Issachar Ben-Ami, *Saint*

Veneration among the Jews in Morocco (Detroit, Mich.: Wayne State University Press, 1998); Yoram Bilu, *Without Bounds: The Life and Death of Rabbi Ya'akov Wazana* (Detroit, Mich.: Wayne State University Press, 2000); and most recently Oren Kosansky, "All Dear unto God: Saints, Pilgrimage, and Textual Practice in Jewish Morocco" (Ph.D. dissertation, University of Michigan, 2003).

29. For a summary of the similarities and differences between Jewish and Muslim saints, see Norman Stillman, "Saddiq and Marabout in Morocco," in *The Sepharadi and Oriental Jewish Heritage,* ed. Issachar Ben-Ami (Jerusalem: Magnes Press, Hebrew University, 1982), 489–500.

30. A.I.U., Maroc II.B.9–13, 10 March 1929, Goldenberg.

31. According to Ben-Ami, ninety Jewish saints are recognized by Muslims in Morocco, and thirty-six Muslim saints are recognized by Jews. See Ben-Ami, *Saint Veneration among the Jews in Morocco,* 131.

32. Henry de Castries, "Les sept patrons de Merrakech," *Hespéris* 4 (1924): 267–268. A Muslim pilgrim to Marrakesh in 1900 describes the pilgrimage circuit to the tombs of the seven saints of Marrakesh in "Description de Marrâkech par El Hasan Ben Mohammed El R'Assâl," trans. E. Michaux-Bellaire, *Archives marocains* 15 (1909): 189–191.

33. A.I.U., Maroc II.B.9–13, 15 March 1929, Camhy. The belief that Muslims prayed to Muhammad rather than to God was a typical Orientalist trope of the period that actually dates back to the Middle Ages. See R. W. Southern, *Western Views of Islam in the Middle Ages* (Cambridge, Mass.: Harvard University Press, 1962), 32.

34. *Times of Morocco,* 25 April 1891.

35. D.A.R., Marrakesh 6, 7 Dhū al-Qaʿda 1301/29 August 1884, Makhzan.

36. *Times of Morocco,* 2 March 1893.

37. See A.I.U., Maroc II.B.9–13, 15 March 1929, Camhy; and A.I.U., Maroc XXVI.E.398–416, 1 December 1938, Goldenberg.

38. Louis Voinot, *Pèlerinages judéo-musulmans du Maroc* (Paris: Larose, 1948), 52.

39. It was forbidden for the bodies of those who died outside the city to be brought back inside the walls for burial.

40. Ben-Ami, *Saint Veneration among the Jews in Morocco,* 250–251.

41. José Bénech, *Essai d'explication d'un mellah (ghetto marocain): Un des aspects du judaïsme* (Paris: Larose, 1940), 181; Ben-Ami, *Saint Veneration among the Jews in Morocco,* 277–279.

42. Ben-Ami, *Saint Veneration among the Jews in Morocco,* 311–312.

43. Ben-Ami, *Saint Veneration among the Jews in Morocco,* 260–263.

44. See A.I.U., Maroc II.B.9–13, 10 June 1934, Abbou, in which the author writes, "The day after the Passover holidays is the moment for pilgrimages par excellence; it is a veritable exodus of Jews from all regions in different directions."

45. A.I.U., Maroc II.B.9–13, 10 June 1932, Goldenberg.

46. See the biographical sketch in Ben-Ami, *Saint Veneration Among the Jews in Morocco,* 226–229; also A.I.U., Maroc II.B.9–13, 10 June 1932, Goldenberg.

47. When the date of a saint's death was not known, the festival was held on another Jewish holiday—often Lag b'Omer, for its association with the sage Shimon bar Yochai, the reputed author of the *Zohar.*

48. A.I.U., Maroc II.B.9–13, 19 December 1933, Abbou.

49. A.I.U., Maroc II.B.9–13, 10 June 1932, Goldenberg.

50. Many of Morocco's Jewish saints are of real or fictional Palestinian origin. See Schroeter, *Merchants of Essaouira,* 95.

51. A.I.U., Maroc II.B.9–13, 10 June 1932, Goldenberg.

52. A.I.U., Maroc II.B.9–13, 10 June 1932, Goldenberg.

53. Cornell, *Realm of the Saint,* 3–31.

54. Samuel Benaïm, *Le pèlerinage juif aux lieux saints au Maroc* (Casablanca: published by the author, 1980), 79. See also Aubin, *Morocco of Today,* 295. According to one report, the Muslim *muqaddim* was responsible for the administration of some of the Jewish saints' tombs. He collected donations to redistribute to the families of the saints for their upkeep. Daniel Saurin and Albert Cousin, *Annuaire du Maroc* (Paris: Librairie du Figaro, 1905), 116.

55. Ben-Ami, *Saint Veneration among the Jews in Morocco,* 240.

56. Schroeter, *Merchants of Essaouira,* 99.

57. Jewish merchants were the primary link between city and countryside throughout North Africa for reasons explained by Schroeter: "The very fact that the Jews were not rooted in rural society, with tribal or kinship ties, meant that they did not constitute a political threat and were therefore more trustworthy in economic matters. Paradoxically this marginality was the guarantee of a neutrality which was in the interest of all parties to maintain under normal conditions." Schroeter, *Merchants of Essaouira,* 86. A similar point is made in Eickelman, *Knowledge and Power in Morocco,* 66.

58. D.A.R., Marrakesh 2, 3 Muḥarram 1283/18 May 1866, al-Mushāwrī to al-Simlālī, re French agent Yitzhaq Sarfati.

59. P.R.O., FO 174: 226, 18 July 1910, Rosen to White, re Mesod Bensauda, agent of the German firm of C. Ficke.

60. P.R.O., FO 174: 282, 10 December 1913, White to Lennox, re Mesaud Haim Rehamiash, prospective agent of the Halford firm at Saffi.

61. Such activities were much lauded by the A.I.U.: "Many Jews roam the countryside . . . buying indigenous goods and selling European goods to the Arabs. The French find in the Jews active assistants, devoted to their beautiful cause." A.I.U., Maroc II.B.9–13, 31 May 1928, Goldenberg. For more on this subject, see Maurice de Perigny, *Au Maroc: Marrakech et les ports du sud* (Paris: P. S. Roger, 1917), 209–211.

62. This was also the case in Essaouira. See Daniel Schroeter and Joseph Chetrit, "The Transformation of the Jewish Community of Essaouira (Mogador) in the Nineteenth and Twentieth Centuries," in *Sephardi and Middle Eastern Jewries: History and Culture in the Modern Era,* ed. Harvey Goldberg (Bloomington: Indiana University Press, 1996), 104–110.

63. The road between Marrakesh and Essaouira was especially treacherous. See P.R.O., FO 174: 193, 28 March 1879, Broome; as well as events described below.

64. The *qā'id* Anflus of Haha was the most notorious offender in the matter of the *nazālas*. He not only initiated their use but also rented them out for $4,000 a month. P.R.O., FO 174: 276, 6 December 1905, Madden to Lowther.

65. Schroeter, *Merchants of Essaouira,* 91.

66. A.I.U. France IX.A.67–73, 8 August 1876, Halévy.

67. As the term suggests, *nazālas* were also meant to serve as hotels (*nazl,* pl. *nuzul:* "inn, hotel"), but according to a British consular agent, "they are nothing of the sort, since no one wishes to stay the night at any one of them." P.R.O., FO 174: 276, 6 De-

cember 1905, Madden. In any event, Ben Taffa and his companions did not stay at the *nazāla,* but instead "took up a lodging in a neighboring house belonging to a Moor."

68. P.R.O., FO 174: 291, 19 March 1875, Anglo-Jewish Association.

69. In a claim concerning the purported robbery of a Jew in Demnat, the *qā'id* Jilali made the following notation in the margin of his register of receipts and expenditures: "This is nothing but a false claim, but we shall pay it just the same in order to execute the orders of our sovereign." Toufiq, "Les juifs de Demnate au 19e siècle," 159.

70. D.A.R., Marrakesh 6, 28 Rajab 1301/24 May 1884, Mawlāy ʿUthmān.

71. D.A.R., Marrakesh 7, 18 Ṣafar 1303/26 November 1885, Umālik. See also D.A.R., Al-Yahūd 1, 15 Rabīʿ I 1303/22 December 1885, al-Khaḍir. According to Umalik, a similar arrangement had been in place under the sultan ʿAbd al-Rahman, but it had lapsed into disuse after his death. Several attempts were required to enforce the ruling in Essaouira, beginning in 1866: Schroeter, *Merchants of Essaouira,* 171, 173. Thc rule was also applied in Mazagan in 1889: P.R.O., FO 174: 293, 30 December 1889, Redman to Green.

72. A.A.E./P., C.P. Maroc 49, 25 November 1885, grand vizier.

73. As has been shown by Pascon and others, these divisions, based primarily on the work of Alan Scham and Ernest Gellner, were themselves quite fluid. See John Hall's introduction to Paul Pascon, *Capitalism and Agriculture in the Haouz of Marrakesh,* ed. John R. Hall, trans. C. Edwin Vaughan and Veronique Ingman (London: Kegan Paul International, 1986), 28–29.

74. Harvey Goldberg, "The Mellahs of Southern Morocco: Report of a Survey," *Maghreb Review* 8, nos. 3–4 (1983): 67.

75. D.A.R., Marrakesh 4, 28 Rajab 1297/6 July 1880, Makhzan.

76. "As for the attacks by the neighboring tribes during periods of interregnum that targeted the *mellah,* they must be understood within the context of the relationship between the city and the countryside, that is to say, between the destitute peasants and the privileged merchants of the cities." Toufiq, "Les juifs de Demnate au 19e siècle," 161–162. Along similar lines, the tribes' mistreatment of Jews was sometimes exaggerated. In Demnat, for example, the city Toufiq is discussing, reports that the tribes had "abused" some of the Jewish women they had kidnapped from the village (and for whom the Jews of Marrakesh had begun collecting ransom money) were later retracted. See P.R.O., FO 413: 22, 24 September 1894, Satow.

77. Several documents deal with this incident, including P.R.O., FO 413: 22, 4 September 1894, Abensur; P.R.O., FO 413: 22, 5 September 1894, Montagu; and P.R.O., FO 413: 21, 11 September 1894, n/a. See also *Le réveil du Maroc,* 12 September 1894.

78. André Joly, "Le siège de Tétouan par les tribus des Djebala, 1903–1904," *Archives marocaines* 3 (1905): 266–300.

79. Edward Burke III, *Prelude to Protectorate in Morocco: Precolonial Protest and Resistance, 1860–1912* (Chicago: University of Chicago Press, 1976), 114.

80. A.I.U., Maroc III.C.10, 12 November 1912, Danon. Kenbib has remarked that El-Hiba's insurrection was unique for its lack of victimization of the Jews. This assertion conflicts with Danon's account, in which he describes the enforcement of the sumptuary laws of *dhimma,* the piercing of the wall of the Jewish cemetery, and the prohibition of Jews' leaving the city (one group caught trying to escape

was arrested and had all their belongings impounded). El-Hiba's soldiers were also said to have forced their way into Jewish homes, where they broke furniture and demanded food and money. Though Kenbib is correct in his assertion that no Jews were killed in the siege, his contention that, among the Jews of Marrakesh, only the large merchants and moneylenders were the victims of the "sacking of their warehouses and burning of their bills of debt" is at odds with Danon's statement that it was precisely the rich merchants who were able to escape damage by keeping their stores closed (most likely by offering bribes), while the *mellah*'s poorer shopkeepers were forced to remain open, and thus suffered the greatest harassment by El-Hiba's men. See Mohammed Kenbib, *Juifs et musulmans au Maroc, 1859–1948* (Rabat, Morocco: Faculté des Lettres et des Sciences Humaines, 1994), 394–400.

81. Paul Pascon, *Capitalism and Agriculture in the Haouz of Marrakesh,* 38.

82. See report in *Le réveil du Maroc,* 10 October 1894.

83. P.R.O., FO 413: 45, 4 May 1907, Lennox.

84. A.I.U., Maroc II.B.9–13, 4 July 1913, Danon.

85. See D.A.R., Marrakesh 6, 4 Shawwāl 1301/28 July 1884, Umālik, in which a member of the Misfiwa tribe who had been imprisoned by his *qā'id* was freed upon securing the purchase of 717 *riyāls* worth of oil by a Jew from Marrakesh.

86. P.R.O., FO 413: 51, 22 October 1908, Madden.

87. In 1896, the chief of a French military mission estimated that the Rehamna constituted "more than one third" of the city's population. Quoted in Helen Titus, "Among Competing Worlds: The Rehamna of Morocco on the Eve of French Conquest" (Ph.D. dissertation, Yale University, 1978), 51 n.8.

88. Titus, "Among Competing Worlds: The Rehamna of Morocco on the Eve of French Conquest," 52.

89. P.R.O., FO 174: 281, 1906–1911, Azulay. Rosillio eventually acquired land in Palestine as well: P.R.O., FO 835: 178, 1948, n/a.

90. Joseph Thompson, *Travels in the Atlas and Southern Morocco* (London: George Philip and Son, 1889), 419.

91. Schroeter, *Merchants of Essaouira,* 91–92.

92. P.R.O., FO 413: 20, 10 July 1893, Ridgeway.

93. Mohammed Ennaji, *Expansion européenne et changement social au Maroc* (Casablanca: Editions Eddif, 1996), 57–58.

94. *Le réveil du Maroc,* 10 October 1894.

95. *Le réveil du Maroc,* 6 February 1895.

96. Ennaji, *Expansion européenne et changement social au Maroc,* 63.

97. Abdellah Laroui, *Les origines sociales et culturelles du nationalisme marocain, 1830–1912* (Paris: F. Maspero, 1977), 391.

98. The provisions of the Madrid conference in 1880 had applied only to land within ten kilometers of Morocco's coastal cities and not to the country's interior. See Pascon, *Capitalism and Agriculture in the Haouz of Marrakesh,* 60.

99. The prisoner died in captivity in 1897, fourteen months after having been captured. See Titus, "Among Competing Worlds: The Rehamna of Morocco on the Eve of French Conquest," 103–105; and P.R.O., FO 413: 25, 19 March 1896, Nicholson.

100. As is well known, Mawlay Hassan made just such a gift to the Glaoua in recognition of the hospitality they had shown to the sultan and his troops at a crucial moment in the *maḥalla* of 1893. The cannon ensured the tribe's supremacy in the At-

las for years to come. See Gavin Maxwell, *Lords of the Atlas: The Rise and Fall of the House of Glaoua, 1893–1956* (London: Arrow, 1991), 31–50.

101. Deverdun, *Marrakech,* 1:525.

102. A.I.U., Maroc XXVI.E.398–416, 23 July 1907, Falcon.

103. *Jewish Missionary Intelligence,* August 1894. The Jews of Essaouira lobbied their governor to ban the local tribes from participating in the city's Fantasia in the wake of the Ahmar kidnapping incident: A.A.E./P., C.P.C. Maroc 2, 6 August 1891, Hugonnet.

104. D.A.R., Marrakesh 2, 27 Jumādā I 1282/18 October 1865, Ibn Danī to al-Ṭāhir.

105. A full narrative of the events of the *ḥāfiẓīya* is presented in Burke, *Prelude to Protectorate in Morocco,* 99–152.

106. The people of Marrakesh were particularly upset when the sultan traveled to the mosque by car (instead of on horseback, as was traditional), because they were unable to see him. *Le réveil du Maroc,* 12 January 1899.

107. Burke, *Prelude to Protectorate in Morocco,* 99–127.

108. Jérome Tharaud and Jean Tharaud, *Marrakech, ou les seigneurs de l'Atlas* (Paris: Librairie Plon, 1920), 132.

109. A.I.U., Maroc XXIV.E.384–393, 17 December 1929, Camhy.

110. Walter Harris, *Morocco That Was* (London: Eland, 1983), 311–312. A.I.U. director Falcon, who disliked both Corcos and Hafidh, suggested that the latter's attitude was pragmatic at best: "His feelings with regard to the Jews are the same as those of his coreligionists: neither hate, nor love, but simply disdain, an atavistic disdain for a race that always bowed its head in front of the greatest calamities and the most flagrant injustices. Mawlay Hafidh thus does nothing for nor against the Jews. When he needs them, he is gentle and pleasant, when he has no need for them, he pays them no attention at all." A.I.U., Maroc VII.B, *déclassé,* 10 October 1907, Falcon.

111. Maxwell, *Lords of the Atlas,* 95.

112. This is certainly the opinion of Maxwell. See *Lords of the Atlas,* 96.

113. A.I.U., Maroc XXVI.E.398–416, 22 December 1908, Falcon.

114. A.I.U., Maroc XXVI.E.398–416, 27 November 1908, Falcon.

115. A.I.U., Maroc XXVI.E.398–416, 8 December 1908, Falcon.

116. A.I.U., Maroc VII.B, *déclassé,* 6 May 1907, Falcon.

117. "Une interview avec un grand chérif," *Le réveil du Maroc,* 5 June 1895. Corcos's association with Ibn Dawud was complicated by the fact that the pasha was infamous for his ill treatment of Marrakesh Jewry. Not merely guilty by association (he was Ba Ahmad's brother-in-law), Ibn Dawud once showed up at the metalworkers' market and announced that the Jews had two days to make him three hundred iron vases. He likewise "volunteered" Jews for the unpopular office of *amīn,* beating and jailing those who refused. According to the A.I.U., Corcos sanctioned this behavior: "The cruelty of Ben Dawud is proverbial in Marrakesh . . . Today, thanks to the friendliness M. Corcos, the head of the [Jewish] community, shows toward him, Ben Dawud is able to inflict any trouble he wishes on our coreligionists with total impunity. If any members of the community complain to the prime minister, the affair is covered up and the plaintiffs are sent away thanks to evidence provided by M. Corcos, who always shows favor to [Ibn Dawud]." A.I.U., Maroc III.C.10, 20 December 1900, Levy.

118. P.R.O., FO 413: 37, 23 November 1904, Nicolson. See also Burke, *Prelude to Protectorate in Morocco,* 104.

119. Burke, *Prelude to Protectorate in Morocco,* 32, 33.

120. A Portuguese memoir of 1539 reported that both Muslims and Jews in Marrakesh received training in the fabrication of arms and ammunition from Europeans: "Mémoire de Joao Affonso aux membres du tribunal de conscience," in *Les sources inédites de l'histoire du Maroc,* première série, *Archives et bibliothèques de Portugal,* ed. Pierre de Cenival, David Lopes, Robert Ricard, and Chantal de La Véronne (Paris: Paul Geuthner, 1934–1953), 3:220. As discussed in chapter 1, Leo Africanus observed Jews carrying guns in the countryside, and several sources in the following centuries concur. For references, see Daniel Schroeter, "The Jews of Essaouira (Mogador) and the Trade of Southern Morocco," in *Communautés juives des marges sahariennes du Maghreb,* ed. Michel Abitbol (Jerusalem: Imprimerie Daf-Chen, 1982), 373 n.46.

121. Germain Mouette, "Histoire des conquestes de Mouley Archy," in *Les sources inédites de l'histoire du Maroc,* deuxième série, *Archives et bibliothèques de France,* ed. Henry de Castries, Pierre de Cenival, and Philippe de Cossé Brissac (Paris: E. Leroux, 1922–1960), 2:176.

122. Schroeter, "Jews of Essaouira," 369.

123. For example, Thomson's Jewish interpreter, David Assor, made a loan of $25 to a Muslim from Demnat at a rate of a half dollar per day with three donkeys, two cows, two guns, and a sword as collateral. Thomson, *Travels in the Atlas and Southern Morocco,* 419.

124. The French put a special guard at the *mellah*'s gate to prevent guns from being brought into other parts of the city. For the same reason, Jews were barred from entering their cemetery, and all burials during the war years had to take place in the presence of an A.I.U. representative: A.I.U., Maroc IV.C.11, 13 August 1914, Danon.

125. Burke, *Prelude to Protectorate in Morocco,* 121–122.

126. Burke, *Prelude to Protectorate in Morocco,* 109.

127. P.R.O., FO 413: 51, 22 August 1908, Madden.

128. This is the opinion of Burke, *Prelude to Protectorate in Morocco,* 103.

129. D.A.R., Marrakesh 1, 1 Shaʿbān 1266/12 June 1850, al-ʿAyāshī.

130. D.A.R., Al-tartīb al-ʿāmm, 27 Rajab 1297/5 July 1880, Makhzan.

131. Schroeter, *Merchants of Essaouira,* 178.

132. Thomson noted that the Jews were the only Moroccans who did not bury their money: *Travels in the Atlas and Southern Morocco,* 377.

133. P.R.O., FO 413: 47, 12 November 1907, Lowther.

134. Françoise Legey, *Essai de folklore marocain* (Paris: Paul Geuthner, 1926), 278.

135. Bénech, *Essai d'explication d'un mellah,* 262.

136. The sentiments of people in the south had not changed from the time of an earlier administrative shakeup, when it was remarked, "The south hates the north, particularly the official classes of Fez and Rabat, who until lately held all the Government posts worth having." P.R.O., FO 413: 35, 15 December 1903, Nicholson.

137. A.I.U., Maroc XXVI.E.398–416, 4 December 1908, Falcon.

138. A.I.U., Maroc VII.B, *déclassé,* 5 May 1907, Falcon. The evacuation is confirmed in P.R.O., FO 413: 46, 15 August 1907, n/a. It followed the Rehamna demand for the eviction of Europeans from properties owned by the tribe that had been rented out by the Makhzan: P.R.O., FO 413, 45, 5 June 1907, Ghanjaoui.

139. A.I.U., Maroc XXVI.E.398–416, 14 May 1907, Falcon.

140. Jonathan Katz, "The 1907 Mauchamp Affair and the French Civilising Mission in Morocco," in *North Africa, Islam, and the Mediterranean World: From the Almoravids*

to the Algerian War, ed. Julia Clancy-Smith (London: Frank Cass, 2001), 153. Nessim Falcon's anti-Hafidhist sentiments are further evident in his assertion that Mawlay Hafidh was complicit in the Mauchamp murder. Among the accusations he makes in his affidavit are that Hafidh sent unarmed police to quell the riots and that his own servants were in the crowd attacking Mauchamp. See Katz, "The 1907 Mauchamp Affair," 156.

141. Clifford Geertz, "Suq: The Bazaar Economy in Sefrou," in *Meaning and Order in Moroccan Society: Three Essays in Cultural Analysis,* ed. Clifford Geertz, Hildred Geertz, and Lawrence Rosen (Cambridge: Cambridge University Press, 1979), 170.

EPILOGUE

1. Jérome Tharaud and Jean Tharaud, *Marrakech, ou les seigneurs de l'Atlas* (Paris: Librairie Plon, 1920), 134.

2. Fifty-five Jews left Marrakesh for Jerusalem between 1 April 1919 and 31 August 1919, with forty or so more following early the next month: A.A.E./P., Maroc 1917–1940, 6 September 1919, Zagury. Zionist activity in Morocco focused primarily on Fez. See A.A.E./P., Maroc 1917–1940, n/d, n/a.

3. Pierre Flamand, "Quelques renseignements statistiques sur la population israélite du Sud marocain," *Hespéris* 37 (1950): 371. According to Goldenberg, director of the A.I.U. school in Marrakesh in the 1930s, rural immigration more than doubled the Marrakesh *mellah*'s population during the period 1912–1936: A.I.U., Maroc XXVI.E.398–416, 15 March 1936, Goldenberg.

4. *Encyclopedia Judaica,* 1st ed. (Jerusalem: Encyclopedia Judaica, 1971), s.v. "Marrakesh."

5. Josette Sicsic, "Etre juif à Marrakech," *L'arche* 12, no. 297 (1981): 67.

6. Shlomo Elbaz, "Marrakech, la Rouge," in *Les juifs de Maroc,* ed. Alfred Goldenberg (Paris: Editions du Scribe, 1992), 184.

7. Ḥāy al-Salām is still one of the most densely populated areas of the city, and also one of the poorest.

8. Christian Norbert-Schulz, *Architecture, Meaning, and Place: Selected Essays* (New York: Rizzoli, 1988), 31.

9. Mohammed Naciri, "Regards sur l'évolution de la citadinité au Maroc," in *Middle Eastern Cities in Comparative Perspective,* ed. Kenneth Brown, Michele Jolé, Peter Sluglett, and Sami Zubaida (London: Ithaca Press, 1986), 249–270.

BIBLIOGRAPHY

ARCHIVAL SOURCES

Morocco

Direction des archives royales (Mudīrīya al-Wathā'iq al-Malakīya), Rabat

Marrākush, folders 1–12. Correspondence with officials of Marrakesh.
Al-Yahūd, folders 1–2. Correspondence relating to Jewish affairs.
Qurqūz. Correspondence with the Corcos family.
Al-tartīb al-ʿāmm. Unclassified documents.

Bibliothèque générale (al-Khizānat al-ʿāmma), Rabat

D3410: Risā'il muḥtasib Marrākush Mawlāy ʿAbdallāh al-Būkīlī.
D1690: Kunāsh al-dākhil wa al-khārij li-banīqat Marrākush.

Bibliothèque royale (al-Khizānat al-Ḥasanīya), Rabat

K85: Mustafadāt madīnat Marrākush mā bayna 1294–1297.
K146: Mustafadāt madīnat Murrākush wa nawāḥ īhā, 1305–1312.
K425: Mā ṣīrahu al-amīn al-ḥājj ʿAbd al-Raḥmān b. ʿAbd al-Kabīr al-Marrākushī ʿalā sūr al-millāḥ sanat 1314.
K618: Taqīd al-dākhil wa-l-khārij bi-l-raḥba al-Marrākushīya 1413.

Merkaz al-Bahīya (Jewish Community Study Center), Marrakesh

Unclassified rabbinical/notary documents.

France

Archives de l'Alliance Israélite Universelle, Paris

Maroc

Comités locaux et communautés: I, II.B.9–13, VII.B
Situation générale intérieure des juifs: 1.C.1–2, II.C.3–9, III.C.10, IV.C.11
Politique extérieure: I.D.1
Ecoles: XXIII.E.359–384, XXIV.E.384–393, XXV.E.394–397, XXVI.E.398–416, XXVII.E.417–442, XVIII.E.443–470
Personalités importantes: I.J.2

France

Comité central: III.A.8–18, VI.A.43, IX.A.67–73
Souscriptions en faveur des juifs: XXXV.B.306–323

Situation générale intérieure des juifs: I.C.1–4
Politique extérieure: I.D.1–4, IV.D.15–17, VIII.D.42–50
Ecoles: VIII.E.13–18, IX.E.19–33
Rapports et questions générales: VI.F.12
Rapports: XIV.F.25

Archives du ministère des affaires étrangères, Paris

Maroc, 1917–1940.
Correspondance politique, Maroc 1–75.
Correspondance politique des consuls, Maroc 1–2.
Mémoires et documents, Maroc 1–15.
Nouvelle série, Maroc 1–472.
Affaires diverses politiques, Maroc 1–16.
Négociations commerciales, Maroc 1–2.

Bibliothèque nationale, Paris

BN Geog 27: Manuscrits de la Société de Géographie.
BN Geog 29: Photographs de la Société de Géographie.

Great Britain

Public Record Office, London

FO 52: Morocco, General Correspondence, Consuls, 1761–1837.
FO 84: Slave Trade (1853–1892).
FO 99: Morocco, General Correspondence, Series II, 1836–1905.
FO 174: Embassy and Consular Archives, Tangier Correspondence.
FO 403: Confidential Prints, Morocco.
FO 413: Confidential Prints, Morocco.
FO 631: Embassy and Consular Archives, Mogador Correspondence.
FO 635: Morocco, Mogador misc.
FO 828: Embassy and Consular Archives, Marrakech, Register of Correspondence.
FO 831: Reports on Insurrection in Southern Morocco.
FO 835: Embassy and Consular Archives, Casablanca Correspondence.
FO 836: Embassy and Consular Archives, Register of Marrakech Correspondence.
FO 909: Consular Court Records, Marrakech.
FO 925: Foreign Office Maps.

Greater London Record Office

Records of the Board of Deputies of British Jews:
ACC/3121, Class B: President and Secretary's Papers.
ACC/3121, Class C.
ACC/3121, Class E.
ACC/3121, Class F: Finances.

Anglo-Jewish Archives, London and Southampton

MS 137: Papers of the Anglo-Jewish Association, 1871–1983.

Israel

Central Archives for the History of the Jewish People, Jerusalem

MG: Miscellaneous letters and rabbinical documents from Morocco.

NEWSPAPERS

Jewish Missionary Intelligence, London.
Jewish Chronicle, London.
Al-Moghreb al-Aksa, Tangier.
Le réveil du Maroc, Tangier.
Times of Morocco, Tangier.
L'univers israélite, Paris.

UNPUBLISHED THESES

Gottreich, Emily. "Jewish Space and the Moroccan City: A History of the Mellah of Marrakech." Ph.D. dissertation, Harvard University, 1999.

Kosansky, Oren. "All Dear unto God: Saints, Pilgrimage, and Textual Practice in Jewish Morocco." Ph.D. dissertation, University of Michigan, 2003.

Titus, Helen. "Among Competing Worlds: The Rehamna of Morocco on the Eve of French Conquest." Ph.D. dissertation, Yale University, 1978.

PUBLISHED SOURCES IN ARABIC AND HEBREW

Abīṭbūl, Micha'el. *Tujjâr al-sulṭân: Une élite économique judeo-marocaine au XIXème siècle.* Jerusalem: Institut Ben-Zvi, 1994.

Afā, 'Umar. *Al-Ṣaḥrā' wa-Sūs min khilāl al-wathā'iq wa-al-makhṭuṭāt.* Rabat, Morocco: Kullīyat al-Adāb wa-al-'ulūm al-Insānīya, 2001.

Ibn al-Fāsī, Abī Zar'. *Rawḍ al-Qirṭās.* Trans. by Auguste Beaumier. Paris: Imprimerie imperiale, 1860.

Ibn Manẓūr, Muḥammad. *Lisān li-lisān.* Beirut: Dar al-Kutub al-'Ilmiyah, 1993.

Ibn Ṣaghīr, Khālid. "Wathīqa ghayr munshūra 'an millāḥ Marrākush fī-l-qarn al tāsi' 'ashar." *Hespéris-Tamuda* 35, no. 2 (1997): 25–71.

Ibn Zaydān, 'Abd al-Raḥmān. *Itḥāf a'lām al-nās bi-jamāl akhbār 'āḍirat miknās.* 5 vols. Casablanca: Idiyāl, 1990.

Al-Ifrānī, Muḥammad. *Nuzhat al-ḥādī bi-akhbār mulūk al-qarn al-ḥādī.* Edited and with a French translation by Octave Houdas. Paris: E. Leroux, 1888–1889.

Al-Khamlīshī, 'Abd al-'Azīz. "Ḥawal mas'ala binā' al-millāḥāt bi-l-mudun al-maghribīya." *Dar al-Nīyāba* 14 (1987): 21–28; 19–20 (1988): 30–41.

Al-Marrākushī, al-'Abbās b. Ibrāhīm. *Al-I'lām bi-man ḥalla Marrākush wa Aghmāt min al-a'lām.* 10 vols. Rabat, Morocco: al-Maṭba'a al-Malakīya, 1974–1983.

Al-Nāṣirī, Aḥmad b. Khālid. *Kitāb al-Istiqṣā' li-Akhbār duwal al-Maghrib al-Aqṣā.* 9 vols. Casablanca: Dar al-Kitab, 1949. Cited in García-Arenal, "Saintеté et pouvoir dynastique," 1025.

al-Tāzī, 'Abd al-Hādī. *Qaṣr al-badī' bi-Marrākush.* Rabat, Morocco: Wizārat al-Dawlat al-Mukallafat bi-l-Shu'ūn al-Thaqāfīya, 1977.

Bibliography

PUBLISHED SOURCES IN EUROPEAN LANGUAGES

Aafif, Mohamed. "Les harkas hassaniennes d'après l'œuvre d'A. Ibn Zidane." *Hespéris* 19 (1980–1981): 153–168.

Abitbol, Michel, ed. *Communautés juives des marges sahariennes du Maghreb.* Jerusalem: Imprimerie Daf-Chen, 1982.

———. *Temoins et acteurs: Les Corcos et l'historie du Maroc contemporain.* Jerusalem: Institut Ben-Zvi, 1977.

Abu-Lughod, Janet. "The Islamic City: Historical Myth, Islamic Essence, and Contemporary Relevance." *International Journal of Middle Eastern Studies* 19 (1987): 155–176.

Africanus, Leo. *Description de l'Afrique.* 2 vols. Edited and translated by Alexis Epaulard. Paris: Librairie d'Amerique et d'Orient, 1956.

———. *The History and Description of Africa.* 3 vols. London: Haklyut Society, 1896.

Al-Abassi, Ali Bey. *Travels of Ali Bey in Africa and Asia: 1803–1807.* 2 vols. Philadelphia: M. Carcy, 1816.

Allain, Charles, and Gaston Deverdun. "Les portes anciennes de Marrakech." *Hespéris* 44 (1957): 85–126.

Alterman, Hyman. *Counting People: The Census in History.* New York: Harcourt, Brace, and World, 1969.

Aubin, Eugene. *Morocco of Today.* London: E. B. Dutton, 1906.

Ayache, Germaine. "La minorité juive dans le Maroc précolonial." *Hespéris-Tamuda* 25 (1987): 147–168.

Ballon, Hillary. *The Paris of Henri IV: Architecture and Urbanism.* Cambridge, Mass.: M.I.T. Press, 1991.

Barkan, Omer. "Essai sur les données statistiques des registres de recensement dans l'empire ottoman au XVe et XVIe siècles." *Journal of Economic and Social History of the Orient* 1, no. 1 (1957): 9–21.

———. "Research on the Ottoman Fiscal Surveys." In *Studies in the Economic History of the Middle East,* edited by Michael Cook, 163–171. London: Oxford University Press, 1970.

Baudry, Jean. "Une ambassade au Maroc en 1767." *Revue des questions historiques* 36 (1906): 181–198.

Bederman, Sanford. *God's Will: The Travels of Rabbi Mordochai Abi Serour.* Atlanta: Georgia State University, Department of Geography, 1980.

Ben-Ami, Issachar. *Culte des saints et pèlerinages judéo-musulmans au Maroc.* Paris: Editions Maisonneuve & Larose, 1990. Published in English as *Saint Veneration among the Jews in Morocco* (Detroit, Mich.: Wayne State University Press, 1998).

———, ed. *The Sepharadi and Oriental Jewish Heritage: Studies.* Jerusalem: Magnes Press, Hebrew University, 1982.

Benaïm, Samuel. *Le pèlerinage juif aux lieux saints au Maroc.* Casablanca: published by the author, 1980.

Bénech, José. *Essai d'explication d'un mellah (ghetto marocain): Un des aspects du judaïsme.* Paris: Larose, 1940.

Bennison, Amira. "Liminal States: Morocco and the Iberian Frontier between the Twelfth and Nineteenth Centuries." In Clancy-Smith, *North Africa, Islam, and the Mediterranean World,* 11–28.

Ben-Sasson, Haim, ed. *History of the Jewish People.* Cambridge, Mass.: Harvard University Press, 1976.
Ben Srhir, Khalid. *Britain and Morocco during the Embassy of John Drummond Hay, 1845–1886.* Translated by Malcolm Williams and Gavin Waterson. London: Routledge/Curzon, 2005.
Bilu, Yoram. *Without Bounds: The Life and Death of Rabbi Ya'akov Wazana.* Detroit, Mich.: Wayne State University Press, 2000.
Botte, Louis. "Marrakech une année après la conquête." *L'Afrique française* 12 (1913): 429–433.
Bourqia, Rahma. "Don et théâtralité: Réflexion sur le rituel du don (hadiya) offert au sultan au XIXe siècle." *Hespéris-Tamuda* 31 (1993): 61–75.
Bowie, Leland. "An Aspect of Muslim-Jewish Relations in Late Nineteenth-Century Morocco: A European Diplomatic View." *International Journal of Middle Eastern Studies* 7 (1976): 3–19.
Braude, Benjamin, and Bernard Lewis. *Christians and Jews in the Ottoman Empire.* 2 vols. New York: Holmes and Meier, 1982.
Braudel, Fernand. "Espagnols et mauresques." *Annales E.S.C.* 4 (1947): 397–410. Cited in Deverdun, *Marrakech,* 1:442.
———. *The Mediterranean and the Mediterranean World in the Age of Philip II.* 2 vols. Translated by Siân Reynolds. New York: Harper and Row, 1972.
Burke, Edmund, III. *Prelude to Protectorate in Morocco: Precolonial Protest and Resistance, 1860–1912.* Chicago: University of Chicago Press, 1976.
Campo, Juan. *The Other Sides of Paradise: Explorations into the Religious Meanings of Domestic Space in Islam.* Columbia: University of South Carolina Press, 1991.
Castellanos, Manuel Pablo. *Descripcion histórica de Marruecos y breve reseña de sus dinastías.* Santiago: A. Fraile, 1879.
Castries, Henry de. "Les sept patrons de Merrakech." *Hespéris* 4 (1924): 245–303.
———, ed. and trans. *Une description du Maroc sous le règne de Moulay Ahmed El-Mansour, 1596.* Paris: E. Leroux, 1909.
Celarié, Henriette. *Un mois au Maroc.* Paris: Hachette, 1923.
Célérier, Jean. "Le Maroc: Pays du sucre et d'or." *France-Maroc* 79 (1923): 113–115.
Cenival, Pierre de. "L'église chrétienne de Marrakech au XIIIe siècle." *Hespéris* 7 (1927): 69–83.
———. "Les emirs des hintata, 'rois' de Marrakech." *Hespéris* 24 (1937): 245–261.
———. "Le palais d'El Bedi et l'œuvre de Matham: Introduction critique." In *Les sources inédites de l'histoire du Maroc: Pays-Bas,* 4:570–623.
Champion, Pierre. *Rabat et Marrakech.* Paris: H. Laurens, 1926.
Clancy-Smith, Julia. *North Africa, Islam, and the Mediterranean World: From the Almoravids to the Algerian War.* London: Frank Cass, 2001.
Colin, Georges, ed. *Chronique anonyme de la dynastie saadienne.* Arabic text with introduction and notes in French. Rabat, Morocco: F. Moncho, 1934.
Conring, Adoph von. *Marroko: Das Land und die Leute.* Berlin: G. Hempel, 1880.
Cook, Weston. *The Hundred Years War for Morocco.* Boulder, Colo.: Westview Press, 1994.
Corcos, David. *Studies in the History of the Jews of Morocco.* Jerusalem: Rubin Mass, 1976.
Cornell, Vincent. *Realm of the Saint: Power and Authority in Moroccan Sufism.* Austin: University of Texas Press, 1998.
———. "Socioeconomic Dimensions of Reconquista and Jihad in Morocco: Por-

tuguese Dukkala and the Saʿdid Sus, 1450–1557." *International Journal of Middle Eastern Studies* 22 (1990): 379–418.
Cousin, Albert, and Daniel Saurin. *Le Maroc.* Paris: Librairie du Figaro, 1905.
Dakhlia, Jocelyne. "Dans la mouvance du prince: Symbolique du pouvoir itinérant au Maghreb." *Annales E.S.C.* 43, no. 3 (1988): 735–760.
Dan, Pierre. *Histoire de Barbarie et de ses corsaires, des royaumes et des villes d'Alger, de Tunis, de Salé, et de Tripoly.* Paris: P. Rocole, 1637.
Davidson, John. *Notes Taken during Travels in Africa.* London: J. L. Cox and Sons, 1839.
"Description de Marrâkech par El Hasan Ben Mohammed El R'Assâl." Translated by Edouard Michaux-Bellaire. *Archives Marocains* 15 (1909): 189–191.
Deshen, Shlomo. *The Mellah Society: Jewish Community Life in Sherifian Morocco.* Chicago: University of Chicago Press, 1989.
Deverdun, Gaston. *Marrakech des origines à 1912.* 2 vols. Rabat, Morocco: Editions Techniques Nord-Africaines, 1959.
Doutté, Edmond. *Missions au Maroc: En tribu.* Paris: Paul Geuthner, 1914.
Dozy, Reinhart, and Michael De Goeje, eds. and trans. *Description de l'Afrique et de l'Espagne, par Edrisi.* 2 vols. Leiden, Netherlands: E. J. Brill, 1866.
Dundes, Alan, ed. *The Blood Libel Legend: A Casebook in Anti-Semitic Folklore.* Madison: University of Wisconsin Press, 1991.
Eickelman, Dale. *Knowledge and Power in Morocco.* Princeton, N.J.: Princeton University Press, 1985.
———. "Religion and Trade in Western Morocco." *Research in Economic Anthropology* 5 (1983): 335–348.
Elaouf, David. "Une architecture juive?" In Goldenberg, *Les juifs du Maroc,* 303–307.
Elbaz, Shlomo. "Marrakech, la Rouge." In Goldenberg, *Les juifs de Maroc,* 175–185.
Elias, Elias Antoon. *Elias' Modern Dictionary, Arabic-English.* 31st ed. Cairo: Elias' Modern Pub. House, 1990.
El Mansour, Mohamed. *Morocco in the Reign of Mawley Sulayman.* Wisbech, England: Middle East & North African Studies Press, 1988.
El Moudden, Abderrahmane. "Etat et société rurale à travers la *harka* au Maroc du XIXème siècle." *Maghreb Review* 8, nos. 5–6 (1983): 141–145.
Encyclopedia of Islam. 2nd ed. Leiden, Netherlands: Brill, 1960.
Encyclopaedia Judaica. 1st ed. Jerusalem: Encyclopaedia Judaica, 1971.
Ennaji, Mohammed. *Expansion européenne et changement social au Maroc.* Casablanca: Editions Eddif, 1996.
———. *Soldats, domestiques, et concubines: L'esclavage au Maroc au XIXe siècle.* Paris: Balland, 1994.
Erckmann, Jules. *Le Maroc moderne.* Paris: Challamel Ainé, 1885.
Fattal, Antoine. *Le statut légal des non-musulmans en pays d'Islam.* Beirut: Imprimerie Catholique, 1958.
Flamand, Pierre. *Diaspora en terre d'Islam.* Vol. 1, *Les communautés israélites du Sud-Marocain.* Casablanca: Imprimerie Réunies, 1959.
———. *Un mellah en pays berbère: Demnate.* Paris: Librairie generale de droit & de jurisprudence, 1952.
———. "Quelques renseignements statistiques sur la population israélite du Sud marocain." *Hespéris* 37 (1950): 363–397.
Florence, Ronald. *Blood Libel: The Damascus Affair of 1840.* Madison: University of Wisconsin Press, 2004.

Foucauld, Charles de. *Reconnaissance au Maroc.* Paris: Challamel, 1888.
Francisco Jesus Maria de San Juan del Puerto. *Mission historial de Marruecos.* Seville: Francisco Garay, 1708.
Friedman, Ellen. *Spanish Captives in North Africa in the Early Modern Age.* Madison: University of Wisconsin Press, 1983.
Gaignebet, Jean. "Marrakesh: Grand carrefour des routes marocaines." *Revue de geographie marocaine* 7 (1928): 272–304.
Garcia-Arenal, Mercedes. "Mahdi, Murabit, Sharif: L'avènement de la dynastie Sa'dienne." *Studia Islamica* 71 (1990): 77–113.
———. "Sainteté et pouvoir dynastique au Maroc: La résistance de Fès aux Sa'diens." *Annales E.S.C.* 4 (1990): 1019–1042.
———. "Spanish Literature on North Africa in the XVI Century: Diego de Torres." *Maghreb Review* 8, nos. 1–2 (1983): 53–59.
Garcia-Arenal, Mercedes, and Gerard Wieggers. *A Man of Three Worlds: Samuel Pallache, a Moroccan Jew in Catholic and Protestant Europe.* Baltimore: Johns Hopkins University Press, 2003).
Gatell, Joaquin. *Viages por Marruecos, el Sus, Wad Nun y Tekna.* Madrid: Sociedad Geográfica, 1879.
Geertz, Clifford. "Suq: The Bazaar Economy in Sefrou." In *Meaning and Order in Moroccan Society: Three Essays in Cultural Analysis,* edited by Clifford Geertz, Hildred Geertz, and Lawrence Rosen, 123–244. Cambridge: Cambridge University Press, 1979.
———. "Toutes Directions: Reading the Signs in an Urban Sprawl." *International Journal of Middle East Studies* 21 (1989): 291–306.
Gellner, Ernest. *Saints of the Atlas.* Chicago: University of Chicago Press, 1969.
Gerber, Jane. *Jewish Society in Fez, 1450–1700.* Leiden, Netherlands: E. J. Brill, 1980.
Ginsburg, J. B. *An Account of the Persecution of the Protestant Mission among the Jews, at Mogador, Morocco.* London: Edward G. Allen, 1880.
Godard, Leon. *Description et histoire du Maroc.* Paris: C. Tanera, 1860.
Goldberg, Harvey. "The Mellahs of Southern Morocco: Report of a Survey." *Maghreb Review* 8, nos. 3–4 (1983): 61–69.
———, ed. *Sephardi and Middle Eastern Jewries: History and Culture in the Modern Era.* Bloomington: University of Indiana Press, 1996.
Goldenberg, André, ed. *Les juifs du Maroc.* Paris: Editions du Scribe, 1992.
Grabar, Oleg. "Cities and Citizens: The Growth and Culture of Urban Islam." In *The World of Islam,* edited by Bernard Lewis, 89–117. London: Thames and Hudson, 1976.
Hajji, Muhammad. *L'activité intellectuelle au Maroc a l'époque Sa'dide.* 2 vols. Rabat, Morocco: Dar El-Maghrib, 1976.
Haneda, Masashi, and Toru Miura, eds. *Islamic Urban Studies: Historical Review and Perspectives.* London: Kegan Paul International, 1994.
Harris, Walter. *The Land of an African Sultan: Travels in Morocco, 1887, 1888, and 1889.* London: Sampson Low, Marston, Searle, & Rivington, 1889.
———. *Morocco That Was.* London: Eland, 1983.
Harrus, Elias. *L'Alliance en action: Les écoles de l'Alliance israélite universelle dans l'Empire du Maroc (1862–1912).* Paris: Nadir, 2001.
Hava, J. G. *Al-Faraid Arabic-English Dictionary.* Beirut: Catholic Press, 1964.
Herlihy, David. *Medieval Households.* Cambridge, Mass.: Harvard University Press, 1985.

Hikmet, Nazim. *Poems of Nazim Hikmet.* Translated by Randy Blasing and Mutlu Konuk. New York: Persea Books, 1994.

Hirschberg, Haim Z. *A History of the Jews in North Africa.* 2 vols. Rev. ed. Leiden, Netherlands: Brill, 1974–1981.

———. "The Jewish Quarter in Muslim Cities and Berber Areas." *Judaism* 17 (1968): 405–421.

Hodgkin, Thomas. *Narrative of a Journey to Morocco in 1863 and 1864.* London: T. C. Newby, 1866.

Hooker, Joseph, and John Ball. *Journal of a Tour in Morocco and the Great Atlas.* London: Macmillan, 1878.

Höst, Georg. *Nachrichten von Marokos und Fès.* Copenhagen: Verlegts, 1781.

Hourani, Albert, and S. M. Stern, eds. *The Islamic City.* Philadelphia: University of Pennsylvania Press, 1970.

Hsia, R. Po-chia. *The Myth of Ritual Murder: Jews and Magic in Reformation Germany.* New Haven: Yale University Press, 1988.

Humphreys, R. Stephens. *Islamic History: A Framework for Inquiry.* Minneapolis, Minn.: Bibliotheca Islamica, 1988.

Hunwick, John. "Al-Mahili and the Jews of Tuwat: The Demise of a Community." *Studia Islamica* 61 (1985): 155–183.

Jackson, James Gray. *An Account of the Empire of Marocco.* Philadelphia, 1810.

Joly, André. "Le siège de Tétouan par les tribus des Djebala, 1903–1904." *Archives marocaines* 3 (1905): 266–300.

Kadoch, Jacky. Interview by Emily Gottreich. March 1996 and June 2004. Marrakesh, Morocco.

Katz, Jacob. *Tradition and Crisis.* New York: Schocken, 1971.

Katz, Jonathan. "The 1907 Mauchamp Affair and the French Civilising Mission in Morocco." In Clancy-Smith, *North Africa, Islam, and the Mediterranean World,* 143–166.

Kenbib, Mohammed. "Changing Aspects of State and Society in Nineteenth-Century Morocco." In *The Moroccan State in Historical Perspective, 1850–1985,* edited by Abdelali Doumou, translated by Ayi Kwei Armah, 11–27. Dakar, Senegal: Codesria, 1990.

———. *Juifs et musulmans au Maroc, 1859–1948.* Rabat, Morocco: Faculté des Lettres et des Sciences Humaines, 1994.

———. "Les relations entre musulmans et juifs au Maroc, 1859–1945: Essai bibliographique." *Hespéris-Tamuda* 23 (1985): 83–104.

Kerrou, Mohamed, and Moncef M'halla. "La prostitution dans la médina de Tunis au XIXe et XXe siècles." In *Etre marginal au Maghreb,* edited by Fanny Colonna and Zakya Daoud, 201–221. Paris: CNRS Editions, 1993.

Koehler, Henri. *L'église chrétienne du Maroc et la mission franciscaine.* Paris: Société d'éditions franciscaines, 1934.

———. "La kasba saadienne de Marrakech, d'après un plan manuscrit de 1585." *Hespéris* 27 (1940): 1–19.

Koestler, Arthur. "Reports and Comment: Marrakech." *Atlantic Monthly* 12 (1971): 6–25.

Kostof, Spiro. *The City Shaped: Urban Patterns and Meanings through History.* Boston: Little, Brown, 1991.

Lagardère, Vincent. *Les Almoravides jusqu'au règne de Yûsuf b. Tâsfîn (1039–1106).* Paris: L'Harmattan, 1989.

Lambert, Paul. "Notice sur la ville de Maroc." *Bulletin de la Société de géographie de Paris* (November–December 1868): 430–447.
Lane, Edward. *Arabic and English Lexicon.* Vol. 1. Lahore, Pakistan: Islamic Book Centre, 1978.
Lapidus, Ira. *Muslim Cities in the Later Middle Ages.* Cambridge: Cambridge University Press, 1984.
Laredo, Abraham. *Les noms des juifs du Maroc.* Madrid: Consejo Superior de Investigaciones Científicas, Instituto "B. Arias Montano," 1978.
Laroui, Abdellah. *Les origines sociales et culturelles du nationalisme marocain, 1830–1912.* Paris: F. Maspero, 1977.
Laskier, Michael. *The Alliance Israélite Universelle and the Jewish Communities of Morocco: 1862–1962.* Albany: State University of New York Press, 1983.
———. "The Alliance Israelite Universelle and the Struggle for Recognition within Moroccan Jewish Society, 1862–1912." In Ben-Ami, *The Sepharadi and Oriental Jewish Heritage,* 191–207.
Legey, Françoise. *Essai de folklore marocain.* Paris: Paul Geuthner, 1926. Published in English as *The Folklore of Morocco,* translated by Lucy Hotz (London: G. Allen and Unwin, 1935).
Lemprière, William. *A Tour through the Dominions of the Emperor of Morocco.* Newport, England: Tayler, 1813.
Le Tourneau, Roger. "Notes sur les lettres latines de Nicolas Clénard relatant son séjour dans le royaume de Fés." *Hespéris* 19 (1934): 45–63.
Levy, Andre, and Yoram Bilu. "Nostalgia and Ambivalence: The Reconstruction of Jewish-Muslim Relations in Oulad Mansour." In Goldberg, *Sephardi and Middle Eastern Jewries,* 288–311.
Levy, Simon. "Ḥāra et mellāḥ: Les mots, l'histoire et l'institution." In *Histoire et linguistique,* edited by Abdelahad Sebti, 41–50. Rabat, Morocco: Université Mohammed V, Publications de la Faculté des Lettres et des Sciences Humaines, 1992.
Lewis, Bernard. *Jews of Islam.* Princeton, N.J.: Princeton University Press, 1987.
Mackenzie, Donald. *The Khalifate of the West.* London: Simpkin, Marshall, Hamilton, Kent, 1911.
Malka, Elie. *Essai d'ethnographie traditionnelle des mellahs.* Rabat, Morocco, 1946.
Mann, Vivian, ed., *Morocco: Jews and Art in a Muslim Land.* London: Merell in association with the Jewish Museum, 2000.
Marçais, Georges. "La conception des villes dans l'islam." *Revue d'Alger* 2 (1945): 517–533.
Marçais, William. "L'islamisme et la vie urbaine." *L'académie des inscriptions et belles-lettres, comptes rendus* (1928): 86–100.
Marmol Carvajal, Luis del. *L'Afrique de Marmol.* 3 vols. Translated by Nicolas Perrot. Paris: L. Billaine, 1667. A translation of *Descripción general de Africa,* 2 vols. (Granada: Rene Rabut, 1573).
Marty, Paul. "Les institutions israélites au Maroc." *Revue des études islamiques* 3 (1930): 297–332.
Massignon, Louis. "Enquête sur les corporations d'artisans et des commerçants au Maroc." *Revue du monde musulman* 58 (1924): 1–250.
Maxwell, Gavin. *Lords of the Atlas: The Rise and Fall of the House of Glaoua, 1893–1956.* London: Arrow, 1991.

Meakin, Budgett. *The Land of the Moors: A Comprehensive Description.* London: Darf, 1986.
Memmi, Albert. *The Pillar of Salt.* Boston: Beacon Press, 1992.
Messier, Ronald. "Rereading Medieval Sources through Multidisciplinary Glasses." In *The Maghrib in Question: Essays in History and Historiography,* edited by Michel Le Gall and Kenneth Perkins, 174–200. Austin: University of Texas Press, 1997.
———. "Rethinking the Almoravids, Rethinking Ibn Khaldun." In Clancy-Smith, *North Africa, Islam, and the Mediterranean World,* 59–80.
Meunié, Jacques, and Henri Terasse. *Nouvelles recherches archéologiques à Marrakech.* Paris: Arts et métiers graphiques, 1957.
Meyer, Michael. "Where Does the Modern Period of Jewish History Begin?" *Judaism* 24, no. 3 (1975): 329–338.
Miège, Jean-Louis. *Le Maroc.* Paris: Presses universitaires de France, 1950.
———. *Le Maroc et l'Europe: 1830–1894.* 5 vols. Rabat, Morocco: Editions la Porte, 1989.
———. *Une mission française à Marrakech en 1882.* Aix-en-Provence: La pensée universitaire, 1968.
———. "Les missions protestantes au Maroc, 1875–1905." *Hespéris* 42 (1955): 153–186.
———. *Morocco.* Translated by O. C. Warden. Paris: Arthaud, 1952.
Miller, Susan Gilson. "Dhimma Reconsidered: Jews, Taxes, and Royal Authority in Nineteenth-Century Tangier." In *In the Shadow of the Sultan: Culture, Power, and Politics in Morocco,* edited by Rahma Bourqia and Susan Gilson Miller, 103–128. Cambridge, Mass.: Harvard University Press, 1999.
———. "Gender and the Poetics of Emancipation: The Alliance Israélite Universelle in Northern Morocco, 1890–1912." In *Franco-Arab Encounters,* edited by Leon Carl Brown and Mathew Gordon, 229–252. Beirut: The American University of Beirut Press, 1996.
———. "Kippur on the Amazon: Jewish Emigration from Northern Morocco in the Late Nineteenth Century." In Goldberg, *Sephardi and Middle Eastern Jewries,* 190–209.
———. "Un *mellaḥ* désenclavé: L'espace juif dans une ville marocaine; Tanger, 1860–1912." In *Perception et réalités au Maroc: Relations judéo-musulmanes,* edited by Robert Assaraf and Michel Abitbol, 325–349. Casablanca: Najah El Jadida, 1998.
———. "Saints et laïcs dans le Tanger juif du XIXe siècle." In *Mémoires juives d'Espagne et du Portugal,* edited by Aron Rodrigue and Esther Benbassa, 171–193. Paris: Publisud, 1996.
Miller, Susan Gilson, Attilio Petruccioli, and Mauro Bertagnin. "Inscribing Minority Space in the Islamic City: The Jewish Quarter of Fez (1438–1912)." *Journal of the Society of Architectural Historians* 60, no. 3 (2001): 310–327.
Mitchell, Timothy. *Colonising Egypt.* Cambridge: Cambridge University Press, 1988.
Mocquet, Jean. "Voyage de Jean Mocquet au Maroc." In *Les sources inédites de l'histoire du Maroc: France,* 2:400–404.
Mouette, Germain. "Histoire des conquestes de Mouley Archy." In *Les sources inédites de l'histoire du Maroc,* deuxième série, *Archives et bibliothèques de France,* edited by Henry de Castries, Pierre de Cenival, and Philippe de Cossé Brissac (Paris: E. Leroux, 1922–1960), 2:1–201.

———. "The Travels of the Sieur Mouette in the Kingdoms of Fez and Morocco." In *A New Collection of Voyages and Travels,* edited by John Stevens, 27–113. London, 1711.

Naciri, Mohammed. "Regards sur l'évolution de la citadinité au Maroc." In *Middle Eastern Cities in Comparative Perspective,* ed. Kenneth Brown, Michele Jolé, Peter Sluglett, and Sami Zubaida (London: Ithaca Press, 1986), 249–270.

Noin, Daniel. *La population rurale du Maroc.* 2 vols. Paris: Presses universitaires de France, 1970.

Norberg-Schulz, Christian. *Architecture, Meaning, and Place: Selected Essays.* New York: Rizzoli, 1988.

Nordman, Daniel. "Les expéditions de Moulay Hassan: Essai statistique." *Hespéris-Tamuda* 19 (1980–1981): 123–152.

Noy, Dov. *Moroccan Jewish Folktales.* New York: Herzl Press, 1966.

Orwell, George. *The Collected Essays, Journalism, and Letters of George Orwell.* Edited by Sylvia Orwell and Ian Angus. New York: Harcourt, Brace & World, 1968.

Pascon, Paul. *Capitalism and Agriculture in the Haouz of Marrakesh.* Edited by John R. Hall. Translated by C. Edwin Vaughan and Veronique Ingman. London: Kegan Paul International, 1986.

———. *Le Haouz de Marrakesh.* 2 vols. Rabat, Morocco: Editions marocaines et internationales, 1977.

Pascon, Paul, and Daniel Schroeter. "Le cimetière juif d'Iligh, 1751–1955: Etude des épitaphes comme documents d'histoire démographique." In *La maison d'Iligh et l'histoire sociale du Tazerwalt,* edited by Paul Pascon, 113–140. Rabat, Morocco: SMER, 1984.

Périgny, Maurice de. *Au Maroc: Marrakech et les ports du sud.* Paris: P. S. Roger, 1917.

Raymond, André. *The Great Arab Cities in the Sixteenth–Eighteenth Centuries: An Introduction.* New York: New York University Press, 1984.

Raz-Krakotzkin, Amnon. "The Zionist Return to the West and the Mizrahi Jewish Perspective." In *Orientalism and the Jews,* edited by Derek Penslar and Ivan Kalmar, 162–181. Waltham, Mass.: Brandeis University Press, 2005.

Richardson, James. *Travels in Morocco.* 2 vols. London: Charles J. Skeet, 1860.

Rodrigue, Aron. "The Emancipation and Reformation of Women." In *Jews and Muslims: Images of Sephardi and Eastern Jewries in Modern Times,* 80–93. Seattle: University of Washington Press, 2003.

Rosenbloom, Joseph. "A Note on the Size of the Jewish Communities in the South of Morocco." *Jewish Journal of Sociology* 8, no. 2 (1966): 209–212.

Saisset, Pascalle. *Heures juives au Maroc.* Paris: Rieder, 1930.

Saurin, Daniel, and Albert Cousin. *Annuaire du Maroc.* Paris: Librarie du Figaro, 1905.

Savine, Albert. *Dans les fers du Maghreb: Récits de chrétiens esclaves au Maroc, XVIIe et XVIIIe siècles.* Paris: Société des éditions, 1912.

Scham, Alan. *Lyautey in Morocco: Protectorate administration, 1912-1925.* Berkeley: University of California Press, 1970.

Schroeter, Daniel. "La découverte des juifs berbères." In *Relations judéo-musulmanes au Maroc: Perceptions et réalités,* edited by Michel Abitbol, 169–187. Paris: Stavit, 1997.

———. "The Jewish Quarter and the Moroccan City." In *New Horizons in Sephardic Studies,* edited by Yedida Stillman and George Tucker, 67–81. Albany: State University of New York Press, 1993.

———. "The Jews of Essaouira (Mogador) and the Trade of Southern Morocco." In Abitbol, *Communautés juives des marges sahariennes du Maghreb,* 365–390.

———. *Merchants of Essaouira: Urban Society and Imperialism in Southwestern Morocco, 1844–1886.* Cambridge: Cambridge University Press, 1988.

———. "Slave Markets and Slavery in Moroccan Urban Society." In *The Human Commodity: Perspectives on the Trans-Saharan Slave Trade,* edited by Elizabeth Savage, 185–213. London: Frank Cass, 1992.

———. *The Sultan's Jew: Morocco and the Sephardi World.* Stanford, Calif.: Stanford University Press, 2002.

Schroeter, Daniel, and Joseph Chetrit. "The Transformation of the Jewish Community of Essaouira (Mogador) in the Nineteenth and Twentieth Centuries." In Goldberg, *Sephardi and Middle Eastern Jewries,* 99–116.

Schwerdtfeger, Friedrich. *Traditional Housing in African Cities: A Comparative Study of Houses in Zaria, Ibadan, and Marrakech.* New York: J. Wiley, 1982.

Sémach, Y. D. "Une chronique juive de Fès: le 'Yahas Fès' de Ribbi Abner Hassarfaty." *Hespéris* 19 (1934): 79–94.

———. "Un rabbin voyageur marocain: Mordochée Aby Serour." *Hespéris* 8 (1928): 385–399.

Sicsic, Josette. "Etre juif à Marrakech." *L'arche* 12, no. 297 (1981): 66–67.

Slouschz, Nahum. *Travels in North Africa.* Philadelphia: Jewish Publication Society of America, 1927.

Les sources inédites de l'histoire de Maroc. Première série. *Archives et bibliothèques d'Angleterre.* 3 vols. Vols. 1–2 edited by Henry de Castries; vol. 3 edited by Pierre de Cenival and Philippe de Cossé Brissac. Paris: E. Leroux, 1918–1935.

Les sources inédites de l'histoire de Maroc. Première série. *Archives et bibliothèques d'Espagne.* 3 vols. Edited by Henry de Castries. Paris: E. Leroux, 1921.

Les sources inédites de l'histoire du Maroc. Première série. *Archives et bibliothèques de France.* 4 vols. Edited by Henry de Castries. Paris: E. Leroux, 1905–1926.

Les sources inédites de l'histoire du Maroc. Première série. *Archives et bibliothèques des Pays-Bas.* 6 vols. Edited by Henry de Castries. Paris: E. Leroux, 1906–1923.

Les sources inédites de l'histoire du Maroc. Première série. *Archives et bibliothèques de Portugal.* 5 vols. Edited by Pierre de Cenival, David Lopes, Robert Ricard, and Chantal de La Véronne. Paris: Paul Geuthner, 1934–1953.

Southern, R. W. *Western Views of Islam in the Middle Ages.* Cambridge, Mass.: Harvard University Press, 1962.

Stillman, Norman. "The Commensality of Islamic and Jewish Civilizations." *Middle Eastern Lectures* 2 (1997): 81–94.

———. *The Jews of Arab Lands in Modern Times.* Philadelphia: The Jewish Publication Society of America, 1991.

———. "Saddiq and Marabout in Morocco." In Ben-Ami, *The Sepharadi and Oriental Jewish Heritage,* 489–500.

Tharaud, Jérome, and Jean Tharaud. *Marrakech, ou les seigneurs de l'Atlas.* Paris: Librairie Plon, 1920.

Thomson, Joseph. *Travels in the Atlas and Southern Morocco.* London: George Philip and Son, 1889.

Tilly, Charles. "Retrieving European Lives." In *Reliving the Past: The Worlds of Social History,* edited by Oliver Zunz, 11–52. Chapel Hill: University of North Carolina Press, 1985.

Torres, Diego de. *Relación del origen y suceso de los Xarifes y del estado de los reinos de Marruecos, Fez, y Tarudante que tienen usurpados.* Seville: Casa Francisco Perez, 1586. Edited by Mercedes Garcia-Arenal. Madrid: Siglo Veintiuno, 1980.

Toufiq, Ahmed. "Les juifs de Demnate au 19e siècle." In *Juifs du Maroc: Identité et dialogue.* Grenoble: Pensée Sauvage, 1980.

Triki, Hamid, and Bernard Rosenberger. "Famines et épidémies au Maroc aux XVIe et XVIIe siècles." *Hespéris-Tamuda* 14 (1973): 109–175; 15 (1974): 5–103.

Turner, Victor. *Drama, Fields, and Metaphors: Symbolic Action in Human Society.* Ithaca, N.Y.: Cornell University Press, 1974.

Vajda, Georges. *Un recueil de textes historiques judéo-marocains.* Paris: Larose, 1951.

Valence, Paul. "La yeshiba." *Bulletin de l'enseignement publique au Maroc* 26, nos. 1–2 (1939): 3–12.

Valensi, Lucette. *Fables de la mémoire: La glorieuse bataille des trois rois.* Paris: Seuil, 1992.

———. "From Sacred History to Historical Memory and Back: The Jewish Past." *History and Anthropology* 2 (1986): 283–305.

Voinot, Louis. *Pèlerinages judéo-musulmans du Maroc.* Paris: Larose, 1948.

Wehr, Hans. *Dictionary of Modern Written Arabic.* Edited by J. Milton Cowan. 4th ed. Ithaca, N.Y.: Spoken Language Services, 1994.

Westermarck, Edward. *Ritual and Belief in Morocco.* 2 vols. New York: University Books, 1968.

Wheatley, Paul. *The Places Where Men Pray Together.* Chicago: University of Chicago Press, 2001.

Willan, Thomas. *Studies in Elizabethan Foreign Trade.* Manchester, England: Manchester University Press, 1959.

Zafrani, Haim. *Mille ans de vie juive au Maroc: Histoire et culture, religion et magie.* Paris: Maisonneuve et Larose, 1983.

Zerbib, T. "Slave Caravans in Morocco." *Anti-Slavery Reporter* (May–June 1887): 97–99.

INDEX

Italicized page numbers refer to illustrations or tables.

EMILY GOTTREICH is Vice Chair of the Center for Middle Eastern Studies, University of California at Berkeley.

www.ingramcontent.com/pod-product-compliance
Ingram Content Group UK Ltd.
Pitfield, Milton Keynes, MK11 3LW, UK
UKHW022010120125
453522UK00005B/277

9 780253 218636